# READERS' GUIDES TO ESSENTIAL CRITICISM

CONSULTANT EDITOR: NICOLAS TREDELL

*Published*

| | |
|---|---|
| Patsy Stoneman | Emily Brontë: *Wuthering Heights* |
| Susie Thomas | Hanif Kureishi |
| Nicolas Tredell | Joseph Conrad: *Heart of Darkness* |
| Nicolas Tredell | Charles Dickens: *Great Expectations* |
| Nicolas Tredell | William Faulkner: *The Sound and the Fury – As I Lay Dying* |
| Nicolas Tredell | F. Scott Fitzgerald: *The Great Gatsby* |
| Nicolas Tredell | The Fiction of Martin Amis |

*Forthcoming*

| | |
|---|---|
| Paul Baines | Daniel Defoe: *Robinson Crusoe – Moll Flanders* |
| Peter Dempsey | The Fiction of Don Delillo |
| Jodi-Anne George | *Beowulf* |
| William Hughes | Bram Stoker: *Dracula* |
| Matthew Jordan | Milton: *Paradise Lost* |
| Jago Morrison | The Fiction of Chinua Achebe |
| Nicholas Potter | Shakespeare: *Antony and Cleopatra* |
| Stephen Regan | The Poetry of Philip Larkin |
| Nicolas Tredell | Shakespeare: *Macbeth* |
| Gina Wisker | The Fiction of Margaret Atwood |
| Angela Wright | Gothic Fiction |

**Palgrave Readers' Guides to Essential Criticism**
**Series Standing Order**
**ISBN 1–4039–0108–2**
(*outside North America only*)

You can receive future titles in this series as they are published by placing a
standing order. Please contact your bookseller or, in the case of difficulty, write to
us at the address below with your name and address, the title of the series and the ISBN
quoted above.

Customer Services Department, Palgrave Macmillan Ltd
Houndmills, Basingstoke, Hampshire RG21 6XS, England

# The Fiction of Julian Barnes

VANESSA GUIGNERY

Consultant editor: Nicolas Tredell

palgrave
macmillan

First published 2006 by
PALGRAVE MACMILLAN
Houndmills, Basingstoke, Hampshire RG21 6XS and
175 Fifth Avenue, New York, N.Y. 10010
Companies and representatives throughout the world

PALGRAVE MACMILLAN is the global academic imprint of the Palgrave
Macmillan division of St. Martin's Press, LLC and of Palgrave Macmillan
Ltd. Macmillan® is a registered trademark in the United States, United
Kingdom and other countries. Palgrave is a registered trademark in the
European Union and other countries.

ISBN-13: 978–1–4039–9059–4  hardback
ISBN-10: 1–4039–9059–X       hardback
ISBN-13: 978–1–4039–9060–0  paperback
ISBN-10: 1–4039–9060–3       paperback

This book is printed on paper suitable for recycling and made from
fully managed and sustained forest sources.

A catalogue record for this book is available from the British Library.

A catalog record for this book is available from the Library of Congress.

10   9   8   7   6   5   4   3   2   1
15   14   13   12   11   10   09   08   07   06

Printed in China

# Contents

Scammel and John Bayley focusing on intertextual echoes; Pateman on the fragility of truth.

The Brilliant Essayist: *Letters from London* (1995), *Something to Declare* (2002) and *The Pedant in the Kitchen* (2003)

John Walsh and James Wood considering Barnes as essentially an essayist; Moseley's account of the first volume; interesting reviews by Patrick Cockburn, Alain de Botton, Claire Messud and Jane Jakeman.

The Simulacrum of National Identity: *England, England* (1998)

Challenging views of the novel as satire by reviewers, and as farce by the author; perceptive essay by Vera Nünning on the construction of Englishness and the invention of tradition; comparative analysis by James J. Miracky, drawing on the theories of Jean Baudrillard.

In Search of Lost Times: *Cross Channel* (1996) and *The Lemon Table* (2004)

James Wood and Adrian Kempton on the predominance of facts; thoughtful reviews by Michiko Kakutani, Michael Wood and Robert MacFarlane on the nostalgia for the past and for lost loves, and on the mechanisms of memory.

Endings and New Beginnings: *Arthur & George* (2005)

Discussion of Barnes's latest novel, which mixes biography and imagination; consideration of its narrative technique, its echoes of detective fiction and its introduction of a new topic for Barnes, that of racial prejudice.

# ACKNOWLEDGEMENTS

I am most grateful to Julian Barnes for patiently answering my queries and kindly sending me the first proofs of his latest novel, *Arthur & George*, so that an account of it could be included in the Guide. I would like to very warmly thank the series editor Nicolas Tredell for his diligent, attentive and insightful work on the manuscript. Ryan Roberts amicably recommended me to Nicolas Tredell and provided much useful help with the bibliographical references. The Harry Ransom Humanities Research Center of Austin University, Texas, generously granted me the Cline fellowship, thus enabling me to spend one month in Austin and work on Julian Barnes's manuscripts. I am deeply grateful to Emma Cypher-Dournes and Laurent Bury for their close rereading of the Guide and their perceptive suggestions and comments. My most profound gratitude goes to my partner, Patrick Rimoux, for his constant support.

# Introduction: Julian Barnes in 10½ Chapters

Julian Barnes is the author of ten novels, two volumes of short stories, three collections of essays, and four detective novels published under a pseudonym. His books have received considerable critical acclaim worldwide, and several have been nominated for and/or have won prestigious literary prizes. The distinctive feature of Barnes's work taken as a whole is its diversity of topics and techniques, which confounds some readers and critics, but enchants others. While some underlying themes can be identified, such as obsession, love, the relationship between fact and fiction, or the irretrievability of the past, it is clear that in each novel Barnes aims to explore a new area of experience and experiments with different narrative modes. He explains: 'In order to write, you have to convince yourself that it's a new departure for you and not only a new departure for you but for the entire history of the novel.'[1] If Barnes has written several conventional novels which have not always attracted considerable critical attention, he has also proved very keen on formal experimentation. British writer Alain de Botton (born 1969) referred to him as 'an innovator in the form of the novel',[2] and many critics have emphasised the hybridity of most of his books, which blur and challenge the borders that separate existing genres, texts, arts and languages. As Peter Childs points out, 'Barnes is sometimes considered a postmodernist writer because his fiction rarely either conforms to the model of the realist novel or concerns itself with a scrutiny of consciousness in the manner of modernist writing.'[3] To get a better understanding of the recurrent critical debate on postmodernism in Barnes's fiction, a brief and clear definition of this complex notion might be useful, such as that proposed by British writer A. S. Byatt (born 1936): 'an awareness of the difficulty of *realism* combined with a strong attachment to its values, a formal need to comment on their fictiveness combined with a strong sense that models, literature and the *tradition* are ambiguous and emblematic goods combined with a profound nostalgia for, rather than rejection of the great works of the past'.[4] Byatt thus points to several elements of postmodernism which can be perceived in Barnes's fiction: he both resorts to and subverts realistic strategies; his writing is essentially self-reflexive; and he celebrates the literary past but also considers it with irony.

Before examining the specific qualities of Barnes's writing, a general survey of his career might throw light on the diversity of his literary production. The second son of Albert Leonard and Kaye Barnes, both of them French teachers, Julian Barnes was born in Leicester on 19 January 1946. Six weeks later, the family moved to Acton, a western suburb of London, and then in 1956 to Northwood from which Barnes commuted via the Metropolitan Line for seven years to attend the City of London School. This north-western suburban area, known as Metroland, would give its name to Barnes's first novel years later. From 1959, the family spent their summer holidays driving through different regions of France. Though those early holidays were 'filled with anxiety' (p. xii), as Barnes recalls in his preface to *Something to Declare* (2002), the author later developed a passion for France, which he shares with his brother, Jonathan Barnes, who owns a house there and is a Professor of Philosophy at the University of La Sorbonne in Paris. From 1964 to 1968, Barnes studied first philosophy and then modern languages (French and Russian) at Magdalen College, Oxford, where he took his BA with Honours; in 1966–7, he taught English at a Catholic school in Rennes, France. From 1969 to 1972, Barnes worked as a lexicographer for the *Oxford English Dictionary Supplement*, and was in charge of the 'rude words and sports words'.[5] He then read for the bar and qualified as a barrister in 1974 but he never practised because at the same time he started working as a free-lance journalist, which appealed much more to him. He wrote reviews, articles and columns under his own name as well as under pseudonyms. Thus, from 1976 to 1978, he published satirical pieces as Edward Pygge in the 'Greek Street' column of the *New Review* and in 1977 became contributing editor under the direction of the poet, critic and literary editor Ian Hamilton (1938–2001), to whom he would later devote an essay, 'Bitter Lemon Days' (1999). In 1981, another of his pen-names, Basil Seal, restaurant critic for the *Tatler*, was nominated Gourmet Writer of the Year. In 1977, Barnes joined the *New Statesman* as assistant literary editor under Martin Amis (born 1949). There, he met and made friends with columnist Christopher Hitchens (born 1949), as well as the poets Craig Raine (born 1944) and James Fenton (born 1949), and until 1981, reviewed novels and television programmes. In 1979, Barnes married literary agent Pat Kavanagh, to whom most of his fiction is dedicated and whose surname he used as a pseudonym for his detective novels. From 1979 to 1982, he was deputy literary editor of the *Sunday Times*, and from 1982 to 1986, television critic for the *Observer*.

Alongside this work as a journalist, Barnes starting writing fiction: his first short story, 'A Self-Possessed Woman', appeared in *The Times Anthology of Ghost Stories* in 1975, and in 1980 he published his first novel, *Metroland*, which won the Somerset Maugham Award for a debut novel and was turned into a film in 1998. His second novel, *Before She Met Me* (1982), surprised readers with its mixture of horror and comedy and received mixed reviews. As Barnes recalls, both books sold about 1,000 copies in hardback and 'staggered into paperback'.[6] As a consequence, Barnes did not expect much better for his next book, 'an upside-down sort of novel': 'I suspected that *Flaubert's Parrot* might interest a few Flaubertians, and perhaps a smaller number of psittacophiles [parrot lovers].'[7] Yet, it met with huge success and is to this date Barnes's most celebrated book worldwide. It received several prizes in Great Britain and abroad, and was shortlisted for the Booker Prize, which unfortunately Barnes has not yet won for any of his books: 'I don't want to think about it. It's much more important whether one's satisfied with the book oneself and whether it's still in print in ten years' time, and anything on top is a bonus.'[8] In 1983 (one year before the publication of *Flaubert's Parrot*), Barnes had already been selected by the Book Marketing Council as one of the twenty 'Best of Young British Novelists' in a list that included Martin Amis, Pat Barker (born 1943), William Boyd (born 1952), Kazuo Ishiguro (born 1954), Ian McEwan (born 1948), Salman Rushdie (born 1947) and Graham Swift (born 1949). A sample of their work was then published in *Granta*. At the age of forty and thanks to the success of *Flaubert's Parrot*, Barnes stopped his regular activities as a journalist, even if he continues to publish occasional reviews, essays and pieces on painting in *Modern Painters*, the *New Yorker*, the *New York Review of Books*, the *Guardian* or the *Times Literary Supplement*. In 1986, his fairly conventional novel *Staring at the Sun* met critical reservations. From 1981 to 1987, Barnes also published four detective novels as Dan Kavanagh: *Duffy* (1980), *Fiddle City* (1981), *Putting the Boot In* (1985) and *Going to the Dogs* (1987). In 1988, he translated into English a book by German cartoonist Volker Kriegel, *The Truth about Dogs*. Barnes also wrote an unpublished non-fiction work entitled *A Literary Guide to Oxford* in the 1970s, as well as drafts for two screenplays, *Growing Up in the Gorbals* (1987) and *The Private Wound* (1989), based on the novel (1968) by Nicholas Blake (the pseudonym of the poet C. Day-Lewis, 1904–72), all of which can only be consulted at the Harry Ransom Humanities Research Center of Austin University, Texas, which owns all of the writer's papers and manuscripts from 1975 to 2000.

Barnes's second major critical and commercial success came in 1989 with *A History of the World in 10½ Chapters*. From 1990 to 1994, he became the London correspondent of the *New Yorker* and wrote long essays on his own country that were later collected in *Letters from London 1990–1995*. In 1991, he published the delightful *Talking It Over*, which received a prize in France, was turned into a French film in 1996, and was followed ten years later by its sequel, *Love, etc* (2001). His seventh novel, *The Porcupine*, appeared in 1992 and aroused mixed responses. In 1995 Barnes taught a course of creative writing at Johns Hopkins University in Baltimore, and in 1996 he published his first collection of short stories, *Cross Channel*, about the British in France, followed two years later by *England, England* (1998), a farcical novel about the invention of English tradition, which was shortlisted for the Booker Prize. In 2002, Barnes turned his attention to France again through a collection of essays, *Something to Declare*, and his translation into English of the remarkable *In the Land of Pain* (published posthumously in 1930) by French author Alphonse Daudet (1840–97). The latter suffered from syphilis and the book is a stunning collection of notes about his symptoms, his excruciating pain and his various treatments. In the introduction, Barnes wonders: 'How is it best to write about illness, and dying, and death?' (p. v); two years later, he would provide answers in a superb volume of short stories about the theme of ageing and approaching death, *The Lemon Table* (2004). *The Pedant in the Kitchen* (2003) is Barnes's third collection of essays, and *Arthur & George* (2005) is his tenth novel and latest publication to date. Through the years, Barnes has received several awards both in Britain and abroad: the E. M. Forster American Academy and Institute of Arts and Letters award for work of distinction in 1986, the Gutenberg Prize in France in 1987, the Premio Grinzane Cavour in Italy in 1988, the Shakespeare Prize of the FVS Foundation of Hamburg in 1993, and the Austrian State Prize for European Literature in 2004. He was named Chevalier of the Order of Arts and Letters in France in 1988, promoted to Officer in 1995, and finally to Commander in 2004.

In recent years, several scholars have devoted their research to Barnes's fiction so that a range of monographs are now available. *Understanding Julian Barnes* (1997) by Merritt Moseley and *Julian Barnes* (2002) by Matthew Pateman are useful comprehensive accounts of Barnes's books, both providing a thematic and formal analysis. Moseley's monograph examines Barnes's novels and short stories, but also his detective fiction and essays until 1996, while Pateman focuses exclusively on the novels published under Barnes's name up to 2001. *Language, History, and Metanarrative in the Fiction of Julian Barnes* by Bruce Sesto (2001), which focuses on Barnes's novels until 1992 with the exception of *Staring at the Sun*, consists of the author's dissertation, which dates back to 1995 and has undergone no rewriting since. It unfortunately contains several errors and is more of a description than a genuine analysis. Monographs also appeared in foreign languages: I have published three books in French – *Postmodernisme et effets de brouillage dans la fiction de Julian Barnes* [*Postmodernism and Modes of Blurring in the Fiction of Julian Barnes*] (2001), 'Flaubert's Parrot' de Julian Barnes (2001) and *Julian Barnes: L'Art du mélange* [*The Art of Mixing*] (2001) – while Christoph Henke published *Vergangenheitsobsessionen: Geschichte und Gedächtnis im Erzählwerk von Julian Barnes* [*Obsessions of the Past: History and Memory in the Fiction of Julian Barnes*] (2001), in German. Many scholarly essays have appeared over the years, mostly drawing their analysis from the theories of postmodernism, deconstructionism and narratology, and very often focusing on Barnes's most successful novels, *Flaubert's Parrot* and *A History of the World in 10½ Chapters*. Reviews, chapters in books, and interviews can also sometimes usefully complement one's critical perspective on Barnes's work. An extensive bibliography of primary and secondary sources is in progress, assembled by Ryan Roberts, manager of the resourceful Julian Barnes website (www.julianbarnes.com). Roberts's bibliography, which is bound to be extremely rich and of excellent quality, will come as a handy complement to this Guide for readers who want to pursue their analysis of Barnes's work in more depth.

The purpose of this Guide is to provide a comprehensive and accessible conspectus of the essential criticism on Barnes's work, drawing from a selection of reviews, interviews, essays and books. Through the presentation, explanation and assessment of key critical interpretations and perspectives, the Guide will both examine the various issues which have aroused critical interest (narration/voice, history/story, biography, infidelity . . .), and explore the combination of innovative techniques and strategies with conventional modes and codes in Barnes's novels, short stories but also essays. The aim is thus also to give insight into the non-fiction of Barnes, who is often praised as a brilliant essayist, and to suggest some links between his fictional and non-fictional production.

The Guide is composed of 10½ chapters as an echo of Barnes's *A History of the World in 10½ Chapters*, in which the half-chapter entitled 'Parenthesis' – an essay about love and history – implies that the supposedly universal history presented by Barnes is not complete. This Guide's half-chapter, or 'Parenthesis', will therefore focus on the author's production as an essayist but also implicitly suggests the necessarily incomplete nature of any presentation of the essential criticism concerning Barnes's work. The Guide is divided into chapters examining each of Barnes's novels and short-story collections in order of publication. Chapters One and Two focus on Barnes's first two novels, *Metroland* and *Before She Met Me*, drawing from reviews and interviews, but also from the perceptive accounts in Merritt Moseley's and Matthew Pateman's monographs. The issues of retrospective jealousy and imaginary cuckoldry in the second novel are examined through the thoughtful essays of Frédéric Monneyron, Mark K. Millington and Alison S. Sinclair. The third chapter is devoted to detective novels written by Dan Kavanagh, which have been thoroughly scrutinised by Moseley, and reasons for the Barnes/Kavanagh double identity are provided by means of extracts from interviews with the author. Chapter Four concentrates on *Flaubert's Parrot* and offers a wide-ranging account of essential criticism from Philip Larkin's and David Lodge's interrogations as to its genre to Andrzej Gasiorek's categorisation of the book as an intellectual whodunnit, from Patti White's examination of Barnes's repeated use of lists and catalogues to Tania Shepherd's computerised linguistic analysis of the novel, from

James B. Scott's deconstructionist approach to Neil Brooks's poststructuralist reading, from Alison Lee's definition of the book as historiographic metafiction to William Bell's exploration of its subversion of biography. The chapter also centres on the debate between Neil Brooks and Erica Hateley about the book's oscillation between modernism and postmodernism, and on Alison Lee's, David Leon Higdon's and Georgia Johnston's examinations of the figure of the narrator. The fifth chapter includes references to several reviews of *Staring at the Sun*, among them Carlos Fuentes's enthusiastic piece, and perceptive criticism by Ann Hulbert and Alison Hennegan. The three parts of the novel are analysed by Pateman in terms of their dominant social discourses and by Richard Pédot in terms of the relation of knowledge to power. In Chapter Six, the generic instability of *A History of the World in 10½ Chapters* is discussed in several reviews, including those of Joyce Carol Oates and Salman Rushdie. Claudia Kotte, Brian Finney and Merritt Moseley examine the echoes and connections in the novel, while Catherine Bernard, Liliane Louvel and Alan Clinton focus more precisely on the issue of the hybridity of the chapter entitled 'Shipwreck'. Gregory Salyer and Claudia Kotte offer their interpretation of the problematising of historical discourse through a postmodernist perspective. Chapter Seven brings together *Talking It Over* and its sequel, *Love, etc*, and presents helpful reviews by John Bayley and Mick Imlah focusing on intertextual echoes, and by Peter Kemp, Elaine Showalter and James Wood about the theme of love. Several critics allude to the echoes of the film *Jules et Jim* (1962) by the French director François Truffaut (1932–84). In a perceptive essay, Craig Hamilton analyses the narrative technique by which contrasting monologues create a polyphony of voices, while Richard Todd and Erica Hateley concentrate on the love triangle. The French film adaptation of the first novel by Marion Vernoux is alluded to. The eighth chapter, devoted to *The Porcupine*, includes quotes from Barnes's thoughtful essays on the situation of Bulgaria in 1990 and on the reception of his novel there in 1992, testifying to the shifting frontier between fiction and reality. Michael Scammel and John Bayley compare the novel to *Darkness at Noon* (1941) by Arthur Koestler (1905–83), while Pateman draws attention to its concern with the fragility of truth. The 'Parenthesis' focuses on Barnes's essay collections, *Letters from London*, *Something to Declare* and *The Pedant in the Kitchen*, and draws from Moseley's account of the first volume and from several interesting reviews. The question of whether Barnes is a better essayist than novelist, argued by James Wood in particular, is debated. Chapter Nine examines *England, England*, considered by some reviewers as a satire while Barnes views it as a farce. In a perceptive essay, Vera Nünning explores the issues of the construction of Englishness and the invention of tradition, while James J. Miracky offers a comparative analysis of Barnes's novel and *Jurassic Park* (1990) by

Michael Crichton (born 1942), drawing from the theories of Jean Baudrillard (born 1929) on the simulacrum. The tenth chapter deals with the two volumes of short stories, *Cross Channel* and *The Lemon Table*, in which, according to James Wood and Adrian Kempton, facts dominate fiction. Reviewers such as Michiko Kakutani, Michael Wood and Robert MacFarlane draw attention to the nostalgia for the past and the interest in the mechanisms of memory in these collections, and analyse some short stories as elegies for lost loves. The conclusion to the Guide presents Barnes's latest novel to date, *Arthur & George*, which mixes biographical details of the life of Sir Arthur Conan Doyle (1859–1930) with an account of a real legal case, and with fictional passages. The narrative technique is discussed, as well as the echoes of detective fiction and the introduction of a new topic for Barnes, that of racial prejudice.

The essential criticism gathered in these pages aims to convey a diversity of views on Barnes's work which testifies not only to the variety of his subjects and the innovative quality of his experimentation with form, but also to the differing reactions, perspectives and interests of critics.

# CHAPTER ONE

# A Witty *Bildungsroman*: *Metroland* (1980)

*M*etroland was Julian Barnes's first novel, published when he was 34, deputy literary editor of the *Sunday Times* and television columnist for the *New Statesman*. It took him almost eight years to write, partly because, as Barnes himself admits, he was 'lacking confidence' in his own abilities as a novelist: 'so it sat in a drawer for a year at a time and went through a lot of re-writing'.[1] He even took an original step to meet potentially unfavourable reviews: 'I thought "There's only one way I can prepare myself for publication, and that's by writing the worst review I'm likely to get myself." So I wrote it, and really slanged the book.'[2] The literary prize for a debut novel that he won, worth £1000, thus came as a liberation: 'I cared very much about winning the Somerset Maugham Award. . . . It gave me self-confidence.'[3] Moreover, he could be relieved in that reviewers were mainly enthusiastic about this *Bildungsroman* (the term for a kind of novel which gives an account of the main protagonist's development from childhood to maturity). Merritt Moseley suggests that this is quite a typical form for a first novel: 'If a novelist is to write a coming-of-age book, it is probably going to be the first book. Julian Barnes is no exception.'[4]

Several reviewers praised more particularly the first part, 'Metroland 1963', in which Christopher Lloyd, a 16-year-old schoolboy, and his friend Toni Barbarowski are sneering at the suburban middle-class world of their parents. Both live in Metroland, a suburban area at the western end of the Metropolitan Line, which developed in the first half of the twentieth century. Barnes himself lived there for eight years and commuted by train from Northwood to the City of London School from 1957 to 1964. In 1992, Barnes took the trip back to Northwood with journalist Mira Stout and explained how, when the Metropolitan Railway pushed forward, 'a thin corridor of land was opened up with no geographical or ideological unity: you lived there because it was an area easy to get out of'. He chose it as the location of his first novel, less for autobiographical reasons than for its abstract qualities:

■ the point about Metroland (and its writerly attraction) was that it is a bogus place, a concept dreamed up by an expanding railway network in partnership with property developers. It was not an existing area that the railway was designed to service but an invented area designed to service the railway. So it was a nonplace, with nontraditions, where mock Tudor was the appropriately bogus prevailing architectural style.[5] □

The choice of Metroland might also be a discreet – though maybe unconscious – homage to Evelyn Waugh (1902–66), one of Barnes's favourite authors, who portrays a Lady Metroland in his early novels from *Decline and Fall* (1928) to *Put Out More Flags* (1942), and more particularly in *Vile Bodies* (1930) and *Scoop* (1938). Some thirty years later, Barnes's reaction to this ordinary middle-class suburb of his childhood is hesitant and contradictory: ' "Well, I *quite* liked it at the time. I mean, I didn't *hate* it I don't think," he says cautiously. "Yeah, maybe I did. . . .Yeah, I did in fact.Yeah, I did actually. I *did* hate it.That's true; I *loathed* it." '[6] Even though Barnes's response to Metroland resembles that of Chris and Toni, the writer insists on the fictional dimension of the novel: 'The difficulty with the first part was that the spirit of it was autobiographical, and the topography was autobiographical, but the actual incidents were invented, and attached to a much more adventurous character.'[7] He admits that, contrary to his heroes, he didn't want to be a rebel: 'Perhaps I *wasn't* rebellious enough. Or maybe I was saving it all for the novel.'[8]

Chris and Toni appear indeed as rebellious in the first part of *Metroland*, 'a maturely sophisticated treatment of premature sophistication in adolescence'[9] according to Ronald Hayman. Frank Kermode (born 1919) praised the accuracy with which Barnes records the jokes of the teenagers, which are bound to trigger off 'the pleasure of self-recognition' in some readers.[10] The two clever and erudite teenagers cultivate cynicism, irony, rootlessness, affectation and a fondness for all that is French in what Edward Blishen considers 'a brilliantly funny account of overbright adolescence'[11] and what David Williams views as 'a deliciously funny novel with seriousness implied but never obtruding'.[12] In an otherwise unsympathetic review, novelist Paul Bailey (born 1937) praises in this first part the characterisation of Uncle Arthur, 'a humorous old fugger' (*Metroland*, p. 46) who clearly despises his nephew Christopher: 'Arthur's antipathy enlivens the otherwise self-congratulatory proceedings – his viewpoint, however jaundiced, provides somes welcome shade.'[13] The controversial journalist and broadcaster Bernard

Levin (1928–2004) also favours the portrayal of 'mean Uncle Arthur'[14] and points out that he is described in turns of phrase that may remind one of the style of Kingsley Amis (1922–95), for example in a sentence such as: 'he would have watered his water if he'd known how' (p. 159).

In the second part, the 21-year-old Christopher goes to Paris to write his thesis, finds love with Annick and loses his virginity, but misses out on the students' demonstration in May 1968. David Williams was disappointed with this part, which, according to him, 'falters'[15] precisely because the 1968 events remain in the background. The reviewer may have overlooked the fact that this is exactly what Barnes intended in order to show that Chris 'may be one of those unfortunate enough never to experience the exciting moments in life', as David Leon Higdon suggests.[16] The title of the second part, 'Paris 1968', deliberately raises expectations, which are then frustrated. As Matthew Pateman suggests, 'Barnes refuses the expected history . . . giving us instead the personal history of Christopher's falling in love, losing his virginity, meeting his future wife . . . .'[17] On the very first page of this second part, Christopher confesses his unease when asked about his time in Paris. The question 'When was that?' (p. 75) invariably leads him to use circumlocutions: 'I would never mention May for a start' (p. 75) and deliberately remain vague: 'Oh, late Sixties' (p. 75). Christopher's embarrassment is due to his inadequate engagement with the historical 'events' of 1968: 'The point is – well I was there, all through May, through the burning of the Bourse, the occupation of the Odéon, the Billancourt lock-in, the rumours of tanks roaring back through the night from Germany. But I didn't actually see anything' (p. 76). History is thus displaced to the margins while what may look as incidental, Chris's personal story, is given central place. The novel thus stays true to the form of the *Bildungsroman*, focusing on the personal development of the main character, especially his sentimental and sexual education. Merritt Moseley notes the irony in Chris's development: 'having spent an adolescence building up an image of France as the home of alienation and political roughness, Christopher misses all the reality and substitutes a romantic life of nearly complete domesticity'.[18]

In the third part, 'Metroland II 1977', the novel comes full circle as Christopher, aged thirty, is back in suburbia where he has settled with his wife Marion into the bourgeois life he despised as a teenager, while Toni has remained faithful to his ideals of art and truth. This third part led to a controversy as to the interpretation of Chris's return to Metroland. Barnes intentionally devised the ironical circular structure: 'I thought of the development as a structure, an arc', in order to show how people can change: 'I'm obviously saying that people develop in ways they don't expect to.'[19] In an interview with Rudolf Freiburg, the writer explained that he was interested in 'the idea of someone setting out on a journey seemingly in one direction and then ending up back where he started. It was about the compromises that people make in a way without realizing that they're doing so.'[20] In his review of *Metroland*, poet Tom Paulin (born 1949) pointed to the clever circularity of the novel and praised the way in which Barnes 'courageously and ironically presents Christopher basking in his suburban happiness'.[21] Bernard Levin, however, missed the irony when he described the conclusion as finding 'the hero not merely exhibiting the suburban virtues but . . . extolling them' and added: 'it may be that Mr Barnes believes in those values himself and is an honest enough writer . . . to say so'.[22] In his interview with Freiburg, Barnes remarked, on the contrary, that he saw the ending as much more poised, 'ambiguous, or balanced, or unclear so that on the one hand Chris . . . either has – depending how you look at him – become mature, sensible, wise, or has completely sold out and tuned all his values to those of wider society.'[23] He even pointed to the misunderstanding of that 'English political commentator called Bernard Levin'.[24] Other reviewers were deeply aware of the ambiguous conclusion. Thus David Leon Higdon draws attention both to the fact that 'Chris has qualified, if not betrayed his idealism' and to 'Chris's emerging doubts and uncertainties dimly forming themselves'.[25] Merritt Moseley insists that 'nothing about this final section . . . is treated as a triumph'.[26]

In the last part, Barnes introduces the themes of fidelity and cuckoldry that will recur in his later works, which leads Jay Parini to describe the novel as 'a meditation on the meaning of fidelity within the context of marriage in an age of crushing cynicism'.[27] Higdon, for his part, proposes that the most interesting scene in the novel is 'the one concerned with adultery'.[28] Even though Marion's revelation of unfaithfulness and Chris's reaction to it are not, as Moseley suggests, 'the pivot of the book', they are 'important parts of the coming-of-age – or perhaps coming-to-terms – plot of *Metroland*.'[29]

What critics mainly saluted in their reviews of *Metroland* was the mastery of style, the sureness of construction, the accuracy of detail, the effective wit and irony, and the apt descriptions of childhood and adolescence remembered with nostalgia and a sense of loss by the first-person narrator. David Williams applauded the liveliness of the novel, by quoting a phrase from Jonathan Swift (1667–1745): 'Alive and talking to me', while Michael Church pointed to the quality of the dialogue, which 'testifies to a well-trained ear'.[30] The ironic perspective is mainly due to the retrospective narration as, throughout the novel, the narrative voice is that of the 30-year-old narrator, who, according to Moseley, 'is now capable of ironic correction of the ideas and postures of his adolescent self. The first-person narration combines an inhabiting of the mind of the adolescent with an older man's understanding of that mind's shortcomings.' Moseley adds that one of the main achievements of the novel is precisely the management of tone as the wiser and distanced view over one's life allows for irony and sharpness: 'The ironic verbal texture . . . keeps the tone astringent.'[31] British writer William Boyd, who qualified *Metroland* as 'rare and unusual', disagreed with this insistence on irony, arguing instead that Barnes 'seems to respect the foibles and poses of adolescence and young manhood as things to be cherished and valued in their own right rather than merely excuses for a few easy laughs'.[32]

Other critics found the first-person narration unoriginal, considering it, as summed up by Richard Todd, 'a curiously downbeat debut from a writer of Barnes's intelligence'.[33] In a particularly harsh review, Paul Bailey explains that he admires Barnes as a journalist, a columnist and a reviewer whose criticism he finds 'amusing', 'perceptive' and 'shrewd', but adds that he was disappointed with this first novel. Bailey's reproaches relate to two main aspects. First of all, he resents the coming-of-age theme: 'The book is neither daring nor imaginative: it traipses over well-worn territory, the territory of a thousand apprentice works . . . . We have been here before.'[34] David Williams shares some of Bailey's reservations: 'The theme – growing up and the sexual itch – is so old you wonder how Barnes keeps it fresh,'[35] but eventually admits that Barnes does keep it fresh in the first and third parts. Bailey on the other hand is adamant in his judgement and cannot find anything fascinating in the common experiences depicted by the narrator.

The second reproach Bailey addresses to Barnes's novel is its 'curious lack of people', its lack of 'a vivid background of other, possibly more interesting lives'.[36] He suggests that all the secondary characters, be they Chris's parents, brother, sister or girl-friend in Paris, are spectral, insubstantial, flat. Moseley responds to this criticism by pointing out that this is precisely how other people appear to Chris: 'The "lack of people" is not a sign of careless writing but apt characterization of a self-absorbed adolescent, impatient of other people because his categories are so selective and literary that hardly anybody *can* exist for him.'[37] Other critics, however, side with Bailey's opinion on the depiction of secondary characters; for example, Tom Paulin regrets that the relationship between Christopher and his wife Marion is not traced in more detail, while Bernard Levin wishes Annick and Marion had been made more concrete: 'What he has not yet mastered is the art of putting the blood as well as the bones in his characters.'[38] This criticism may once again be directed against the homodiegetic narrator (the narrator who is also a character in the story he is telling) rather than against the author. Christopher is a man of words, who is more interested in language, art and literature than in the 'real thing'.

One can therefore concur with Ronald Hayman that *Metroland* is 'a literary novel' even though 'the literature behind it is well digested'.[39] It

develops intertextuality, which consists in putting one's own text in relation with other texts through quotations, references, allusions, parodies or
pastiches. Nicholas Shrimpton regretted this 'slight weakness for cultural
name-dropping'[40] while Richard Brown noted that *Metroland* 'owes a
great deal to the language and traditions of English poetry', feeling
beneath the narrative the influence of the 'steady, empirical treatment and
suburban stoicism' of the poems of Philip Larkin (1922–85).[41] If English
echoes may be perceived by some readers, homage is essentially made to
French literature, culture and language, which might explain the enthusiasm of French critics for *Metroland* when it was eventually translated
into French and published in 1995, i.e. fifteen years after its publication
in England and nine years after *Flaubert's Parrot* appeared in French,
receiving great acclaim. Several French reviewers pointed to the numerous intertextual references and allusions in *Metroland*, which I myself
tried to elucidate.[42] The literary erudition and affected rebellion of the
two teenagers impel them to idealise certain French writers – for example, Gérard de Nerval (1808–55), Théophile Gautier (1811–72), Charles
Baudelaire (1821–67), Paul Verlaine (1844–96) and Arthur Rimbaud
(1854–91). The literary background they blatantly display not only
reveals the characters' pedantry, but also throws light on various aspects
of their personality and evolution. Matthew Pateman sees the protagonists as being 'constructed through literary engagement'[43] and analyses
more particularly the epigraphs to each part and their symbolic significance, suggesting that the progression of the epigraphs reflects the evolution of the main protagonist 'from complexity to simplification, from the
desire to search to the desire to accept'.[44]

Many reviewers perceived also in *Metroland* the first signs of Barnes's
great admiration for Gustave Flaubert (1821–80). As the novel was
published in 1987 in the United States and 1995 in France, i.e. several
years after the success of *Flaubert's Parrot*, American and French critics in
particular pointed to the several allusions to Flaubert. In the first part,
during a Sunday visit to Uncle Arthur, whom Christopher barely toler-
ates, the rebellious teenager chooses to display a symbolic book: 'a small
pocket edition of Flaubert's *Dictionnaire des Idées Reçues*' (*Metroland*, p. 47),
later described in *Flaubert's Parrot* as 'a catalogue of clichés' (p. 86) and 'a
handbook of fake advice' (p. 87). By bringing this book, Christopher
openly reveals his low opinion of Uncle Arthur, who is beset by
prejudices, but also reveals his own personality marked by a 'coruscating
idealism' and 'a public pose of raucous cynicism' (p. 15).

Then, at the end of the second part of the novel, Christopher enumerates the objects he is taking back to England, and a novel by Flaubert is
included: 'In my pocket was the book I'd just started: *L'Education
Sentimentale*' (p. 130). This novel, first published in 1859, deals with the
sentimental education of the main protagonist, Frédéric Moreau, who

goes to Paris in the first half of the nineteenth century, lets the 1848 insurrection pass him by and falls in love instead with Madame Arnoux, a married woman, with whom the relationship remains platonic. Christopher himself indeed goes through his sentimental education in Paris in the troubled year of the student revolution of 1968, but unlike Frédéric, he does lose his virginity with Annick, who is about the same age as he is, and unmarried. Richard Todd analyses this intertext and points to the similarities and differences between the two novels, particularly the differing status of Madame Arnoux and Annick as delineated above. He also notes that Flaubert's novel is a third-person narrative while *Metroland* is a first-person narration, which greatly modifies the perspective; he remarks, however, that the Paris described by Flaubert 'is just as Bohemian as the pre-revolutionary city of 1968'. Todd finally marks the opposition between the '*deus ex machina* role of Frédéric's uncle' whose death enables the young man to inherit the estate, and 'the eccentric and stingy lifestyle of Christopher's Uncle Arthur'.[45]

In the same essay, Todd laments the fact that not much attention has been paid to *Metroland*'s relationship to *Bouvard and Pécuchet* (1881), Flaubert's unfinished book, but he himself declines to elaborate this thesis. *Bouvard and Pécuchet* focuses on the two eponymous heroes, former copyists who decide to retire to the countryside and try to learn all there is to know about various subjects such as history, sociology, botany etc. . . . Their encyclopaedic attempts inevitably lead to failure and ridicule as they cannot achieve exhaustive coverage of any given subject. French reviewer Renaud Matignon claims that *Metroland* is *Bouvard and Pécuchet* in reverse although his explanation is too laconic to be utterly convincing. He suggests that in Flaubert's book, our knowledge helps us pierce through the two protagonists' nonsensical attitude, while in *Metroland* our ignorance constitutes our truth.[46] I would argue that Toni and Christopher's attitude towards the world in general, their pedantry, their seriousness resemble, to a certain extent, the attitude of Bouvard and Pécuchet in that the futility and vanity of their attempts are exposed. Like Flaubert's protagonists, Toni and Chris adopt a superior stance towards their families and friends, pretending to have access to a knowledge others are deprived of, but their supposed erudition proves to be hollow and useless.

The two teenagers' admiration for French culture goes further than literature to include language as well, an aspect which I have attempted to analyse in an essay.[47] In *Metroland*, the use of French words or expressions and the bilingual puns enable Christopher and Toni to cultivate their marginality while exposing further their pedantry. The non-francophone reader may, however, feel excluded as no translation into English is provided, and the frequency of such occurrences may irritate some, as was the case with reviewer Frank Goodman.[48] The protagonists indeed sometimes mix French words with literary references, as in their mottoes: *écraser l'infâme* and *épater la bourgeoisie* (p. 15), 'crush the infamous' and 'shock the bourgeoisie', two expressions which are never translated in the whole novel and which are respectively borrowed from Voltaire (1694–1778) and Charles Baudelaire. The followers of Dada and the surrealists would later appropriate the second expression. Toni and Christopher then create their own idiolect, or language, when they anglicise the French verbs in sentences such as 'How about écrasing someone?' (p. 17) or 'Think I épated him much?' (p. 18). They also deliberately ostracise their fellow pupils when making monolingual puns in French which only they understand. These forays into French have been considered by critics as very playful and clever but also as epitomising the teenagers' snobbery and pretentiousness. One could suggest that Christopher's attachment to all that is French is due to his impatience with Britain and his need to create for himself an identity that would not be strictly English. Indeed, he cultivates rootlessness and can only look up to Toni, whose parents are Polish Jews. Christopher's adoption of French culture, literature and language is a way for him to approach such class. According to Moseley, in *Metroland*, 'France is an idea, as well as a style, a language, a pose, an image of the right sort of life, and a rebuke to Metroland.'[49] France is also very much linked to Christopher and Toni's ideal of art and devotion to art. Elizabeth Kastor rightly identified the subject matter of the novel as being 'about people growing up, when art seems more real than life',[50] and Christopher does admit he dreams 'about finding the key to some vital synthesis of art and life' (p. 128). Even though partly ironic on the part of the narrator, Christopher and Toni's idealistic discourse on art may reflect Barnes's own beliefs and hopes that would haunt him in his later novels.

In 1998, *Metroland* was turned into a film directed by Philip Saville and starring Christian Bale (Christopher), Lee Ross (Toni), Elsa Zylberstein (Annick) and Emily Watson (Marion). Most reviewers found the adaptation dull and morose, unable to convey the wit and cleverness of the novel. The film is based on flashbacks as it starts in the late seventies with Chris, aged thirty, living in suburbia with his wife and baby. As Toni comes to visit them, Christopher remembers with nostalgia his life in Paris in 1968 and his teenage years in Metroland, which triggers off the flashbacks. Reviewer David Gritten found it a 'lame adaptation' because the director chose 'to discard what made the book appealing'. He argues that the first part of the novel, 'the strongest, funniest part', is wasted in the film as the teenagers are portrayed as 'not particularly sharp or clever'. Gritten also suggests that Toni is reduced 'to a philandering opportunist'[51] and deprived of the sense of otherness that gave him his identity in the novel.

Asked about whether he liked the film adaptation of *Metroland*, Barnes pointed to the difficulty of film adaptation and the necessity to drift away from the novel: 'Film is a radically different medium, and the book should therefore be destroyed and reinvented if it is to be a real film, as opposed to an illustrated adaptation.' Displaying the greatest courtesy, he declined to complain about the film: 'There's no more disobliging sight than a writer happily taking money from the movies and then bitching about the result.' Barnes did not comment any further and merely praised the performance of the two main actresses: 'I thought both Emily Watson and Elsa Zylberstein were terrific in *Metroland*.'[52]

Even though the adaptation of *Metroland* was disappointing, there is some satisfaction to be found in the fact that the rights were bought and that a film was indeed directed 18 years after the publication of the novel. With mostly favourable reviews and the satisfaction of winning the Somerset Maugham Award, Barnes was thus launched in the literary world and considered a promising young novelist. If, according to some critics, the form of this first novel, a *Bildungsroman*, was to some extent predictable and unoriginal, readers could wonder what would come next and which form his second novel would take. Would it follow logically from the coming-of-age story and adopt a traditional vein or would it go down a completely different track in terms of both theme and form? This is what the second chapter will try to establish.

# CHAPTER TWO

# When Horror Meets Comedy: *Before She Met Me* (1982)

In 2000, Julian Barnes told Nicholas Wroe: 'After my first book I have not been an autobiographical writer.'[1] Thus, one should not look for any autobiographical hint in the pathological case of retrospective jealousy that *Before She Met Me* records. The novel, written at times in crude language and mixing horror, wry humour and melodrama, focuses on Graham Hendrick, a history teacher who divorces his first wife Barbara and marries Ann, a former actress, whom his novelist friend Jack had introduced to him. Graham starts watching all the films Ann has made in the past, no matter how bad, and becomes obsessed by the relationships she had before he met her, both on and off the screen. His obsession and retrospective jealousy gradually deepen until he becomes convinced that Ann also had an affair with his friend Jack. Deeply wounded and out of his mind, Graham eventually kills Jack and commits suicide in front of Ann.

The dark and disturbing tone of *Before She Met Me* is very different from the amusing and fresh atmosphere of *Metroland*, thus already hinting that Barnes would create a different atmosphere with each new novel. Several reviewers, however, perceived similarities between the main protagonists of both novels. David Leon Higdon saw Graham as 'an older, more disillusioned version of Christopher' and suggested that *Before She Met Me* 'could have been a sequel to *Metroland*' even though Barnes's second novel is 'more thematically ambitious, more psychologically concentrated, and certainly darker' than *Metroland*.[2] Richard Brown concurred that Graham 'might be Chris Lloyd 10 years on',[3] as did Bill Greenwell who felt that the reader might find 'Christopher revisited in Graham' and see Jack Lupton as 'an older Tony'.[4] Matthew Pateman also found that Jack was 'similar in his capacity as foil for the straight man to Toni in *Metroland*'.[5] Despite these echoes in characterisation, the two books differ greatly in theme and tone, and Anthony Thwaite insists that *Before She Met Me* is far from 'the amiable nostalgia of *Metroland*'.[6]

Because of its originality, reviewers were mainly taken aback by this unsettling second book and proved divided in their appreciation of the novel. Two main aspects that had been highlighted upon the publication of *Metroland* recurred in some reviews. First of all, several critics pointed once again to the cleverness and wit displayed by the author: Bill Greenwell praises the 'irresistible blend of wit and intelligence',[7] and Anthony Thwaite, in a lukewarm review, concedes that Barnes is 'very witty' and that the 'whole thing is extremely clever'.[8] However, a few reviewers also suggested that Barnes's wit was too visible and marred the novel. The second aspect concerned Barnes's characterisation of his protagonists. Mark Abley in particular proves extremely fierce in his assessment of the characters, whom he judges 'paper-thin'.[9] Isabel Raphael for her part considers Jack and Barbara as 'caricatures of "types" ',[10] while Bill Greenwell, in an otherwise enthusiastic review, finds that 'Ann's film career is comically, but not convincingly contrived, and Jack's wife, Sue, is flimsily characterised, merely servicing the plot.'[11] Richard Todd rightly reacted against these views by suggesting that this limited characterisation is due to the fact that the focus is via Graham, i.e. we see everything through his eyes: 'Criticisms that all the characterizations except Graham's own are thin and two-dimensional fail to take on board the imposing technical task the novel sets itself of revealing the breakdown of a single consciousness while moving skilfully in and out of it.' Thus, the reader is manipulated in his vision of the various protagonists: for example, 'we are being coerced unawares into viewing Barbara through Graham's eyes as a nagging stereotype'.[12] Merritt Moseley for his part believes that all characters are aptly constructed: 'each is understood, and understandable'. According to him, Barbara is 'a rounded character who does as she does for comprehensible reasons. The minds of Ann and Jack are more thoroughly revealed; their growing impatience with Graham . . . is artfully traced. Ann is a deep characterization.'[13] Characterisation is a key issue in discussions of Barnes's novel as it is usually linked to plot and to the overall credibility of the book. Philip Larkin wrote a sympathetic letter to the author, predicting 'great success' for him with this book, but admitted to finding it 'only half convincing' primarily because 'lecturers don't meet starlets': 'so much is credible that one wants it to be finally convincing. Only, regrettably, it isn't.' Despite these remarks, Larkin read the book twice, judged it 'gripping & moving',[14] and named it one of his books of the year.

Larkin was not the only reader who had mixed views about the novel. Reviewer Gary Krist, for example, finds on the one hand that 'the book lacks credibility in places', particularly after Graham succumbs to retrospective jealousy, from which point 'the novel becomes unconvincing'.

On the other hand, Krist judges the book 'an intelligent and addictive entertainment'.[15] John Mellors also contrasts the novel's entertaining qualities and its lack of credibility, and concludes with a fierce judgement caused by his high expectations: '*Before She Met Me* is an ambitious book, promising much but in the end proving a disappointment.'[16] This view is shared by Mark Abley, who judges the plot 'preposterous' and remarks: 'it takes more than intermittent felicities . . . to make a convincing novel'.[17] It should be noticed that these remarks seemed particularly harsh and unjustified to other critics. Isabel Raphael, for example, found the book 'entirely gripping', savouring the tension that 'builds relentlessly towards a shocking climax',[18] while Bill Greenwell judged Graham's breakdown 'genuinely distressing'[19] and Richard Todd considered the ending 'gruesome because plausible'.[20]

What most critics and reviewers saluted in *Before She Met Me* was the original blend of horror and comedy. Barnes renews the genre of the classical tragedy, which employs stock characters (husband, wife and lover) by proposing a variation on the love triangle (husband, wife and her past) and by mixing tragedy and comedy. As Barnes suggested, it 'has a sour and comic edge to it'.[21] Many reviews thus point to the comic dimension of the book despite its morbidity. In his letter to Barnes, Larkin judged the novel 'amusing and enjoyable', 'very funny, and very observant'.[22] Michiko Kakutani insisted, for her part, on the mixture of comedy and horror and concluded her review approvingly: 'it's rare to come across a novel that's so funny and odd, and at the same time, so resonant and disturbing'.[23] Anthony Thwaite described the novel as an 'elegantly hardboiled treatment of the nastier levels of obsession, full of controlled jokes when almost everything else has got out of control.'[24] Frank Kermode found the progression of Graham's self-inflicted disease 'horribly funny, and idiosyncratic without seriously departing from the tradition of the modern English farcical novel'.[25] The mixture of farce and tragedy may already be anticipated in the second untranslated epigraph to the novel, borrowed from *Les Fourberies de Scapin* [*The Trickeries of Scapin*] (1671) by French playwright Molière (1622–73): '*Il vaut mieux encore être marié qu'être mort*' ['Better wed than dead'] (p. 5). The irony of this cynical quote as a prelude to *Before She Met Me* lies in the fact that the main protagonist, after having been married twice, commits suicide on the last page.

Reviewers often tend to gauge a writer by comparing his work to others' and pointing to possible influences or echoes. Barnes is no exception. Thus, Gary Krist commends in *Before She Met Me* the 'uneasy hybrid of comedy and melodrama' and suggests that Barnes has 'mixed subgenres, devising something halfway between the academic romps of Kingsley Amis or David Lodge [born 1935] and the violent, steamy tales of James M. Cain [1892–1977]'.[26] Moseley points out similarities to Kingsley

Amis's son Martin, and their mutual friend Ian McEwan: Barnes 'writes with a mixture of the comic and the macabre, the lurid and the jocose, which invites comparisons with his friends and contemporaries Martin Amis and Ian McEwan'. As Moseley remarks, both Amis and McEwan were well known at the end of the seventies for the outrageous and shocking plots of some of their novels, such as, respectively, *Dead Babies* (1975) or *The Cement Garden* (1978), and '*Before She Met Me* is another such novel of unease, growing menace, and mental disturbance.'[27] In an interview with Amanda Smith in 1989, Barnes acknowledged that the novel was 'a rather nasty book about unpleasant sexual feelings, jealousies and obsessions. It was meant to have had a rather sour and hard-driving edge to it. I think it's my funniest book, though the humor is rather bleak and in bad taste usually.'[28] Barnes even admits to having been delighted on hearing that one of his friends who had read the book had felt depressed for three days afterwards.[29] Moseley, together with several other critics such as Greenwell, Kakutani, and French reviewers who discovered this novel with delight only in 1991, warmly applauded Barnes's achievement: 'Writing a book this funny which nevertheless turns out to be this savage, without tonal inconsistency or unintended humor, is quite an impressive accomplishment.'[30]

The main theme of the novel, jealousy, 'the green-eyed monster',[31] has been widely discussed by critics, who have frequently pointed out inter-textual echoes, first among which was *Othello* (1604) by William Shakespeare (1564–1616). Graham is ironically and contemptuously nicknamed 'little Othello' (p. 67) by his friend Jack, suggesting that Graham carves out a pathetic figure compared with the larger-than-life Shakespearean hero. If Graham's first wife, Barbara, provides the first spur to jealousy by luring him into going to watch one of Ann's films, then, as David Leon Higdon suggests, 'Graham needs no Iago; he is Iago to his own Othello.'[32] Jealousy feeds on itself as Shakespeare had already pointed out in his play: 'It is a monster / Begot upon itself, born on itself.'[33] Some reviewers referred to more contemporary depictions of obsessive jealousy, such as, for example, *The End of the Affair* (1951) by Graham Greene (1904–91), which figures in *Before She Met Me* as one of Ann's books, given to her by one of her lovers (p. 61). Mark Abley picked up on this intertextual echo but judged that 'the comparison is all to Barnes's disadvantage' as, according to him, *Before She Met Me* lacks the 'passion, tenderness, complexity and moral seriousness of Greene'.[34] Others referred to Harold Pinter (born 1930) and more particularly his 'more subtle, if less pungent'[35] play *Old Times* (1971), focusing on the rivalry over Kate between Anna, a former room mate, and Deeley, her husband, who both invent recollections of their own in order to claim ownership of Kate.

To those who would complain that jealousy is an old theme, better dealt with elsewhere, one could counter that the originality of *Before She Met Me* lies in the fact that it is written in the wake of the sexual liberation of the sixties, which did not eliminate all difficulties in relationships between men and women. David Montrose delineated very aptly the theme of the novel as 'the problem of jealousy in an age of sexual freedom'.[36] Barnes himself pointed to the misconceived ideas dating back to that period of sexual liberation: 'There seems now a major flaw in the hopeful Sixties assumption that the more people you sleep with, the more relaxed you become about the whole thing: that an increase in sexual traffic produces a decrease in the unpleasant emotions sometimes aroused by the business.'[37] On the contrary, those emotions persist and Barnes qualified his novel as 'a sort of anti-'60s book. It's against the idea that somehow the 60s sorted sex out . . . suddenly everyone started sleeping with everyone else, and that cured the lot. . . . I just wanted to say, it's not like that; that what is constant is the human heart and human passions.'[38] This certainly explains why Higdon situated the novel in a deeply rooted novelistic tradition, qualifying it as 'a twentieth-century husband's version of the great nineteenth-century novels of estrangement, adultery and jealousy'.[39]

Barnes, however, does not merely reproduce models of the past; he transforms tradition by making Graham's jealousy retrospective. The novel not only describes concrete examples of this pathology but also contains metatextual pauses during which the main protagonist ponders over his own disease, trying to dissect its causes. This is an issue Barnes has struggled with and to which he attempted to provide provisional answers in an article entitled 'Remembrance of Things Past' (1983). After giving a series of examples, he explains in particular that retrospective jealousy, or 'retro-jealousy' as he calls it, usually 'broadens out into a wider obsession. That previous affair, that earlier lover turn out to be mere nominees for wider areas of baffled resentment: a kind of foolish rage against the immutability of the past and a metaphysical whinge at the fact that things can actually happen despite your absence.'[40] This obsessional rage is precisely what Graham suffers from and what turns his jealousy into a disease of the mind.

Asked about the reason why jealousy figures so much in his work, Barnes answers that it is 'novelistically attractive' as a theme because it is 'dramatic', 'frequently irrational, unfair, boundless, obsessing and horrible for all parties. It's the moment when something deeply primitive breaks the surface of our supposedly grown-up lives [like] the crocodile's snout in the lily pond. Irresistible.'[41] The allusion to the crocodile in Barnes's answer may remind the reader of the first epigraph to the novel, which clearly indicates that what is to follow will concern mechanisms of the brain in its deepest recesses. The passage, which Barnes originally found quoted by a friend of his, the famous Hungarian writer Arthur Koestler,[42] is taken from a medical journal whose bibliographical references are given with the utmost precision – 'Paul D. MacLean, *Journal of Nervous and Mental Diseases*, vol. CXXXV, No. 4, October 1962' (p. 5) – as though already announcing the meticulousness of the history lecturer. The long quotation records that man is endowed with three brains, the lower one reptilian, the second inherited from the lower mammals and the highest one late mammalian. Throughout the novel, the main protagonist reflects on the mechanisms of the human brain and Jack develops a version of that theory of the lower brains or 'the Sawn-Offs' (p. 75), 'the ones that control our emotions, make us kill people, fuck other people's wives, vote Tory, kick the dog' (p. 74), and the higher brains or 'Four-Eyes' (p. 75), which are 'socially acceptable' (p. 74). If Jack tries to reassure Graham by telling him that 'Most people don't kill other people. Most people have got the Sawn-Offs well under their thumb' (p. 75), the reader may foresee the triumph of the primitive brain when confronted with the title of the last chapter, 'The Horse and the Crocodile' (p. 161), which actually echoes the last sentence of the epigraph – 'when the psychiatrist bids the patient to lie on the couch, he is asking him to stretch out alongside a horse and a crocodile' (p. 5). Barnes explained in an interview that he chose this quotation as an epigraph because it 'absolutely fitted the novel . . . which is about a civilized man who finds that the horse and the crocodile have not gone away'. Because of this persistent reptilian mind, 'things which begin optimistically can turn into complete tragedy'.[43] As Moseley suggests, the first epigraph raises 'important questions of freedom and determinism'[44] since one wonders whether Graham will be able to keep his emotions under control or not. Matthew Pateman argues that the epigraph 'locates Hendrick within a strongly materialist conception of the self – a conception where the self is given [by] (or at least heavily determined by) biological and neuro-physiological factors'. Pateman adds that the novel keeps questioning 'the degree to which the brain is controller or controlled'.[45] Bill Greenwell, in his review of the novel, draws attention to this 'battle between our rational and irrational selves, the perennial and unfathomable failure to reconcile our instincts, emotions and intellect'.[46] Eventually in the novel, the horse and the crocodile take control, and Graham is convinced that this was his predetermined fate. Pateman concludes that Graham's choice 'is for a resigned acceptance of what he sees to be the natural narrative conclusion of his predicament',[47] whereas the tragic end is actually the result of a pathological form of jealousy.

French scholar Frédéric Monneyron was particularly interested in the mechanisms of Graham's brain as beset by jealousy, and devoted a whole chapter to *Before She Met Me* in his study of jealousy in literature, *L'Écriture de la jalousie* [*Writing Jealousy*] (1997).[48] Offering a psychoanalytical interpretation of the novel, he applauded the way in which Barnes laid bare the foundations of jealousy, revealed the phantasms attached to it and gave access to the unconscious of the main protagonist. According to Monneyron, Barnes's main achievement in the book lies in the way he juxtaposes jealousy and its interpretation, and offers the reader means to set him/herself free from it. Monneyron explains that in his desire for a total fusion with Ann, Graham cannot stand her absence and compensates for it by the phantasmatic creation of an imaginary rival and by erotic self-satisfactions such as masturbation. In his sexual dreams, he fantasises about Ann with her past lovers, which is a way of imaginatively possessing the intimacy of his partner and his rivals. Graham's obsession thus becomes pathological until his retrospective jealousy towards unidentified past rivals turns into a more traditional jealousy towards an identified present rival, Jack Lupton. Monneyron differentiates between the story proper, or diegesis, in which the resolution of jealousy can only be achieved through the murder of the rival, and the narrative discourse or narration, which offers the reader elements of interpretation of Graham's pathological attitude. He concludes from several introspective passages that Graham's jealousy originates from his infancy and is based on an idealisation of the mother, a forbidding of any desire for the mother by the father, and the ensuing threat of castration.[49] The scholar adds that Graham's jealousy is also marked by specific phantasms that have been identified by Sigmund Freud (1856–1939) in his analysis of its pathological forms. These concern, on the one hand, phantasms of infidelity towards Ann that have been suppressed or projected onto his partner (p. 45), and on the other hand, homosexual phantasms towards Jack, for example when he is about to murder him: 'In a funny way Graham was just as fond of Jack as he'd always been' (p. 165).

The psychoanalytical interpretation of the narrative, which is supported by the resemblance between Graham and Jack's regular conversations and a course of psychoanalytic treatment in which Graham would be the patient and Jack the analyst, releases some of the tension of the diegesis. Humour has the same function, as, according to Monneyron, it contributes to creating some distance between the reader and the grim events that are narrated. Barnes thus caricatures and stereotypes some of Graham's attitudes in order to ridicule them and to introduce comedy in a tragic plot. Monneyron also explains that Barnes displays irony towards the psychoanalytic interpretations that may be applied to his novel, by deriding a systematic and rigid use of the theory. For example, Jack reminds his audience of Freud's remark warning against any excessive resort to symbols: 'Sometimes a cigar … is only a cigar' (p. 138), and mocks the very foundations of the interpretation of dreams: 'Freud's interpretations of dreams were either obvious ("Woman walks up Kraustrasse, buys herself a black hat; the old buffoon charges her

5,000 krone to tell her she wants her husband to be dead") or unverifiably fantastic' (p. 139). Such passages bring comic relief and enable the reader to consider Graham's pathological jealousy, but also psychoanalytic interpretations of his attitude, from a distance.

Another insightful essay on the mechanisms of jealousy in *Before She Met Me* was written by Millington and Sinclair, who focused more particularly on the portrayal of the betrayed husband in works of literature that point to the organising principle of patriarchal societies, in which men exert their sexual authority and social power over women. Millington and Sinclair suggest that there are two models, or paradigms, for such portrayals, which they trace back to the English writer Geoffrey Chaucer (*c*.1343/4–1400) and the Italian writer Giovanni Boccaccio (?1313–75): either the husband is presented as a cuckold and is mocked for being much older than his wife and sexually impotent, or he is characterised as a man of honour who responds powerfully to his fate, usually by killing the unfaithful wife and her lover. In *Before She Met Me*, the two paradigms are not only mixed but also sometimes subverted. Thus, Graham originally seems to fit the model of the cuckold because he is older than Ann, less experienced sexually, and feels inadequate. Echoing Monneyron's interpretation of the novel, Millington and Sinclair suggest that Ann's sexual experience turns her 'into a kind of mother-figure which may create problems for Graham's sense of control over his own identity'.[50] On the other hand, Graham does not fit the model of the laughable cuckold as Ann seems satisfied with her sexual relations with him, and her supposed infidelity only pertains to the time before he met her. Graham thus departs from the model as exemplified by Chaucer and Boccaccio because he never receives any public humiliation as a result of Ann's unfaithfulness and therefore cannot be made a comic figure, to other characters at least.

After a while, moreover, Graham no longer corresponds to the model of the cuckold and seems to switch to that of the man of honour as he resorts to violence and kills Jack, just as Othello meant to kill his supposed rival, Cassio. However, Graham departs from the paradigm of the man of honour in that he then kills himself instead of Ann. According to Millington and Sinclair, this is the sign that Graham still feels inadequate and unable to cope with his grief, unless it is a way for him to inflict an emotional attack on Ann, who is made to witness his suicide powerlessly. Graham thus shares common points with both models, but also diverges from them in original ways. In Millington and Sinclair's view, his ultimate violent reaction against others and himself is 'characteristic of a patriarchal society which does not cope with male problems flexibly but which tries to control and deny them'.[51] Both critics suggest that patriarchy prevents men from expressing their emotions and therefore from dealing adequately with their own sufferings.

Part of Graham's suffering is more precisely due to the fact that he can no longer differentiate his own phantasms and fears from reality, an aspect that has been analysed by Matthew Pateman and myself.[52] Being a history lecturer, Graham should be adept at selecting and interpreting sources of information, but this proves impossible for him so that his version of history is deeply subjective. When reconstructing Ann's past and looking for proofs of her infidelity, Graham makes no selection among the archives: he includes the films in which Ann appeared as well as those in which her supposed lovers played a role, the reviews of these films, photographs, advertisements, coins from foreign countries Ann visited, matchboxes from places where she went. The reader may feel the irony in the following remark: 'There was no point in getting jealous unless you were accurate about it' (p. 60). However, Graham's so-called accuracy and lack of discrimination as a researcher undermine the validity of his conclusions: 'Sometimes he wasn't sure what constituted evidence' (p. 59). Pateman suggests that Graham's 'historical narrative is a montage of disparate forms, his self is an auto-generative self-fulfilling bricolage'.[53] Graham ends up constructing Ann's biography, hence perverting his role as a historian and resorting to the strategies of the fiction writer. He is clearly obsessed with uncovering the truth, just like any historian or detective, but inevitably becomes aware of the irretrievability of the past, a typically postmodernist topic.

The flaw in his method lies in the fact that Graham, despite being a historian, confuses art and life, fiction and reality, his wife as constructed by his imagination and her real self. As John Mellors remarks, the book is the 'illustration of an educated rational being's disintegration when illusion takes over from reality'.[54] Graham's doubts are partly provoked by his own dreams, during which Ann's past lovers luridly describe her sexual life. Instead of vanishing in the morning, the dreams persist in the daytime. Graham first attempts to convince himself of the ontological dichotomy and incompatibility between dreams and reality: 'Dreams couldn't be true, could they: that was why they were dreams' (p. 84). But he also attributes a revelatory function to his dreams, suggesting that they can reveal truths about past reality – he calls them 'post-monitory dreams' (p. 84). Thus, when in one of his dreams, actors tell him that Ann was keen on making love with four men at the same time, he starts wavering: 'What if it were true? It couldn't be true. . . . No, it couldn't be true. But what if it referred to a sort of truth?' (p. 90). Graham takes such fantasies as sources of information, pieces of evidence, if not facts, and thus invalidates the very concept of truth.

Graham's confusion of art and life is also due to his inability to differentiate between Ann's sexual activity on screen and off screen, both of which he considers as acts of adultery. If he first opposes two categories of films, with on the one hand fictive sexual acts and on the other hand effective sexual acts, the two categories then tend to become indistinguishable: '[They] were beginning to get blurred in his head' (p. 92). The ultimate stage consists in looking in the novels of his friend, the fiction writer Jack Lupton, for clues as to his affair with Ann. This confusion of reality and fiction constitutes what Brian McHale in *Postmodernist Fiction* (1987) calls a 'violation of ontological boundaries'.[55] Graham no longer makes any distinction between what is fact and what is fiction so that his biography of his wife is warped. As Pateman wrote, 'Graham's construction is a total fabrication, an arbitrary narrative threaded between disparate states and forms that he believes to be true: he invents his own referent.'[56]

We may add that Ann also creates her own referent when she willingly decides to transform the past – 'I'm sorry to rewrite your past for you' (p. 67) – and obliterate her affair with Jack: 'I've decided we never had an affair' (p. 66). However, Ann and Jack's attitude cannot be confused with that of Graham as, according to Pateman, they 'knowingly lie'.[57] They indeed still know the ontological difference between reality and their own invention, a knowledge which is not shared by Graham. Their attempt to rewrite the past will nevertheless fail as Graham will be convinced of finding evidence of their affair within Jack's own novels. Once again, the frontiers between reality and fiction blur: Jack's supposedly fictional books actually reveal the truth because, as Moseley puts it, he 'lacks the imagination to make up his novels and must rely on disguised versions of his friends and altered retellings of his own life'.[58]

Even though *Before She Met Me* may appear to revert to traditional strategies in its narration and characterisation, the debate which it triggers on the blurring of ontological frontiers between fiction and reality, as epitomised by the coexistence of a history lecturer and a fiction writer, is typically postmodernist. As Bruce Sesto wrote, 'The paradox implicit in having, as central character, a historian who predicates his theoretical conclusions on cinematic "fiction" rather than on empirical "fact" embodies the contemporary novel's concern with the problematical relationship between fiction and historiography [the writing of history]'.[59] This debate as to the relationships between fiction and history, art and life, already announces the main topic of Barnes's next novel, to be published two years later, *Flaubert's Parrot*.

If some aspects of *Before She Met Me* may remind the reader of *Metroland* and foreshadow *Flaubert's Parrot*, the novel is, however, marked by a style, a tone, a general atmosphere that differ greatly from Barnes's other books. One should note that *Before She Met Me* was released in 1982, when Barnes had already published two detective novels under the pseudonym of Dan Kavanagh and was to publish another two in the years to come. In France, *Before She Met Me* appeared in 1991, nine years after its publication in Great Britain, and at the same time as *Putting the*

*Boot In*, Dan Kavanagh's third detective novel, so that journalists often reviewed the two books simultaneously and spotted similarities between them. Thus, Nicole Zand in *Le Monde* compared *Before She Met Me* to an investigation by a detective, before reviewing Kavanagh's detective novel.[60] In England, back in 1982, Anthony Thwaite had remarked that *Before She Met Me* 'seems to follow on from his pseudonymous "Duffy" novels',[61] while the American scholar Merritt Moseley described *Before She Met Me* as 'combining the social observation, comedy, and verbal dexterity of *Metroland* with the queasy moral atmosphere and proximity to violence of *Duffy*'.[62] The next chapter will attempt to define the specific features of these detective novels, which seem to stand apart in Barnes's production.

# CHAPTER THREE

# Barnes/Kavanagh, a Janus-faced Writer: *Duffy* (1980), *Fiddle City* (1981), *Putting the Boot In* (1985) and *Going to the Dogs* (1987)

In 1980, Julian Barnes published both his first novel under his own name, *Metroland*, and his first detective novel, *Duffy*, under the pseudonym of Dan Kavanagh, using the surname of his wife, literary agent Pat Kavanagh, to whom almost all Barnes's books are dedicated. Kavanagh published four detective novels from 1980 to 1987 – *Duffy* (1980), *Fiddle City* (1981), *Putting the Boot In* (1985) and *Going to the Dogs* (1987) – and a short story, 'The 50p Santa. A Duffy Detective Story' (1985). Before focusing on the Kavanagh books proper, the reader may wonder why Barnes should have decided to publish his detective fiction under a pseudonym. It is relatively common for a journalist to use pseudonyms and Barnes alternatively took the name of Edward Pygge, author of satirical pieces in the 'Greek Street' column of the *New Review* from 1976 to 1978, Edwina Pygge, PC49, Fat Jeff, Russell Davies, Marion Lloyd or Basil Seal. Basil Seal is the name of the roguish protagonist of Evelyn Waugh's *Black Mischief* (1932) and *Put Out More Flags* (1942), a name which Barnes used for his activities as a restaurant critic for the *Tatler*, who was Gourmet Writer of the Year in 1981 and actually became so well known as to be referred to in *Going to the Dogs* – at one point, a female protagonist, Lucretia, for whose wealthy family Duffy is investigating, addresses the following remark to the detective: 'I'm reading a fairly good restaurant critic called Basil Seal in a magazine called the *Tatler*' (p. 592). Through a literary strategy of internal focalisation, Duffy is shown, for his part, to denigrate the critic's job that Barnes had nevertheless occupied for several years: 'Lucretia returned to Basil Berk writing about the Golden Sausage in the *Wankers' Monthly*' (p. 592). Barnes, hiding behind Kavanagh, himself protected by Duffy, proves here particularly derisive towards his double. In an interview, Barnes remarked: 'Basil had a lot of terrible prejudices and didn't care what he said.'[1]

These pseudonyms proved useful because they enabled the author to create new personalities for himself and to write particularly scathing articles. For example, his pieces written in the *New Review* as Edward Pygge, which Simon Banner qualified as 'celebratedly waspish',[2] benefited greatly from the fact that people did not know who their author was: 'you definitely didn't want it to come out who you were, because then you wouldn't hear so many stories'.[3] These articles also testify to the writer's ventriloquism, as Barnes himself suggested: 'I suppose in a way it was another fictional voice.'[4] It is interesting to note that Barnes stopped using pseudonyms for his journalistic activities in the 1980s when he became a full-time novelist, as if his former experiments in ventriloquism had worked as a prologue to his fictional creations. These games of hide-and-seek also reveal the author's knack for mischievous manipulations, hoaxes and tricks, which can often destabilise the reader.

Barnes's most famous pseudonym is of course that of Dan Kavanagh, whose detective novels feature a recurrent hero, Nick Duffy, a bisexual ex-policeman who was sacked for a sex case and became a security agent and private detective. Critic Alan Clinton draws a parallel between the bisexual surname of the author – 'Dan' is male, but 'Kavanagh' is the name of Barnes's wife – and the bisexuality of the main character. Barnes justified the bisexuality of his detective from the setting of the first novel: '*Duffy* was set in Soho around the sex industry, and I thought it would be interesting, if you were moving in a morally ambiguous world, to have a character who was sexually ambiguous as well.'[5] Alan Clinton argues, however, that 'the bisexuality of Detective Duffy can be read in another sense as a somewhat autobiographical representation of Barnes's own ambivalence as a writer', being both a 'serious' novelist and the author of popular detective fiction.[6] With his detective production, Barnes changes not only his name but also his personality as the modes and conditions of writing are themselves modified. While it took Barnes eight years to write *Metroland*, the first draft of *Duffy* was composed in just nine days and was revised in three days. That was part of Barnes's experiment, who wanted to test 'what it would be like writing as fast as I possibly could in a concentrated way'.[7] He found out that the strain was different for Kavanagh's and Barnes's books: 'Writing Kavanagh novels is a sort of relaxation after two or three years spent writing novels under my own name.'[8] Circumstances of composition are also different since Kavanagh does not use the same typewriter as Barnes and he leaves London to go to the cottage of Ruth Rendell (born 1930) – who also takes a pseudonym, that of Barbara Vine, to write some of her detective fiction – in order to compose his novels: 'They come out of a different part of the brain', Barnes insists.[9] As a consequence, he created apocryphal lives for Kavanagh and wrote on the dust-jacket of each book the biographical notes of his double, each time different and facetious. If the date of birth of Kavanagh – 1946 – and the place where he lives – North Islington – are indeed those of Barnes, all other information is invented. Thus, Kavanagh was befittingly born in County Sligo in Ireland and his adolescence is variously described as boisterous, uncompromising or quiet. The name of his invented mother, Betty Corrinder, recurs in an anecdote about a woman of easy virtue in *Flaubert's Parrot* (pp. 193–4). The author is said to have been a deckhand on a Liberian tanker but also a rodeo cowboy, waiter-on-roller-skates, bouncer in a gay bar, baggage handler, bar pianist in Macao, goalkeeper, steer-wrestler and assistant marshal at Romford greyhound stadium. Kavanagh's French publisher proved extremely cautious as the biographical notes are followed by a sentence in parentheses: 'Biographical note given by the author and published with no guarantee as to its accuracy.' To the journalists who were baffled by such contradictory and lurid notices, the Janus-faced writer would mischievously say: 'Anything you need to add, please invent.'[10] This attitude fits in with the usual ironic and humorous attitude of Barnes, who is found playing a new hoax on the reader.

Apart from this playful state of mind, Barnes explains his split personality in the following way: 'I knew I wanted to write several thrillers and I didn't know what would come in what order, and I didn't want to be the author of *Metroland* and three thrillers all under the same name.'[11] Part Dr Jekyll, part Mr Hyde, Barnes–Kavanagh insists on keeping his two identities separate, using his surname for his supposedly 'noble', high-brow, mainstream or literary novels. Kavanagh has, for his part, drawn attention to the potentialities of the thriller: 'I believe that the traditional novel, as practised in England and Ireland, is an exhausted genre. True creativity lies in those hitherto despised domains of "sub-literature" – the ballad, the folk poem, the thriller – just as the true energy of a nation comes, not from its soft capital city, but from its extremities, from its despised and downtrodden citizens.'[12] The detective novel as a genre is often considered as part of popular and low-brow literature, even though in recent years several writers have tried to abolish this hierarchy between 'serious' and popular genres by mixing them. Kavanagh's detective novels, however, do not seem to overlap with Barnes's more literary books. As Martha Duffy suggested, they 'read fast and gamy, and – rare for a learned man who takes to writing suspense – they contain virtually no literary allusions'.[13]

During a public meeting in October 1987 on the subject of the detective novel, in which Ruth Rendell also took part, Kavanagh turned up and the secret of his identity, ill-kept until then anyway, was fully revealed. A few days earlier, a photograph of Kavanagh crossing Archway

Bridge in London had actually appeared on the front page of the *London Review of Books*.[14] During the public debate, both Rendell and Kavanagh gave the same reason for their use of an alter ego for their detective novels, i.e. 'the freedom to indulge in more direct social criticism'.[15] Kavanagh indeed presents characters who come from underprivileged social backgrounds, often blighted by drugs and racketeering, and depicts a corrupt, brutal, racist and intolerant society. In *Duffy*, the most successful of the four, the eponymous detective finds himself involved in the circles of prostitution and pornography of the seedy Soho sex clubs. Reviewers praised the realism of the evocations of London, which compensated for what David Montrose considered an 'unexceptional plot'.[16] In *Fiddle City*, which Montrose found less impressive than *Duffy* even though fascinating in some ways, Duffy investigates illicit drug traffic going through Heathrow airport, renamed 'Thiefrow' or 'Fiddle City' (p. 204). Richard Brown praised the way in which both *Duffy* and *Fiddle City* provide 'vivid low-life detail'.[17]

In *Putting the Boot In*, football and finance are fiercely opposed as property developers attempt by any means to transform the site of the football stadium into a shopping mall, a leisure centre and blocks of flats. The theme of the novel reflects Barnes/Kavanagh's keen interest in sports, and in football in particular. Barnes, who was born in Leicester but left the city six weeks later, is indeed a great fan of Leicester City Football Club, a mid-table team whose lack of achievement makes supporting them 'a form of suffering'.[18] In his review of *Putting the Boot In*, French journalist François Rivière particularly saluted Kavanagh's attention to verisimilitude, which he finds rare in the British detective genre.[19] Montrose, on the contrary, judged the book 'an outright disappointment' and described it as 'a lacklustre picture of lower division football coupled with a familiar plot'.[20] In an interview with a Romanian scholar, Barnes revealed that he was well aware of the criticisms directed against his detective fiction: 'one of the complaints about my thrillers was that they were all atmosphere, character and menace, and not enough plot'.[21] Eventually, in *Going to the Dogs*, Duffy has to penetrate the mystery of a privileged family, corrupted by drugs, and the novel highlights the gulf which lies between the idle parvenus of Braunscombe Hall and the working-class background of the detective. In the four books, even though most parts of each novel focus on Duffy, whose point of view is predominant, the device of a third-person or heterodiegetic narrator allows for suspense and the withholding of information.

As Barnes himself indicated, Kavanagh's detective novels are more focused on social reality and actual life than Barnes's books: 'Maybe because in the detective novels I have more freedom to speak of actual life.'[22] This sense of freedom when writing detective novels has repeatedly been underlined by the author. For example, he mentioned that not using his own surname gave him 'a curious liberating effect'. It allowed him to adopt a different, maybe more provocative and undoubtedly freer tone, and to deal with subjects that are often shocking: 'you could indulge any fantasies of violence you might have'.[23] He gives as an example the episode in *Duffy*, as soon as the end of the first chapter, when Kavanagh has a cat spit-roasted, a sadistic act in a country deeply protective of animals, which he would not have dared portray in a Barnes novel. The Kavanagh novels are clearly characterised by the recurrence of violent scenes involving torture, aggression, pornography and an endless violation of ethical laws, even though Merritt Moseley argues that the level of violence in the Duffy books, while shocking to British readers, is 'fairly low by American standards'.[24] The style of the four novels reflects the underprivileged social background in which the detective lives and works, with its array of thugs, criminals and drug-addicts. It is marked by a blatant oral dimension and a colloquial and even vulgar tone. Duffy often resorts to police slang, for example when he repeatedly refers to the force as 'the blues' (p. 59) or the area where he works as 'my patch'.

In his chapter entitled 'Duffy' – the only extensive analysis of the detective novels, which have not attracted much critical attention until now – Moseley argues that the four books meet the conventional expectations of the detective novel. He also underlines the clear separation between Barnes's two literary identities and the two types of narrative strategies he employs:

■ One might hypothesize that the traditionalist side of Julian Barnes, the part of him that appreciates straightforward narration, the management of suspense, and a fairly clear moral taxonomy among the characters, has gone into the making of the Duffy books, leaving him free in his other novels to experiment, to rearrange or dispense with narrative chronology, to be playful about the relationship between art and life.[25] □

This is actually what Alexander Stuart had hypothesised a few years before: 'Perhaps the straightforward storytelling of the "Duffy" books frees Barnes to experiment more widely with his more literary books?'[26] Mark Lawson, for his part, suggests that the literary split may be seen by future biographers as 'indicative of the tension between the cerebral and the accessible'.[27] Richard Brown argues that the Duffy novels were beneficial to Barnes, as they 'helped give Barnes some street-credibility and may also have served to keep his desire to be sensational out of the mainstream fiction'.[28] Charles Moritz is one of the rare critics who pointed to similarities between Barnes and Kavanagh, who 'have in common a narrative smoothness and a satirical edge'.[29]

More specifically, the private detective's quest for truth and his sometimes debatable methods of approaching it may remind the reader of

Graham Hendrick's pathological investigation into the truth of his wife's past in *Before She Met Me*, but they also foreshadow the obsession with truth of Barnes's later protagonists in *Flaubert's Parrot* or *Staring at the Sun*. The detective pattern becomes a narrative model in many contemporary novels which are concerned with the retrospective retrieval of the past, and Duffy's inquiries thus bear some relation to the investigations of some of Barnes's protagonists. Moreover, Duffy's ambivalent relation to truth may announce Barnes's own relativist theories, as developed in the 'Parenthesis' of *A History of the World in 10½ Chapters*. Indeed, in *Duffy*, the private detective confesses to having 'a slightly flexible approach to the truth': 'Most of the time you stuck to the truth as closely as you could, but were prepared to bend with the breeze if necessary. Sometimes, for instance, it might be necessary to tell a little lie, fiddle your notebook just a bit, in order to make sure that a much bigger lie didn't get to pass itself off as the truth' (p. 48).

Despite a few echoes in theme, style and tone – mostly of *Before She Met Me* – the four detective novels differ greatly from the books by Barnes. The dichotomy between the two types of writing is blatant and even claimed by the author: 'Kavanagh wanted to experiment with the conventions of the thriller genre and a "streetier style" without disappointing readers of Julian Barnes.'[30] The verb 'experiment' here sounds odd as it is usually applied to the Barnes books and does not really fit in with the straightforward and conventional narration that critics perceived in the Duffy books. On the other hand, the notion of a 'streetier style' is absolutely convincing as the corrupt and gruff London underworld is aptly rendered. François Rivière particularly values Kavanagh's depiction of Cockney London and its morals, and compares his talent to that of famous thriller writers such as Edgar Wallace (1875–1932), James Hadley Chase (1906–88), Peter Cheyney (1896–1951) and Dick Francis (born 1920). He also suggests that the world staged in *Putting the Boot In* oscillates between that of P. G. Wodehouse (1881–1975) and the comic book *Andy Capp* by Reg Smythe (1917–88).[31] Moseley, for his part, compares the character of Duffy to the 'fictional American detectives of the hard-boiled school associated with Raymond Chandler [1888–1951]' and dismisses any similarity to Hercule Poirot and Miss Marple, the detectives created by Agatha Christie (1904–66), or to Roderick Alleyn, the gentlemanly police officer who features in the novels of Ngaio Marsh (1895–1982).[32]

Within the narration itself, Duffy is presented in contrast or in comparison with famous detectives. Thus, even though Duffy's method entails discreet infiltration and thorough knowledge of a place, for example when he investigates the Soho sex clubs in *Duffy*, he shares none of the mysticism of Chief Inspector Maigret in the novels of Georges Simenon (1903–89), on which he ironises: 'you didn't stand in the middle of Soho, mystically sniffing the air like Maigret, and then head off and run a villain to ground' (p. 60). Despite this mischievous remark, one should note that Barnes admires Simenon greatly, to the extent that he wrote an essay on the Belgian writer, later collected in *Something to Declare* (pp. 99–108), and even impersonated the voice of Simenon for a series of four Maigret episodes released by BBC Radio 4 in December 2002. Simon O'Hagan praised Barnes's performance and expressiveness as Simenon, adding that Barnes delivers his lines 'with the surest of bedside-manner touches'.[33]

If Duffy shirks from an identification with Maigret, he welcomes on the other hand the comparison with Raymond Chandler's protagonists, for example through a clever intertextual allusion to the American writer's famous quote from his essay 'The Simple Art of Murder' (1945) – 'But down these mean streets a man must go who is not himself mean, who is neither tarnished nor afraid' – which recurs slightly modified in *Fiddle City*: 'Down these chow main streets a man must go' (p. 272). The intertextual hint is, however, ironic as Duffy does not strictly correspond to Chandler's ideal portrait of the detective as one who is neither 'mean' nor 'tarnished', but is 'a man of honor' and 'the best man in his world'.[34] Duffy's concept of a moral code is more flexible. As Moseley suggests, Duffy 'is both finely ethical and legally slippery', an ambivalent attitude which is mainly due to his social status.[35] As the narrator of *Duffy* explains, Duffy was made to resign from the force after having been framed by fellow policemen who arranged to find him in bed with a young man aged nineteen. If his former girlfriend Carol, a police officer, sometimes helps him with his criminal investigations, Duffy is neverthe-less regarded with suspicion by the police. As Moseley remarks, he 'occu-pies a legal shadowland'[36] since he sometimes needs to act illegally or to fiddle evidence in order to solve crimes and arrest villains, not an unusual stance for hard-boiled detectives. As stated in *Duffy*, he is not 'idealistic about the law, or about how it was implemented'; on the contrary, 'Duffy's moral outlook had always been pragmatic' (p. 275). Despite this adaptability, Duffy also believes in absolutes that cannot be borne – murder, bent coppers, rape and heroin (p. 275) – which explains why he is still trying to maintain a fairly coherent moral code, 'fixing the record in favour of justice' (p. 48).

Moseley draws attention to characteristics that place Duffy firmly in the 'hard-boiled' tradition, more particularly 'the marginal existence, the alienation and estrangement'.[37] Duffy is indeed a solitary figure, living on his own and beset by obsessive habits and phobias. For example, his phobia of clocks and watches leads him to banish them from his one-room flat and to arrange for 'a Tupperware box in the bathroom marked "Watches" for those who stayed the night' (p. 36). Sexually dissatisfied, he has one-night stands with men and women alike in the first two novels, and maintains an intimate friendship with his former girlfriend, Carol. Duffy is also firmly characterised by identifying features such as the gold stud in his left ear (p. 36), which will be jerked from his ear with pliers by Gleeson in *Fiddle City*.

Kavanagh also sticks to the hard-boiled conventions by writing openings which are both striking and violent, foreshadowing the investigation to come. These thresholds to the novels enable Kavanagh to wink at his attentive reader through echoes between or within his books. Thus, the opening sentence of *Duffy* – 'The day they cut Mrs McKechnie, not much else happened in West Byfleet' (p. 3) – is paralleled by that of *Fiddle City* – 'The day they crashed McKay, not much else happened on the M4' (p. 181). The anaphora (the repetition of the same words at the beginning of sentences) goes as far as the near homonymy (the same sound and spelling) of the characters involved (McKechnie, McKay), while the act of violence (cut, crashed) is committed by mysterious and frightening anonymous agents (they) and is too elliptical to be fully understood at first reading. The end of each sentence eventually broadly situates the scene of the crime (in West Byfleet, on the M4). In *Putting the Boot In*, the first sentence – 'There are too many ways of breaking a footballer's leg' – appears both as the beginning of the first part (p. 355) and as the first sentence of the second part (p. 365), the repetition doubling the outrageous nature of the message. Finally, *Going to the Dogs* starts with an ambiguous sentence – 'There was a body in the library' (p. 543) – which invokes the title of Agatha Christie's second Miss Marple novel, *The Body in the Library* (1942), thus alluding to English country house detective fiction. The author here manages to lure the reader, as the body, which anybody would picture as human, turns out in the last sentence of the chapter to be that of a dog, echoing both the figurative title of the book and *Duffy*, in which the cat is found spit-roasted in the last sentence of the first chapter.

Even though the four novels make a coherent whole, the reader may note an evolution in the characterisation and the themes over the years, foreshadowing the writer's distancing of himself from the genre. In *Putting the Boot In*, Duffy is constantly preoccupied with AIDS and, as a consequence, no longer has carefree sex. The atmosphere is thus slightly different from that of the two preceding novels, in which Duffy was portrayed as promiscuous and in which sex scenes were numerous. Moseley draws attention to the artful construction of the novel, divided into five parts named after the different stages of a football game. While parts One – 'Warm-Up' – Three – 'Half-Time' – and Five – 'Extra Time' – focus in the present, on Duffy playing a football game with the Western Sunday Reliables, parts Two – 'First Half' – and Four – 'Second Half' – deal retrospectively with Duffy's investigation into the various violent and illegal assaults made on the Athletic football team to provoke its relegation. Past and present are thus intertwined and bring variation to the set form of detective fiction. Originality also springs from the fact that the case, though partly solved by Duffy, leads to no prosecution whatsoever. According to Moseley, these changes may reflect 'Barnes's impatience with the standard format', which may have come to feel 'too constricting' for him.[38] Kavanagh's next novel, *Going to the Dogs*, also drifts away from the standard crime thriller, through social commentary on class clashes and a closer focus on the personality and life of the main protagonist. As Moseley suggests again, 'this refusal to hew to the rigidities of the detective format, may be a symptom of Barnes's growing impatience with the Duffy pattern'.[39] According to the critic, such keen interest in peripheral issues makes *Going to the Dogs* 'the most consciously artistic, the most witty, the most self-aware of the Duffy series' but also 'the least satisfying crime thriller', which may explain why it has been the last Kavanagh book to date.[40]

Since 1987, Kavanagh has not published any new detective novel and it was up to Barnes to explain this silence. Therefore, in April 1991, Barnes indicated that Kavanagh, jealous of Barnes's success, was sick and resting in hospital.[41] He would confirm that in January 1996: 'Poor old Dan. He is very sick. He hasn't written anything for years. He's jealous of my success,'[42] before eventually announcing his retirement for being 'not really interested in the procedural or psychological side of crime'.[43] Barnes also confessed to finding a 'recyclable hero more tiresome than he expected'[44] and realised that it was not 'easier to write a series of novels with running characters, but . . . almost more hampering' because of the constraints in terms of characterisation.[45] If he does not disown his thrillers, Barnes nevertheless admits he never rereads them and therefore has no definite opinion on them. Some critics interpreted Kavanagh's retirement as a sign that the writer did not feel he could renew the genre any more, but Barnes gave a more practical reason: 'The serious answer is that he [Kavanagh] existed when I had more energy to burn off fictionally than I do now. When I get into my study these days, the thing I want to write is the next Barnes.'[46] It is certainly no coincidence that Kavanagh should have stopped writing after 1987, that is after Barnes's overwhelming success with his third novel, *Flaubert's Parrot*, which will be examined in the next chapter.

# CHAPTER FOUR

# Postmodernist Experimentation: *Flaubert's Parrot* (1984)

*Flaubert's Parrot*, Julian Barnes's most celebrated book worldwide, marked a decisive step in the writer's career, garnering acclaim from readers, critics and scholars alike. The book was shortlisted for the Booker Prize in 1984, won the Geoffrey Faber Memorial Award in 1985 and the Prix Médicis in the non-fiction category in France in 1986. It was the first novel by Barnes to be translated and it enabled the writer to publish his two earlier novels in the United States and later have them translated into many languages. To this date, *Flaubert's Parrot* remains the book that reviewers and journalists inevitably refer to when presenting the author or his later novels. Asked whether he minded being still best known for *Flaubert's Parrot* despite having published so many books since, Barnes answered in the negative and gave another literary example: 'Kingsley Amis was once asked if *Lucky Jim* was an albatross around his neck, and he said it was better than not having a bloody albatross at all. That's my perspective.'[1]

In an interview, Barnes said he could date the beginning or 'moment of ignition' for *Flaubert's Parrot* very precisely.[2] This took place in September 1981 in Rouen. He had been commissioned to write a guide to the houses of French writers and artists, which never came to fruition, but among the places he visited were the Flaubert museum and Flaubert's house in Croisset where he saw the two parrots that gave him the idea for a story.[3] When *Flaubert's Parrot* appeared some three years later, it proved baffling to reviewers, who found it hard to define, being a hybrid book which challenges any attempt at categorisation, classification and genre taxonomy. The paratexts (which Gérard Genette defines as 'thresholds' to the text and which are liminal devices such as the title, subtitle, epigraph, dedication, preface, cover, blurb . . .)[4] tend to confuse the reader rather than clarify the genre. The front cover of the Picador paperback edition,

of 1985, shows extracts from various reviews, and three of its distin-
guished authors – John Irving (born 1942), John Fowles (born 1926) and
Graham Greene – refer to *Flaubert's Parrot* as a novel. The American
edition (Knopf, 1984) defines it as 'a novel (in disguise)', while the
French edition (Stock, 1986) daringly printed 'novel' on the front cover.
In the Picador edition, the biographical note on the author counts
*Flaubert's Parrot* among Barnes's novels. However, in the blurb that many
would read before buying the book, one reviewer refers to *Flaubert's
Parrot* as 'part novel, part stealthy literary criticism'. Moreover, the
epigraph to the book guides the reader towards a biography: 'When you
write the biography of a friend, you must do it as if you were taking
*revenge* for him' (p. vii),[5] while the table of contents mixes several genres,
as the titles of chapters reveal: 'Chronology', 'Bestiary', 'Train-spotter's
Guide', 'Dictionary', 'Examination Paper' (p. ix). One should be
extremely wary about paratexts and titles, as the narrator himself suggests
within the book when he refers to *Mémoires intérieurs* (1959) by François
Mauriac (1885–1970): 'He writes his "*Mémoires*", but they aren't his
memoirs' (p. 108).

Reviewers and critics were therefore at a loss and most of them
insisted on the hybrid dimension of the text, qualifying the book as 'a
kind of collage',[6] 'a *tour de force* of fiction, criticism, and biography
combined',[7] 'a clever, if at times gamesy, compendium of genres'.[8] In a
private letter, Philip Larkin told Barnes that, in his 'extraordinary and
haunting book', he had used Flaubert 'to write a – a what? Search me, O
Lord, as someone says. I should hate to have to review it.'[9] David Lodge
argued that the form may actually derive from a much older genre:
'Deconstructionists hailed it as an exemplary poststructuralist text. More
traditional literary scholars might categorize it as a Menippean satire' – a
genre that takes its name from its supposed originator, the third-century
BC Greek Cynic philosopher Menippus. Lodge draws his definition of
Menippean satire from the Russian critic and literary theorist Mikhail
Bakhtin (1895–1975), who saw it as 'characterized . . . by "an extraordinary freedom of plot and philosophical invention," "sharp contrasts and
oxymoronic combinations," and "a wide use of inserted genres" '.[10]
Asked about the genesis of the book, Barnes answered: 'I had always
wanted to do something about Flaubert, but I knew I did not want to
write any sort of biography or any sort of work of criticism.'[11] This
impatience with these latter categories may explain why Barnes chose
instead to combine an array of genres. In another interview, however, the
writer claimed that he could not 'think of *Flaubert's Parrot* as anything
except a novel',[12] even though he later conceded that it was 'an upside
down, informal piece of novel–biography'.[13]

Andrzej Gasiorek's originality consisted in qualifying the book as an
'intellectual whodunnit'[14] – reminded maybe of Dan Kavanagh's own

production – as the narrator, Geoffrey Braithwaite, uses the methods of the sleuth who follows all possible tracks, accumulates information and tries to solve a mystery, that of Gustave Flaubert's life, but also that of the stuffed parrot. Thus, the detective genre is subverted, as the object which forms the basis of the investigation looks ludicrous, being no valuable work of art, but just a stuffed parrot. Moreover, the narrator starts his enquiry in the first chapter but completely ignores it in the central thirteen chapters before coming back to it in the final chapter. There, one of the first sentences is full of irony and self-mockery: 'it took me almost two years to solve the Case of the Stuffed Parrot' (p. 216) – the capital letters grant a solemn aspect to a case that nevertheless seems trivial. The genre of the detective novel is all the more subverted as no resolution to the enigma of the parrots is proposed. The novel ends with a sentence which stands alone as a paragraph and marks the triumph of indeterminacy: 'Perhaps it was one of them' (p. 229).

Another unexpected qualification for the novel appeared in France where the Medicis literary jury awarded *Flaubert's Parrot* a prize as an 'essai', which certainly seems surprising for a book containing a fictional framework and fictive characters. However, Barnes countered in an interview that 'essay' in English is 'strictly non-fictional', as opposed to 'essai' in French, which is 'a much broader term' and can refer to 'something broadly imaginative'.[15] James Fenton, one of Barnes's friends, whose poem 'A German Requiem' is partly reproduced within *Flaubert's Parrot* (p. 133), chose a much vaguer term to qualify the book: 'we can very easily forget that the book in front of us is a novel at all. It doesn't *look* like a novel, particularly. It looks like a *thing* . . . like a dictionary, a set of lecture notes, an examination paper and – yes – a short story or two, a disquisition, an argument.'[16] The indeterminate word 'thing' reminds one of a practice common since the 1970s which consists in rejecting genre taxonomy and referring to books simply as 'texts', a practice alluded to with mockery and irony by the narrator: 'Contemporary critics who pompously reclassify all novels and plays and poems as texts' (p. 98). And indeed, after many hesitations, Spanish scholar Ramón Suárez ended up qualifying the book as simply 'text'.[17]

*Flaubert's Parrot* thus appears as ungraspable as far as genre taxonomy is concerned. It resembles the piglet smeared with grease and released into the dance, which Braithwaite refers to in the first chapter (p. 5). Such debates, however, throw doubt on the relevance of generic classification, which tends to erase the singularity of texts rather than highlight their wealth and depth: 'It's a pity you have to classify', Barnes regretted.[18] The writer even specified that such taxonomic concerns should never hamper composition but appear later, for publication: 'When you're actually writing a book, you've got a sense of a complete freedom from categorization.'[19] Calling *Flaubert's Parrot* a novel may, after all, be appropriate since the form is flexible and changing – as the term 'novel' itself suggests – and is very often composed of a mixture of other genres. Mikhail Bakhtin thus argued that the novel takes part in what he calls the 'carnivalisation of literature', meaning that it mixes genres, styles and languages in a heterogeneous whole. This is precisely what occurs in *Flaubert's Parrot*, an aspect which has drawn the attention of various critics and is one of the most recurrent features of postmodernist literature. Far from feeling bound by conventions or strict rules, Barnes appears to advocate innovation and attempts to renew the outmoded, worn-out, exhausted forms and genres of the past by mixing them. *Flaubert's Parrot* therefore exhibits a proclivity for hybridity, multiplicity and decompartmentalisation, and the mixture of genres enables the narrator to approach Flaubert in original and varied ways and to avoid the pitfalls of each individual genre. At the time of the book's composition, Barnes was very well aware of what such heterogeneity entailed: 'I found myself excitedly wondering how far I could push the constraints of traditional narrative: how far I could distort and fragment the narrative line while still keeping (I hoped) a continuous and rising expectation in the reader.'[20]

Taking into account the risk of dislocation, Patti White analyses more particularly Barnes's repeated use of an unusual form in *Flaubert's Parrot*: the list. She explains that lists and catalogues testify to a rigorous quest for exhaustiveness, but questions the relevance of such forms, 'forms inevitably foregrounding the struggle to maintain a secure categorical border and stabilize an enclosed data pool constantly threatened by structural collapse or chaotic intrusion'.[21] White argues that the obsessive ordering of data, similar to the encyclopaedic approach of the two copyists in Flaubert's *Bouvard and Pécuchet*, paradoxically creates chaos because such data are trivial and anecdotal, and therefore cannot lead to a coherent and total apprehension of Flaubert. William Bell concurs, suggesting that the list itself is 'a form of randomness'.[22] Patti White – but also French scholar Catherine Bernard in an insightful essay[23] – goes on to compare Braithwaite's task to that of the museum or the encyclopedia, which attempt to impose order and coherence upon a set of disparate fragments. This simile is implicitly provided in the first chapter through the description of the two Flaubert museums, in which the heterogeneity of objects prevails (pp. 15, 21). White's conclusion is original as she argues that even though constructed out of fragments, 'the work functions as an integrated whole', as 'a realization not of a Flaubert biography, but of a coherent and comprehensible narrative project whose subject is finally itself'.[24] Frank Kermode, in his review of the novel, also insisted on this sense of coherence: 'the book does feel disorderly at times, but it is true to the laws of its own being'.[25]

Tania Shepherd, on the contrary, was mainly struck by the chaotic, discontinuous and seemingly haphazard composition of the novel and has therefore attempted to highlight the underlying organisation of *Flaubert's Parrot* through a computerised linguistic analysis of this non-narrative text, which enabled her to identify simple and complex lexical repetitions. Having established that neither temporal sequence nor causality can justify the succession of chapters, she verified that the first and last chapters can be considered as the 'initiating and closing kernels'[26] of the same narrative about the quest for a stuffed parrot, which is, however, never fully developed in the intervening chapters. She then posited that the biographical subject matter introduced in the second chapter, 'Chronology', functions as a paradigmatic axis which is recycled in various non-narrative forms in the next twelve chapters, with the sequence apparently based on mere juxtaposition. Shepherd noted, however, that these chapters could not be read in random order because of the insertion of three types of material: first, the fictional story of the narrator and his wife, which is slowly revealed by fragments and whose gaps are filled step by step; then, the repeated allusions to Flaubert's *Dictionary of Accepted Ideas*, which prepare the reader for an understanding of chapter 12, 'Braithwaite's Dictionary of Received Ideas'; and finally, the verbatim repetition of quotations from Flaubert, which establishes links between disconnected chapters. Her analysis confirms the novel's discontinuity and atypical organisation.

Both White and Shepherd have shown through their analysis that the narrator's fragmented and discontinuous approach fails to provide a totalised and coherent knowledge of Flaubert. In an essay,[27] I suggested that this impossible synecdochal journey from the part to the whole is inscribed within postmodernist aesthetics, which favours fragmentation, multiplicity and the refusal of totalisation: details about Flaubert's life and work are juxtaposed, and fail to stand for the whole of the writer's life and work. As James B. Scott explains, the unstable and fragmentary dimension of the book derives not only from the chaotic mixture of genres, but also from the blurring of ontological frontiers between fiction and non-fiction: '[the] medley of prose genres . . . deconstructs the conventional distinctions between fiction and non-fiction'.[28] While Plato insisted on the necessary separation between these two heterogeneous types of writing, Braithwaite intertwines the two, as suggested by his enumeration: 'Three stories contend within me. One about Flaubert, one about Ellen, one about myself' (p. 94), to which one may add the one about Louise Colet. Such a quote highlights the blurring of fiction and history, with the historical couple, Flaubert and Colet, being placed side by side with the fictitious couple, Geoffrey and Ellen Braithwaite, whose literary models, Charles and Emma Bovary, are also invented. Within the novel, some passages resemble a chronicle containing a series of historical facts referring to actual places in France (Rouen, Croisset, Trouville, Barentin . . .) and people who existed (Maxime du Camp,

Louise Colet, Louis Bouilhet . . .). At the same time, however, *Flaubert's Parrot* is placed within an imaginary framework as Braithwaite and his wife are fictional protagonists. The allusions to their fictitious life are certainly too rare and elliptical to let anyone qualify the book as an auto-biography even though Patti White suggests that a 'fragmentary and incomplete Braithwaite autobiography nests within his fragmented biog-raphy of Flaubert'.[29] In any case, the life of the Braithwaites gives its structure to the book as Barnes himself indicated: 'if you withdrew the fictional infrastructure, it would just sort of collapse. It wouldn't be worth reading.' The writer adds: 'the whole impetus of the novel is aiming towards the chapter called "Pure Story" . . . without it, the elements of the book would still be there, but it would be like taking the tentpole out of a tent . . . the fabric would still be there, but it wouldn't look like a tent, it would just be a load of fabric lying on the ground'.[30] While most reviewers and critics praised the author's compassion for his protagonist and the way in which he communicates 'genuine emotion without affec-tation or embarrassment',[31] the American novelist John Updike (born 1932) is one of the rare dissenting voices, who was not moved by Braithwaite's constantly deferred tragedy. He blames the book for being too literary and artificial, and for thwarting the reader's curiosity as to Braithwaite's secret: 'The blatant forestallment of revelation begins to nag as well as tease; as one disparate chapter of mock scholarship succeeds another . . . readerly fatigue and irritation set in.' Updike wishes that 'pure event' had taken over and argues that the fictional chapter, 'Pure Story', comes too late.[32]

The ontological status of this fictional but 'pure' story is ambiguous, as underscored by the polysemy of 'pure'. Does 'pure story' mean 'not corrupted', as opposed to Emma Bovary's corrupted one; 'purely imagi-nary', as opposed to all the chapters relating to real people and places; or 'true story', as understood by French translator Jean Guiloineau, who entitled the chapter 'Une histoire vraie [A true story]'?[33] This interpre-tation is corroborated by a previous assertion of the narrator: 'Ellen's is a true story: perhaps it is even the reason why I am telling you Flaubert's story instead' (p. 95). The narrator seems to invert the ontological status of stories and to subvert generic conventions as Ellen's fictional story would be more authentic than Flaubert's real story. The reader's confu-sion is furthered by the constant intertwining of fictional data on the Braithwaites and supposedly factual chapters on Flaubert which never-theless yield contradictory information. James B. Scott analyses this 'deconstruction of prose genre taxonomies' that shatters the promise of any fixed meaning: 'the reader is at all times caught between the poles of true and not true, so that even the conventional signification patterns (biography presents fact; fiction presents fancy) no longer function'.[34] According to William Bell, the effect of juxtaposing the stories of

Flaubert and of the Braithwaites is 'to sow confusion and to force on the
reader a re-examination of what s/he believes historiography to be'.[35]

The irretrievability of the past, the inaccessibility of truth and the indeterminacy of signs are among the recurrent issues debated in most critical pieces on *Flaubert's Parrot*, and all of these issues figure prominently in
discussions of postmodernism in literature. As Neil Brooks rightly
remarks, '*Flaubert's Parrot* seems to put itself very self-consciously within
the field of postmodern explorations about textuality and history.'[36] In
his poststructuralist reading of the novel, Scott situates the book within
the postmodernist discourse which posits the 'indeterminacy of meaning'
and elusiveness of truth. Scott explains how Barnes 'deconstructs conventional narrative structures'[37] by offering contradictory views on Flaubert
and highlighting the imprecision of language in which signifiers (i.e. the
materially perceptible components of the sign – sounds or visible mark-
ers such as letters and words) open onto a plurality of signifieds (i.e.
the conceptual components of the sign). Thus, words such as 'giant' or
'fat' (p. 101) do not refer to the same reality in the nineteenth century
and today, just as the narrator cannot know for sure that the redcurrant
jam of Flaubert's time has the same colour as ours. Alison Lee develops
similar poststructuralist and deconstructionist arguments when she points
out how the narrative shows that 'there is no single truth any more than
there is a single parrot', taking as an example not only the end of the
book but also the plurality of meanings of the word 'parrot'.[38] Scott
argues that such uncertainty makes the past irretrievable and unknow-
able, and Braithwaite's quest never-ending and tantalising. He reflects that
the lack of closure and the infinite deferral of any fixed meaning epitomised by the novel actually mirror the condition of human consciousness and of empirical reality. In his own analysis, Merritt Moseley argues
that Barnes actually does not go as far as Scott's radical scepticism about
truth and reality: 'Barnes's position is more tentative or more ambiguous
than the postmodern skepticism about referentiality and knowledge.'[39]
Even though Braithwaite doubts the possibility of knowing the past, he
never denies its reality. When attempting to define his book, Barnes says
it is about 'the shiftiness of the past, and the uncertainty and unverifia-
bility of fact'.[40] At the beginning and throughout *Flaubert's Parrot*,
Braithwaite is indeed obsessed by the following epistemological question: 'How do we seize the past?' (pp. 5, 100, 113), suggesting that the
narrator does not consider historical or biographical knowledge as an
unproblematic category, but questions the ways in which we come to
know the past.

Several critics have thus situated *Flaubert's Parrot* within what theorists
such as Linda Hutcheon and Alison Lee have called 'historiographic
metafiction',[41] i.e. novels that represent historical characters and events

but at the same time keep reflecting within the text on issues relating to the retrieval of the past. Whereas nineteenth-century novelists such as Sir Walter Scott (1771–1832) sought to convey historical knowledge in a lively way without questioning its value and validity, in postmodernist fiction, the historical novel becomes 'a means for inquiring into the epistemological problems of historiography' to quote Elisabeth Wesseling.[42] In *Flaubert's Parrot*, as Gasiorek demonstrates, 'Barnes's preoccupation with the inaccessibility of the past leads him to focus less on the past itself – the object of historical enquiry – than on the modes by which it is apprehended.'[43]

In her analysis, Alison Lee focuses on the unbearable split within Braithwaite: 'while as a character Braithwaite is obsessed by concerns we might associate with Realist reading – detail, authority, intention, reference – as a narrator, he constantly undermines his own obsessions'.[44] Thus, Braithwaite accumulates referential facts and resorts to the rigourous conventions of history-writing or biography when he gives bibliographical references, such as 'Maxime du Camp's *Souvenirs littéraires* (Hachette, Paris, 1882–3, 2 vols). . . . On page 306 of the first volume (Remington & Co., London, 1893, no translator credited)' (p. 88), or the long and detailed references to Musgrave's books on nineteenth-century France (pp. 102–3). These precise references are supposed to assert the validity and reliability of the discourse, but look odd in a work of fiction and disrupt our reading of a continuous narrative. Moreover, they foreground the discursive nature of the representation of the past and the fact that Braithwaite can have no direct access to the past as he can only seize it through textualised documents. After showing that the past is inaccessible to us except in textual form, that documents are bound to be fragmentary and that the historian or biographer necessarily selects information, emplots data and fills in the gaps in the record, Braithwaite redefines the past as 'autobiographical fiction pretending to be a parliamentary report' (p. 101), thus suggesting its discursive and narrative dimension and disputing any claim to exhaustiveness, objectivity and scientific truthfulness. Braithwaite's approach therefore consists in using the codes of traditional genres such as biography or historiography and then subverting them by revealing their inadequacy, which corresponds to the postmodernist method as delineated by Hutcheon: 'What postmodern parody does is to evoke what reception theorists call the horizon of expectation of the spectator, a horizon formed by recognizable conventions of genre, style, or form of representation. This is then destabilized and dismantled step by step.'[45] In an insightful essay, William Bell analysed in detail how Barnes manages 'both to engage with traditional features of biography and to keep them at arm's length'.[46] Among these features, Bell chooses that of the chronology and focuses on the second chapter, which has drawn much critical attention. There, the narrator imitates the style and the typography of traditional chronologies with the indication of the most important dates in the writer's life, followed by a short development, usually in noun phrases. The originality consists in juxtaposing three chronologies, the first insisting on Flaubert's successes, the second highlighting his failures and the third entirely composed of quotations from Flaubert. As Bell suggests, 'whereas chronology functions in many lives as a semi-explicit, necessary and all-embracing principle, here it is super-explicit, isolated and made to seem arbitrary'.[47] The sense of arbitrariness derives from the juxtaposition of contradictory information, which reveals the active role of the biographer in his presentation of facts. For example, the first chronology suggests that Flaubert died at his most successful and while he was still full of creative energy (p. 21), while the second contrarily chooses a very pessimistic approach (p. 27), and the third ends on Flaubert's oscillation between a desire to create and a feeling of wariness (p. 34).

Braithwaite thus lets contradictory information coexist but, in an interview, Barnes denied that such juxtaposition might be 'confusing', arguing instead that it was 'illuminating': 'I don't think that . . . all the facts, all the statements there are incompatible with one another in terms of human life and human psychology.'[48] The coexistence of different versions is, however, a way to undermine the certainties of conventional biography. Barnes remarked: 'I regard biography with some suspicion as a genre. I am frequently made uncomfortable and even disapproving of the certainties with which biographers describe lives',[49] which certainly explains why he should experiment with the form and also why he never completed the biography of Kingsley Amis he had been asked to write.[50] In *Flaubert's Parrot*, the narrator subverts other biographical conventions, for example by 'inventing when the evidence runs out',[51] as in the third chapter, 'Finders Keepers', where Braithwaite uses fiction to compensate for the disappearance of Flaubert's correspondence with the English governess Juliet Herbert. William Bell concludes his demonstration by showing that Barnes's handling of biography is not destructive but creative: 'his conception of biography might be understood not as denying a traditional form but as contributing to a renewal of that form' so that '*Flaubert's Parrot* fulfils the purpose of biography, *but in a different way*', which is typical of postmodernist experimentations.[52]

If most critics highlighted the postmodernist features of *Flaubert's Parrot* in relation to the past, some have argued that the book oscillates between modernism and postmodernism. Thus, Neil Brooks remarks that Braithwaite takes a modernist approach to texts as he seeks 'stable hierarchies and master-narratives' which can bring 'order and intelligibility' to his life and lead to 'the consummate modernist fulfillment, an epiphany of "pure" understanding'.[53] However, Brooks sides with Lee and Scott in noting that Braithwaite's totalising dream and positivist stance are countered by acute relativism, indeterminacy and rival versions of the same stories, all characteristic features of postmodernism. In an original and stimulating earlier essay, Brooks had already approached this dichotomy between modernism and postmodernism in relation to *Flaubert's Parrot* by exploring one of the intertexts of the book, namely *The Good Soldier* (1915) by Ford Madox Ford (1873–1939). Barnes repeatedly refers to it as one of the greatest – though underrated – twentieth-century novels, and he devoted a long and impressive essay – ' "O Unforgetting Elephant" ' (1997) – to Max Saunders's biography of Ford. In *The Good Soldier*, the narrator John Dowell writes the story of his unfaithful wife and her lover in an attempt to come to terms with her death. After a detailed account of the similarities between the two books in terms of plot, self-deluded narrators and strategies of deferral and digression, Brooks points to a fundamental difference: while *The Good Soldier* is 'a classic modernist novel',[54] *Flaubert's Parrot* is a typical postmodernist production. Brooks demonstrates that after his wife's death, Ford's narrator can rely on the persistence of codes of propriety and of tradition. The very act of telling his 'saddest story' – the subtitle of Ford's novel – enables Dowell to restore some kind of order to his life. On the other hand, Braithwaite 'discovers in postmodern society that even stories cannot tell tales that provide a secure foundation'.[55] *Flaubert's Parrot* reveals that the codes modernist texts could rely on are no longer available in a postmodern era. Asked about this intertext, Barnes retorted that the main difference between Braithwaite and Dowell is that the latter 'is unable to tell his story or defers telling his story because he doesn't really understand it. He is the classic example of what people call the unreliable narrator.' On the other hand, 'Braithwaite quite deliberately at one point tells you he is a reliable narrator and that everything he tells you about Flaubert is true.' His constant deferring of the tragedy of his life is therefore due not to his lack of understanding but to 'emotional blockage'.[56]

Inspired by Brooks's article, Australian scholar Erica Hateley argues that *Flaubert's Parrot* 'maintains a strong modernist aesthestic despite its seeming postmodern sensibilities'.[57] Hateley interprets the novel as revisiting what she views as 'that most modern of modernist literary modes': the *Künstlerroman*, which, one should note, had nineteenth-century precursors, for example *The Masterpiece* (1886) by Emile Zola (1840–1902). The *Künstlerroman* is a novel which focuses on the development of an artist or writer, and in *Flaubert's Parrot*, Braithwaite, while supposedly devoting a book to Flaubert, goes through a 'process of individuation' and produces his own text tinged with autobiography.[58] Hateley notes that Braithwaite's modernist project consists in giving a coherent and total view of Flaubert but is confronted with the plurality and contradiction that are specific to postmodernist culture. If most critics have highlighted Braithwaite's ultimate failure in his totalising project,

Hateley proves more optimistic: she argues that Braithwaite's Flaubertian quest, though incomplete, has enabled him 'to deal with the death of his wife and in turn enact his own artistic development', 'to reconcile the deficiencies of his own past, and therefore move forward'.[59] Many critics have argued contrarily that Braithwaite never comes to terms with his past or with his wife's suicide and that 'his full confession brings no consolations',[60] but Hateley's case for the purgative or cathartic power of writing is interesting.

Several critics have focused on the figure of Braithwaite as he is certainly a typical postmodernist self-conscious narrator in so far as he exposes the constraints upon his research and comments on his own choices as he goes along. The irony consists in choosing an intrusive narrator in a book devoted to Flaubert, who specifically claimed the necessity for an impersonal type of narration. In realist fiction, the narrator is often presented as a stable, reliable and omniscient figure, whom Lee defines as 'an unproblematically constituted, individual "subject" who is the prime mover of events, and from whom essential meaning emanates'.[61] David Leon Higdon suggests that Barnes, but also Graham Swift, have created a new type of narrator, 'the *reluctant narrator*, who is reliable in strict terms, indeed often quite learned and perceptive, but who has seen, experienced or caused something so traumatic that he must approach the telling of it through indirections, masks and substitutions'.[62] Braithwaite sums up the characteristics of such a narrator: 'a contemporary narrator hesitates, claims uncertainty, misunderstands, plays games and falls into error' (p. 99), adding a self-reflexive remark: 'As for the hesitating narrator – look, I'm afraid you've run into one right now' (p. 100). The main rhetorical figure he uses is aposiopesis, i.e. a sudden break in writing which suggests unwillingness or inability to proceed, and which appears whenever Braithwaite starts talking about his private life: 'I remember...But I'll keep that for another time' (p. 82); 'I...I...' (p. 100); 'My wife...Not now, not now' (p. 120). Braithwaite's hesitations and frequent digressions reflect his difficulties in confronting his wife's adultery and suicide, and his literary investigation into Flaubert's life and works is a way of postponing telling the story of his marital life, which has parrotted that of Charles and Emma Bovary. Neil Brooks suggests that the repeated deferral of this painful topic reflects Braithwaite's 'inability to deal with the emotional issues [he] seeks to address unemotionally'. Brooks argues that Braithwaite wants to convince the reader he can 'objectively and dispassionately relate all the facts',[63] including his wife's death, which, as I have analysed in an essay,[64] is reported coldly and impersonally. As Higdon had already revealed, Braithwaite 'strives for a Flaubertian detachment, objectivity and impersonality',[65] but Brooks remarks that this only reveals his incompetence and ignorance as to affairs of the heart.

Most of all, Braithwaite fears the reader's reaction to his painful confession, and, as I sought to demonstrate in an essay,[66] he oscillates throughout the novel between a desire to share his experience with the reader or narratee, to establish an intimate relationship, and a reluctance to entirely confide in him. The book constantly moves to and fro between intimacy and distance, so that the reader sometimes feels involved in the fiction and sometimes feels distanced from it, but is undoubtedly made aware of the fact that the narrator manipulates him/her, guides his/her judgements and controls his/her reactions. As Polish scholar Tomasz Dobrogoszcz suggested, Braithwaite 'is shown as an ambiguous figure – a strong creator having strict control over the narrative, and at the same time a reluctant vacillator, hesitant and hankering after the reader's trust'.[67] Gasiorek also emphasised the way in which Braithwaite directs the reader's response in a very authoritative manner, thus impeding free interpretation: 'the reader's approach . . . is effectively forestalled because it is directed down certain paths'.[68] At times, the narrator conducts some form of Socratic dialogue, directly addressing the reader and even imagining the questions and objections he/she may voice (pp. 109, 159), but, as Gasiorek underlines, 'Braithwaite's strategy only appears to invite dialogue and to solicit a response, for his narrative, in keeping with his monomania, is monologic.'[69]

Georgia Johnston, for her part, analysed in particular the way in which Braithwaite manipulates the reader by hiding his gendered bias and perpetuation of a patriarchal system. For example, Braithwaite pretends to allow for different perspectives on Flaubert when he concedes 'admittedly we hear only Gustave's side of the story' (p. 159) and decides to write 'Louise Colet's version' in the eleventh chapter. He exploits his talents as a ventriloquist to give voice to a silenced woman, and yet, according to Johnston, displays a sexist attitude by portraying Colet as 'miserable with and without Flaubert, as the inferior artist, as [a] mistress who is vengeful, possessive, small-minded'.[70] Braithwaite's wife, Ellen, fares no better as her husband proves unable to confront her story and understand her: 'My wife: someone I feel I understand less well than a foreign writer dead for a hundred years' (p. 201). He does not even grant her a voice but reveals her through the reflection of a fictional creation, Emma Bovary. As Johnston suggests, this approach confirms the patriarchal ideology and creates a bond between Braithwaite and Flaubert, 'relegating women to the textual, securing men in the authorial'.[71]

Braithwaite actually manages to defer his personal confession about his wife by devoting the largest part of the book to Flaubert so that *Flaubert's Parrot* reads like a vibrant and original homage to the French writer, jangling with 'cross-fertilizing, self-seeding, memory-jogging, imagination-releasing resonances', to quote reviewer David Coward.[72] Barnes's fondness for the work of Flaubert is well known as he devoted many essays to his favourite writer, most of which are collected in *Something to Declare*. In *Flaubert's Parrot*, Flaubertian intertextuality is so extensive that Braithwaite's voice sometimes tends to disappear beneath or behind that of Flaubert. Chapters such as 'The Flaubert Bestiary' and 'Examination Paper' almost take the form of a collage of quotations from Flaubert's correspondence so that Braithwaite's role seems limited to that of a compiler, or a parrot, Flaubert's parrot. 'Braithwaite's Dictionary of Accepted Ideas' reveals the scope of the narrator's ventriloquism as the chapter consists of a parody and a stylistic pastiche of Flaubert's *Dictionary of Accepted Ideas*. Braithwaite has so fully incarnated and impersonated Flaubert's voice that some passages could be seen as cases of plagiarism, the narrator merely repeating or parroting the writer's words, without inverted commas. The third chronology of Flaubert's life is a great achievement in confusion as some readers believed it was a pastiche of Flaubert's style, while it is entirely composed of quotations from Flaubert's correspondence in the form of metaphors and comparisons, thus forming an original autobiography. As Gasiorek suggests, 'Braithwaite is modelling himself on Flaubert,' adopting his ironic tone and mimicking his disingenuousness.[73] This deliberate confusion of voices suggests that the notion of paternity or author–ity has disappeared and that the words themselves are more important than the identity of the writer. This mimicking effect is furthered by the fact that the Braithwaites' story seems to parrot that of Charles and Emma Bovary in Flaubert's famous novel. As Higdon wrote: 'he and his wife have already been written'.[74]

It should be noted, however, that *Flaubert's Parrot* does not read as a submissive and repetitive text, but is an act of genuine and original creation in which Barnes respectfully celebrates Flaubert but also evinces his great talents as a novelist and stylist. As Neil Brooks claims, '*Flaubert's Parrot* suggests that repetition need not be mere mimicry, but can be a profoundly creative act.'[75] Thus, Braithwaite tactfully and originally handles grief and emotion, culminating in the highly moving chapter called 'Pure Story'. He makes Louise Colet's unheard and unsung voice palpable. The metaphors are finely developed and well related to twentieth-century reality, while the style is precise, elegant, and has a specific Barnesian touch to it. Terence Rafferty praised the book for performing 'a couple of literary marriages straight out of critics' dreams: he's written a modernist text with a nineteenth-century heart, a French novel with English lucidity and tact'.[76] *Flaubert's Parrot* thus oscillates between repetition and difference, between the awareness of past literature and a desire to go beyond and make something new and hybrid. Barnes is in no way constrained by the heritage of Flaubert or by past conventions, but manages on the contrary to create a voice of his own and a form of his own. The book ends on an enigmatic note, suggesting that the quest for the parrot, for Flaubert's voice and past, for the truth of his own life, has not been completed but, as James B. Scott remarked, to such a 'Grail-questing knight' as Braithwaite, 'the search is all'.[77] *Flaubert's Parrot* thus reminds the reader that, to quote David Coward, 'there are questions to which there are no answers',[78] foreshadowing the main topic of Barnes's next novel, *Staring at the Sun*, whose original title was *Question and Answer*. Reviewers and readers were bound to wonder what to expect next, whether Barnes would continue in the postmodernist, experimental and moving vein of *Flaubert's Parrot* or whether he would revert to the conventional narrative strategies of his earlier novels. This is what the next chapter will attempt to find out.

# CHAPTER FIVE

# An Ordinary Miracle: *Staring at the Sun* (1986)

Julian Barnes started writing *Staring at the Sun* in 1982, and had already completed a third of the book when he decided to compose a short story about Flaubert, which grew into a whole book. As a consequence, he put aside *Staring at the Sun* for 18 months and came back to it only after the success of *Flaubert's Parrot*. Reviewers and readers were mainly disconcerted by this new novel, which is strikingly different in theme, form and style from the experimental *Flaubert's Parrot*. However, in an interview with Patrick McGrath, Barnes pointed out the link he perceived between the two novels:

■ The connection that I see between the two is technical rather than thematic, in that *Flaubert's Parrot* is a book that went off in all directions, and one of the ways of tying it all together was to use repeated phrases and ideas like thin bits of gossamer, to keep it vaguely bound together. That developed in *Staring at the Sun* into actual images, and incidents, and stories, which, as the story continues, take on more depth and significance. At first, they're just odd stories, but by the end they become metaphors.[1] □

If the echoes may indeed remind the reader of the repetitions in *Flaubert's Parrot*, the structure follows on from *Metroland* as the novel, divided into three parts, ranges from 1941 to 2021 and tells the story of Jean Serjeant's seemingly ordinary life from childhood through adolescence to adulthood and old age. The first part relates Jean's childhood, her fascination with the Royal Air Force pilot Thomas Prosser, grounded and billetted with the Serjeants in 1941, and her unhappy marriage to a dull policeman, Michael. The second part deals with the birth of her son Gregory, and her decision to leave her husband and live alone with Gregory. Having stared at the sun with Prosser, Jean is now staring at the son, a paronomasia (pun, play on words) or near homophony ('sun' and 'son' sound the same) which reflects the evolving focus of the novel. The third part, more speculative and philosophical, proposes an alternative point of view, that of Gregory, who keeps asking the General Purposes Computer questions about God, life and death. Reviewer Ann Hulbert rightly pointed to the 'uncharacteristic spirit of Barnes's new novel',[2] which offers a series of ordinary miracles and invites the reader to probe beneath the apparent simplicity of the prose. Thus, the book achieves a precarious balance between ordinariness and lyricism through the creation of eloquent metaphors and the use of a seemingly simple but actually polysemic language. As Christopher Lehmann-Haupt argues, 'if this new book lacks the artistic trickiness of its predecessors, there is a quieter game being played in its pages. That game lies in the language, with words and phrases echoing musically throughout the novel until the homeliest of phrases is raised up to a kind of poetry.'[3]

Upon publication of the novel, the reviews were mixed, but on the whole more sympathetic in the United States than in Great Britain. However, British journalist Simon Banner called *Staring at the Sun* Barnes's 'most ambitious [novel] to date' and found his major achievement in 'the memorable creation of the initially appallingly naive but, by 2020, wry and incisive Jean'.[4] Alison Hennegan praised the way Barnes confounds the reader's expectations and provides 'many exhilarating and satisfying flights of fancy',[5] and Mira Stout called the book 'arguably Barnes's strongest novel'.[6] Mark Lawson on the other hand was unrelenting, judging the book 'a crippling disappointment', short on narrative action, lacking a unifying theme, and with Barnes being an 'indifferent fictional ventriloquist'. According to Lawson, Barnes's voice 'ambushes all his creations'[7] so that none of his characters is granted a specific voice of his/her own. This criticism is shared by Hulbert, who finds that in the second part 'there are moments when the standards of articulateness simply seem confused, and Jean sounds more like her author or his previous protagonists than like herself'.[8] David Lodge, for his part, was not won over by the third part, in which Gregory, judged 'colorless' by both Lodge and Merritt Moseley,[9] appears as 'a mere mouthpiece for philosophical speculations' which seem 'to have strayed into the novel from *Flaubert's Parrot*'. Lodge concludes that *Staring at the Sun* is 'an honorable failure, and affords the reader who appreciates good prose many incidental pleasures'.[10] Confronted by such criticism, Barnes reacted in a highly defensive way, telling Andrew Billen: 'As soon as you say you were disappointed, I get deeply protective about the novel. I say: Carlos Fuentes liked it – so sod you. This is the writer's response. It's like criticising your fourth child.'[11]

And indeed, the most memorable review is certainly that of Mexican writer Carlos Fuentes (born 1928), who names the novel 'a marvelous literary epiphany' and salutes 'the universal English voice of Julian

Barnes'. He argues that Barnes is 'at the forefront of a new internationalization of British fiction' along with his fellow writers Peter Ackroyd (born 1949) and Bruce Chatwin (1940–89): 'he breaks barriers of conventional time and genres, creates characters from ideas and language, and stares not only at the sun but at the reader's intelligence'. Fuentes comments: 'Julian Barnes's brilliant new novel flashes between the extremes of enchantment and disenchantment, questioning where we might find our proper places as men and women in the coming century.' More precisely Fuentes shows how Jean moves from enchantment with Prosser and Uncle Leslie, both of whom she loses, to disenchantment with her husband Michael.[12]

The title of the book and the image of the RAF pilot Tommy Prosser seeing the sun rise twice while flying his Hurricane fighter, 'an ordinary miracle he would never forget' (p. 2), provide the central metaphor and theme of the novel according to Alison Hennegan: 'the ordinary nature of the miraculous and the miraculous nature of the ordinary'.[13] Flights and aeroplanes function as metaphoric *leitmotifs*, moving from Prosser's Hurricane fighter to Gregory's model aircraft, from Jean's first flight – supposed to cure her whooping cough – to Prosser's last flight towards death, climbing into the sun, from Jean flying to her own idiosyncratic version of the Seven Wonders of the World to Gregory and Jean's ultimate flight at the end of the novel when they watch the sun set twice, thus echoing the opening of the novel in reverse. While Prosser's staring at the sun rising twice was an ordinary miracle and an act of defiance, Jean and Gregory's watching the sun set twice, at the end of their lives, amounts to an acceptance of death. The lyricism and enchantment of the introductory description which gives the novel its title were praised by several critics, with the notable exception of Matthew Pateman, who judged it 'bathetic' and contrasted it to the end of the novel: 'The movement from the ridiculous to the sublime is mirrored in the structure of the book where the bathos of the opening section is weighed against the pathos of Jean's flight and twice-seen sunset on the final page.'[14] The terms 'ridiculous' and 'bathos' sound odd when applied to such a lyrical passage, unless Pateman perceived an underlying irony in the description of the episode. Hennegan provided several interpretations for the image of flight in the novel – 'soaring aspiration, cowardly retreat, necessary escape, a defiance of nature explicable by natural laws'[15] – while Hulbert saw it as a reflection of the narrative structure of the novel: 'Flight is the reigning image in the narrative and also of the narrative, which itself skims over expanses of space and time, doubles back, lands smoothly in unusual places, then takes off again to follow Jean's runic observations.'[16] Fuentes argues, for his part, that the novel repeats the myth of Icarus, whose wings of waxed feathers melted when he flew too close to the sun, leading to Icarus's death. In Barnes's novel, the winged Icarus,

Prosser, climbs into the sun before dying and is replaced by a 'wingless, sedentary Icarus', Gregory.[17]

If Prosser and Gregory are central figures, *Staring at the Sun* is remarkable in that, for the first time in his literary career, Barnes offers a woman's perspective: 'Writing a book from a woman's point of view seemed to be part of the necessary education of being a novelist.'[18] Moreover, he linked this narrative choice to the main theme of the book: 'I began to think about a book on courage – in war, in facing life alone and in front of the big questions that bother us all. . . . Then I realised my first novel was about a man and told in the first person, the second about a man in the third person, and I thought a woman would be a good progression.'[19] Hennegan argues, however, that the novel transcends gender despite the presence of 'feminist jokes, arguments, ripostes and graffiti . . . embedded in the fabric of the book'. Even though Jean's life seems to contain 'the familiar raw material of a modern conventional form, the female and feminist *Pilgrim's Progress*',[20] the novel addresses issues that concern men and women alike, such as courage, death or eternity. In an interview, Barnes revealed that the novel had four separate roots, which were intertwined: he wanted to write a novel from a woman's point of view, with courage as a theme, first set in the Second World War, but which covered a hundred years.[21]

Barnes repeatedly said in interviews that he wanted to situate the novel before and during the Second World War because it was the period just before he was born and therefore the one people talked about when he was growing up. As David Lodge rightly points out, Barnes's choice to imagine the war through the eyes of a woman has been shared by other writers of his generation, such as David Hare (born 1947) in his plays *Licking Hitler* (1978) and *Plenty* (1978), or Ian McEwan in his screenplay *The Imitation Game* (1980). Their common purpose consists in 'contemplating, with a consciousness raised by the feminism of the 1970s, the plight of women in the 1940s, caught up in a war generated by men and managed by men'.[22] Thus, unlike Rachel, Gregory's feminist girlfriend, Jean accepts men's domination: 'War, of course, was men's business. Men conducted it, and men – tapping out their pipes like headmasters – explained it' (p. 17).

As Barnes wanted to cover a hundred years, the novel had to end in the future but Barnes believes that 'the future is going to be remarkably like the present'. The technology may evolve but 'the human heart, sometimes unfortunately, remains constant'.[23] Because the novel is partly set in the future and epitomises the role of computers, Barnes expected to see the words 'Orwellian vision' appear in reviews,[24] but critics also mentioned the heritage of Aldous Huxley (1894–1963) and his *Brave New World* (1932). Most, however, highlighted the lack of intertextuality in the book, which contains hardly any literary references apart from the mention of a marriage manual, *Married Love* (1918) by Marie Stopes (1880–1958) (pp. 38–40). Following the highly intertextual *Metroland* and *Flaubert's Parrot*, in which art seems more real than life, the decision to banish literary allusions was deliberate on the author's part: 'I wanted to write a book in which no one reads books.'[25] Barnes opted instead for an impressionistic approach, based on images as Hulbert suggests: 'Barnes strips away the layers of literary reference and allows his narrative to progress more by suggestive images than by arguments.'[26] Despite the intertextual discretion of the novel, Carlos Fuentes perceived implicit parallels between Jean's attempts to fill in the vacuums in her life and modern society, and the attitudes of the heroines of *Madame Bovary* and 'A Simple Heart' by Flaubert: 'Mme Bovary is defeated by the holes she finds in life and fills the vacuums with poison. But Jean does not overcome her dull husband and her second-rate life by swallowing arsenic; she prefers, like Flaubert's own simple heart, the servant Félicité, to digest her remarkable and unremarkable, sad, rewarding life,'[27] which might very well be a form of courage.

Barnes named courage as the main theme of *Staring at the Sun*, and indeed courage and the lack of it, or fear, figure prominently in the novel and take up several forms, which Merritt Moseley enumerates in his study. Military courage and the lack of it are epitomised by Prosser, whom Jean judges 'brave' (p. 102) but whom his RAF ground crew and his widow would consider 'windy' (pp. 48, 127). Uncle Leslie, for his part, is despised by his family for having run away from the war, being 'a bit of a spiv' (p. 55), and on his deathbed he confesses: 'I was always a bit windy. . . . Always running away. Always running. I was never brave' (p. 129). But courage is not only military, as Barnes explained: 'We do tend to think of courage as a male virtue, as something that happens in war, something that consists of standing and fighting. But there are 85,000 other sorts of courage, some of which come into the book – banal forms of courage – to live alone, for example, social courage. Then, the sort of sexual courage that we see in the relationship of the two women, Jean and Rachel.'[28] Thus Jean's courage consists in leaving her husband after twenty years of marriage when she is pregnant, and bringing her child up on her own; it also includes going to bed with her son's girlfriend but does not actually extend to having sex with her, as Jean apologises: ' "I don't suppose I have the courage to go to bed with you properly, dear" ' (p. 127). Courage is also the way in which Leslie faces cancer and death – 'Leslie . . . had died with courage' (p. 134) – and the way in which Jean seems to stare at death at the end of the book while Gregory is crying. The issue of courage is thus often linked to those of death and suicide. Prosser ends up committing suicide in his aeroplane, staring both at death and at the sun, thus belying the twenty-sixth maxim of French moralist La Rochefoucauld (1613–80), which possibly inspired the title of the novel: 'Le soleil ni la mort ne peuvent se regarder fixement' – 'Neither the sun nor death can be stared at steadily.' Gregory, terrified of death and deprived of the certitude of God's existence, considers suicide and asks the computer: 'Is suicide valid?' (p. 179), and his mother: 'Is suicide permissible?' (p. 185). As Moseley argues, 'the crucial decision is whether to go on living: to do so, without the consolation of God – to look at the sun without a sheltering hand – is courage'.[29] Throughout the novel, the narrator and the focalisers constantly question the meaning of the words 'brave' and 'courage', and propose new definitions of the terms.

There were few academic responses to the novel apart from chapters in the monographs by Moseley, Pateman and myself, and a fascinating article by French scholar Richard Pédot. These pieces focused more specifically on the novel's questioning of the possibility and status of knowledge and the importance of the epistemological theme. The narrator of *Staring at the Sun* insists that the craving for definite knowledge is shared by all human beings – 'The mind longs for certainty' (p. 98) – and therefore by the protagonists of the novel. In order to assuage this craving, the supposedly democratic twenty-first-century world in which the protagonists live has devised a 'General Purposes Computer' or GPC (p. 144), whose aim is to 'put the whole of human knowledge on to an easily accessible record' (p. 144) and to achieve the utopia of total history. A later function of GPC, added in 2008 and called TAT, an ironic and explicit acronym for 'The Absolute Truth' (p. 146), even suggests the possibility of attaining a unique and total truth, the dream of all positivist historians, which Gregory and Jean will, however, be denied. As the novel progresses, suspicions accumulate as to the possibility of attaining truth and certainty on any subject. Scholars start complaining that 'the concept of "Total Knowledge" was at odds with what they referred to as "Correct Knowledge" ' (p. 145). Thus, the image of the programmatic title, which, according to Pédot, sounds like the 'metaphor of a journey to the very centre of life and truth',[30] is actually misleading as the reader is denied any access to ultimate truth and knowledge.

Despite the protagonists' thirst for certainties, *Staring at the Sun* charts their progressive waning, as Gregory remarks: 'First you had the questions and you sought the answers. Then you had the answers and you wondered what the questions were. Finally, you realized that question and answer were the same, that the one enclosed the other' (p. 189). The ternary, or three-part, rhythm of the sentences reflects the ternary structure of the novel, from childhood to adulthood to old age, and the scholars mentioned above analysed the three stages of the novel in relation to the characters' attitude towards questions and anwers. I based my analysis on the evolution of the epigraphs as, despite the lack of any literary paraphernalia in *Staring at the Sun*, Barnes took up again the strategy initiated in *Metroland* of starting each of the three parts with an epigraph which gives hints as to the mood and theme of the following pages.[31] For Richard Pédot, the ternary structure corresponds to an epistemological division into three periods or 'three patterns in the relation of knowledge to power, each generating its own form of dissent or eccentricity'.[32] Matthew Pateman, for his part argues that the novel proposes three literary and social narratives that promise 'closure and knowledge',[33] but none actually keeps that ambitious promise.

The epigraph to the first part, taken from the correspondence of the Russian dramatist and short-story writer Anton Chekhov (1860–1904), introduces a first question or riddle: 'You ask me what life is? It is like asking what a carrot is. A carrot is a carrot, and nothing more is known. / *Chekhov to Olga Knipper, 20 April 1904*' (p. 3). It is certainly no coincidence that a novel fraught with unanswered questions about vast themes such as life, death and religion, should open with an existential one and that it should be followed by a firm and peremptory, but also ironic and sarcastic tautology which leaves the question unanswered. According to Pédot, this first stage corresponds to the ancient world, when one was sure of the questions one wanted to ask but not of the answers. This parallels Jean's position as a child and teenager when she struggles with questions which adults refuse to answer. The figures of authority are essentially masculine and deny any possibility of contradiction or uncertainty, as epitomised by Jean's father, a grocer, 'the sort of man who knew that a pound of flour was a pound of flour' (p. 19), just like 'a carrot is a carrot' (p. 3). Thus, in the ancient world and in Jean's adolescent world, the order of words corresponds to the order of things, in a perfect balance between signifier (the materially perceptible component of the sign – sound or visible mark), and the signified (the conceptual component of the sign). Pateman, for his part, calls the first movement, situated in the past, a literary historical narrative whose dominant social discourse is marriage. Even though Jean is beset by doubts about the love she is expected to feel for Michael and the decision to marry him, she opts for the comfort or illusion of certainty: 'of course it was right. Michael was the answer, whatever might have been the question' (p. 36). For a while, Jean's self-delusion leads her to believe that marriage does indeed bring closure – 'Getting married was an end' (p. 62) – and knowledge – 'I thought I knew the answers when I married' (p. 121). The second part will chart Jean's disillusionment with marriage and resound with echoes of previous and later works by Barnes.

According to Pédot, the second section corresponds to the modern world, in which the answers suddenly appear inadequate and throw doubt on the validity of questions. Thus, Jean's marriage to Michael seems an inadequate answer and the male language of authority is destabilised and brutally rejected by Rachel and her feminist theories. If the epigraph to the first part was precisely dated, the epigraph to the second, a graffito, is less precise but likewise takes the form of a facetious question: '*Three* wise men – are you serious? / *graffito, c.1984*' (p. 65). This cryptic and sarcastic formula will recur within the section itself, some sixty pages later, when the narrator reproduces a list of bland statements and rhetorical questions uttered by Rachel, who never stops chastising men: 'Rachel said: "*Three* wise men – are you serious?" ' (p. 123). Pateman identifies the second part, set in the 1980s, as a literary narrative of the contemporary whose dominant social discourse is polemical politics as epitomised by Rachel, but Jean is uncomfortable with this prescriptive and mono-discursive vision of the world.

Compared with the facetious question which provides the epigraph to the second part of the novel, the epigraph to the third part is more philosophical, reflecting the overall tone of this part: 'Immortality is no learned question. / *Kierkegaard*' (p. 137). No date is attributed, as though the notion of temporality had become obsolete. The assertive form has replaced the interrogative mode even though the epigraph contains the noun 'question', and essential questions remain unanswered. Similarly to the second epigraph, the sentence of the Danish philosopher Søren Kierkegaard (1813–55) recurs within the text, without being identified, when Gregory wonders about death and suicide and remembers a sentence quoted by the General Purposes Computer: '*Immortality is no learned question*: TAT had quoted this to him at some point' (p. 186). Through the epigraphs, the novel thus marks a chronological progression starting from life and ending with death and immortality: all of these metaphysical riddles find no resolution in the book. Pateman calls the third section, set in the future, a literary dystopian narrative whose dominant social discourse is information technology. However, the General Purposes Computer can provide facts but neither opinions nor speculations. All speculative discourse is met with 'NOT REAL QUESTION' (pp. 149, 161, 175, 176, 179) and knowledge is therefore incomplete. Pateman deduces that the novel 'seems to tend towards a "postmodern" notion of knowledge that prioritizes heterogeneity, dissensus, and openness'.[34] Pédot also argues that the third period is that of the postmodern world, in which the game of questions and answers itself is deemed irrelevant. Pédot concludes that each system or epistemological period is destabilised by a protagonist who eventually eludes it, thus obeying the injunction, '*Be always escaping*' (pp. 40, 183), that Jean read in her marriage manual: 'Uncle Leslie had run away from the war . . . . She had run away from Michael, and from marriage; from Rachel too, she supposed. Now Gregory was wondering whether to run away from the whole thing' (p. 183).

The couplet *Question and Answer*, which is so relevant to the novel, was actually its first title and it appears when Gregory defines the monotonous work of the General Purposes Computer, in an almost psalmodic rhythm: 'GPC was just a ramshackle, human old thing, trained to give answers. Question and answer, question and answer, question and answer' (p. 189). At one point, Barnes told Michael Ignatieff: 'My books are about posing the questions in the right way and not giving answers.'[35] Gregory himself is aware of the importance of asking GPC the right question: 'the problem is not what is the answer but what is the question' (p. 162), thus paraphrasing 'the American writer who asked, *in extremis*, "What is the answer?" and, receiving no reply, continued, "In that case, what is the question?" (p. 153). As Hulbert rightly suggests, 'the real challenge lies not in discovering any one right answer, but in recognizing the paradoxical importance and pointlessness of all the right questions'.[36] The book is indeed fraught with odd questions, starting with the incongruous riddles shared by Jean and Uncle Leslie. Eccentric uncles figure regularly in Barnes's fiction – Uncle Arthur in *Metroland*, Uncle Leslie in *Staring at the Sun*, Uncle Freddy in *Cross Channel* – all refusing to conform to expected norms and social codes. Then, questions become more abstract and existential. According to Fuentes, the main riddle posed by the novel is the following: 'are ordinary human beings condemned to ordinary, humdrum lives, or is there still a possibility of enchantment?'[37] More broadly, this novel questions nothing less than the meaning of life, the status of death and the existence of God. In the last part, Gregory even compiles a list of fourteen possible solutions to the question of God's existence (pp. 162–5), starting with two self-contradictory hypotheses, a rhetorical device which is also called a palinode (i.e. a text which retracts what has just been stated): '1 That God exists. / 2 That God does not exist' (p. 162). Gregory cannot decide the answer to this question, divided between TAT, which, being asked 'Do you believe in God?', replied with the irritating 'NOT REAL QUESTION' (p. 175), and his mother, who, being asked 'Is religion nonsense?', answered self-confidently: 'Yes, dear' (p. 185). The reader may remember that Jean experienced an unconventional epiphany when visiting the Grand Canyon, as, instead of being overwhelmed by 'the power of God and the majesty of his works' (p. 98), she realised that she had no religious sense whatsoever: 'The Canyon stunned her into uncertainty' (p. 98). As for Barnes, he says he was brought up without religion and admits: 'I don't believe in God, but I miss Him.'[38] As might be expected, *Staring at the Sun* does not provide any definite answer but acknowledges man's need for God, who keeps fear at bay. Moseley sums up this point: 'God is the hand we put before our eyes because we cannot stare directly at the sun.'[39]

The issue of God and religion will recur in Barnes's next novel, *A History of the World in 10½ Chapters*, but in a more humorous, subversive and maybe more efficient way. The epistemological question as to the possibility of ever achieving complete knowledge, introduced in *Before*

*She Met Me,* developed in *Flaubert's Parrot* and approached in *Staring at the Sun* through the focus on endless interrogations and on the role of technology in a future world, will also be confronted in Barnes's next novel from the broader perspective of a history of the world. Characterised by a conventional form and structure, *Staring at the Sun* may have disappointed readers who had been seduced by the formal experimentation of *Flaubert's Parrot,* but it seriously addresses important issues which constantly preoccupy Barnes – truth, knowledge, death – even though it does so from the point of view of an ordinary woman rather than an intellectual. The fact that critics and scholars have not paid much attention to the novel – to the extent that Bruce Sesto ignored it in his monograph – may be due to some internal flaws but also certainly to its uncomfortable position in between Barnes's masterpieces, *Flaubert's Parrot* and *A History of the World in 10½ Chapters,* whose ambitious programme and original form will be discussed in the next chapter.

# CHAPTER SIX

# A Re-vision of History: *A History of the World in 10½ Chapters* (1989)

*A* History of the World in 10½ Chapters is an ambitious tragicomic novel composed of various stories randomly ranging over centuries and involving different characters in each chapter. It is usually considered as Julian Barnes's second postmodernist masterpiece after *Flaubert's Parrot*, displaying as much heterogeneity in style, form and approach, and attracting as much critical attention. The two books are also linked in that Barnes's original idea was to take up again Braithwaite's narrative voice: 'I was going to write *Geoffrey Braithwaite's Guide to the Bible*. Which would be the entire Bible, restructured for handy modern use, with the boring bits cut out, written by an agnostic skeptic rationalist.' Barnes dropped the idea but something of it 'transmuted itself into a woodworm's account of the Ark'.[1] When Barnes's new novel was published, reviewers were mainly concerned with its generic hybridity – part history, part fiction – which some found disconcerting even though it was certainly one of its many achievements. Thus David Sexton remarked: 'Barnes writes books which look like novels and get shelved as novels but which, when you open them up, are something else altogether,'[2] while D. J. Taylor argued that the book was 'not a novel, according to the staider definitions'.[3] Having already gone through this debate with *Flaubert's Parrot*, Barnes was slightly irritated that it should emerge again with his new book: 'My line now is I'm a novelist and if I say it's a novel, it is.'[4]

Some critics, daunted by the lack of a single plot, the disruption of chronology and the absence of narrative cohesion, referred to the book as a collection of tales, stories or short stories, encouraged by the fact that a few chapters had been published independently in the *New Yorker*. Thus, Robert Nixon, unconvinced by the novelistic genre, concludes that 'Barnes has come up with a confident collection of short stories somewhat bewildered by its packaging as a novel,'[5] while Merle Rubin and Robert Irwin hesitate, suggesting that the book is 'less a novel than a collection of linked stories and essays',[6] 'more than just a collection of short stories and essays, not quite a novel'.[7] Barnes adds to the confusion by entitling the seventh chapter 'Three Simple Stories' in homage to Gustave Flaubert's *Three Tales*, the first of which, 'A Simple Heart', inspired *Flaubert's Parrot*. The writer nevertheless rejects the appellation of 'short stories' as the book consists of various strands which are carefully woven into all the chapters through echoes, repeated phrases, details and themes: 'it was conceived as a whole and executed as a whole. Things in it thicken and deepen.' Barnes added with irony: 'if you don't like it, it's a collection of short stories. If you do, it's a novel.'[8]

The title of the book itself creates a horizon of expectation about which critics disagree. While Kate Saunders argues, 'with misplaced assurance' according to Merritt Moseley,[9] that the novel fulfils the horizon of expectation – '*A History of the World in 10½ Chapters* is just what the title promises – a fictional history of the world, or the gospel according to Julian Barnes'[10] – American writer Joyce Carol Oates (born 1938) counters that the generic hints are actually deceiving: 'Barnes's fifth book is neither the novel it is presented as being nor the breezy pop-history of the world its title suggests.'[11] The book does, however, draw inspiration from historical events, such as the shipwreck of the *Medusa* in 1816, that of the *Titanic* in 1912, the earthquake in Arghuri in 1840, the tragedy of the 937 passengers on board the *Saint Louis* in 1939, the hijacking in October 1985 of the cruise ship *Achille Lauro*, and the nuclear catastrophe at Chernobyl on 25 April 1986. The author's note at the end of the book confirms that Barnes consulted historical sources and required the help of someone who did research for him. But the result is not a historical book as it mixes history with fictional forms. As Salman Rushdie suggests, 'what [Barnes] offers us is the novel as footnote to history, as subversion of the given'.[12] The book thus brings together several genres, such as the fable, the bestiary, the epistolary form, the essay, travel writing, legal proceedings, art analysis and a new genre Barnes calls 'love prose' (p. 228). The book also presents a variety of stylistic registers, and mixes contradictory versions, narrative voices and focalisations as each chapter proposes new narrators and points of view on history and stories, thus producing a dynamic polyphony which is that of history: 'The history of the world? Just voices echoing in the dark' (p. 242). Barnes justified this multiplicity as an essential part of his craft: 'Exploring all the available points of view is part of a novelist's job.'[13]

The generic and narrative instability of the book can be interpreted as the sign of a constant quest for new forms, as Barnes acknowledges: 'I'm very interested in form and in seeing what happens when you bend traditional narrative and fracture it', but the novelist was well aware of the risks of 'stretching [the book] to the point at which you hope the chewing gum doesn't snap'.[14] Throughout the composition of the novel, he would wonder: 'how long can I stretch the narrative line like a piece of elastic without it breaking?'[15] However, the chewing gum does not snap thanks to the recurrence of motifs, sea voyages, catastrophes, woodworms, analogies between characters, echoes, plot links, verbal repetitions and thematic coherence, which German scholar Claudia Kotte analyses in detail in two perceptive essays.[16] Brian Finney also examines the connections in the novel and suggests that they 'assert in narrative form that certain patterns of human interaction reappear over the expanse of history'.[17] As Kathleen Ferris concludes in chapter 4: 'Everything *is* connected, even the parts we don't like, especially the parts we don't like' (p. 84). Richard Locke is, however, not convinced by this sense of coherence, arguing instead that there are 'too few unifying actions or organically developing themes or arguments. The effect is not *collagiste* or symphonic: the presumably tragic–comic *concordia discors* remains discordant.'[18] Merritt Moseley disagrees with this interpretation, suggesting that collage 'is not a helpful analogy' whereas 'symphony' is, since such a musical composition 'has themes and motifs, and the repetition and patterning of these provide its unity'.[19] Moseley then proceeds to analyse some of these repeated motifs. Throughout the book, the generic, stylistic and narrative blurring challenges classification and categorisation, and thus resists history's inexorable logic of division between pure and impure, clean and unclean, weak and strong, winners and losers. Through its polymorphous form, the book celebrates plurality and hybridity, while remaining accessible and pleasurable to readers. As Joyce Carol Oates remarks, it is 'post-modernist in conception but accessibly straightforward in execution'.[20]

Some chapters have drawn the attention of critics more than others, and this is particularly the case with 'Parenthesis'. Placed between the eighth and ninth chapters, 'Parenthesis' is not granted any number but acquires the status of the half-chapter of the title. According to Lionel Kelly, who borrows the term from French philosopher Jacques Derrida (1930–2004), it is a '*parergon*, a discourse outside the main frame'.[21] According to Kotte, it 'challenges our culturally encoded numerical system, where decimal numbers suggest systematic order, unity, and coherence'.[22] An eloquent non-fictional essay on love and history, it stands apart and raises questions as to the identity of the narrative voice. In an interview, Michael Ignatieff asked Barnes: 'How autobiographical was that "Parenthesis"?', to which the writer answered: 'Entirely.' The beginning and the end of the half-chapter, therefore, present the author, lying in bed with his wife, trying to sleep. To give a clue to the reader, Barnes refers to 'Burial of the Count of Orgaz' (1586–88), a painting by

El Greco (1541–1614), and focuses on the mourner who 'looks directly out of the picture': 'Tradition claims that the figure is El Greco himself. I did this, he says. I painted this. I am responsible, and so I face towards you' (p. 227). This last assertion could be slightly modified and attributed to Barnes in 'Parenthesis': 'I wrote this. I am responsible, and so I face towards you.'

Barnes no longer hides behind the masks of his pseudonyms or narrators, but assumes responsibility for his reflections about love and history: 'I just emerge from the wings.'[23] Barnes also confessed to Alexander Stuart: 'You have all these masks as a fiction writer and every so often you think, "Well, actually, no, I'll just write the truth".' The half-chapter is therefore supposed to be 'direct and simple', a haven from the horrors of history which have been described all through the novel: 'what do we put against this horrible 24-wheeler called history that's thumping along with a tiny little trailer called politics behind it? And if we don't think that religion is true, it would be very nice, because we're novelists, to think that art was the answer. But art doesn't work for everyone, so love seems to be the one you accept.'[24] In his monograph, Matthew Pateman analyses the difficulties arising from such debatable statements about religion, art and love, together with the contradictions inherent in Barnes's conception of history.[25] As Isabelle Raucq-Hoorickx suggests in her narratological analysis of the book, in 'Parenthesis', 'the novel starts deconstructing itself' as the narrator or implied author invites his reader to 'see the world through another point of view' (p. 243), that of love.[26] The half-chapter, echoing in some ways the fragmentary meditations of *A Lover's Discourse: Fragments* (1977) by French semiotician Roland Barthes (1915–80), is thus an ambitious and powerful piece, which attracted much criticism, for example that of Salman Rushdie, who had reservations about it: 'here one wishes that Barnes the essayist had stepped aside for Barnes the full-blooded novelist; that instead of a disquisition on love, we could have been given the thing itself'.[27] British novelist Jonathan Coe (born 1961) shared this view, judging the piece 'too florid and too cool at the same time',[28] and Moseley conceded that it was 'vulnerable to charges of sentimentality or of old-fashioned liberal humanism'.[29] Spanish scholar María Lozano considered, for her part, that love was presented here as a central catastrophe – 'a violent story of cannibalism, violence and randomness' – thus echoing the historical discourse of the other chapters.[30] The generic and narrative specificity of 'Parenthesis' confirms the hybridity of the book but its reflections also weave the threads of all the chapters together.

Another striking example of hybridity is the fifth chapter – 'Shipwreck' – which has drawn the attention of several scholars, in particular Catherine Bernard, Liliane Louvel, Alan Clinton, Gregory J. Rubinson and myself. There, Barnes inserts the reproduction of a painting by Théodore Géricault (1791–1824), *The Raft of the Medusa* (1819), and the frontiers between the visual and the textual tend to blur. The aim of the chapter is to demonstrate how catastrophe can be turned into art, be it pictorial or textual. This original chapter, which Louvel calls 'iconotext' or 'text-image',[31] is composed of a first historical part which relates the actual shipwreck near Senegal in 1816, based on the account of two survivors, Savigny and Corréard. It is followed by a reproduction of Géricault's painting, and eventually ends with a second part which offers an account of the genesis of the work of art and a pictorial analysis of it. Catherine Bernard explains that the insertion of a colour photograph of the painting marks the violent intrusion of the visual within the textual, and the confrontation of two different semiotic systems (systems of signs).[32] Louvel confirms this interpretation and suggests that the painting supplements the text in that it both replaces it and adds to it.[33] The photograph, reproduced on a double page, oscillates between the inside and the outside of the book just as some figures in the painting seem to go over its edge. The fractured aspect of the figures in the picture combines with the temporal and spatial dislocation and with the referential indeterminacy of the scene – the title 'Scene of Shipwreck' is too vague to identify a specific place, time and event – so that the painting reads as a metaphor of the hybrid and discontinuous construction not only of the fifth chapter but also of the whole book.[34]

The second part of the chapter consists of the textual description and interpretation of the painting, also called *ekphrasis*. The hybridity is thus reinforced by this representation of a representation, which testifies to a double transfer: from the actual catastrophe to the painting, and from the visual representation to the textual analysis. In both cases, the issue is hermeneutic, i.e. pertaining to interpretation: Géricault interpreted the historical facts, introducing many anomalies as pointed out in the chapter, while the narrator and the reader of 'Shipwreck' interpret the pictorial signs. In both cases, interpretation is presented as multiple and unstable, and this is epitomised by the coexistence of two eyes, the ignorant eye mirroring the uninitiated reader, and the informed eye reflecting the ideal reader. The schizophrenic narrator thus shares his glance between his 'two eyes, ignorant and informed' (p. 132), and constantly moves from one perspective to another. The bifocalisation leads to a frustrating uncertainty as to the meaning of the ship on the horizon, either a sign of hope and rescue or one of 'hope being mocked' (p. 132) since the vessel is not coming towards the shipwrecked. Indeterminacy prevails as the narrator remarks: 'do we end up believing both versions? The eye can flick from one mood, and one interpretation, to the other: is this what was intended?' (p. 133). If Géricault's work began with 'truth to life' (p. 126) because he read Savigny and Corréard's account and met them, the allegiance then became 'truth to art' (p. 135) as 'The incident never took place as depicted' (p. 135). Gregory J. Rubinson argues, however, that Géricault's painting, like Barnes's history, is very informative: 'though it departs from documentary realism, it offers us a kind of knowledge about its subject unavailable in strictly realist modes of representation'.[35] Drawing from the theories of the German philosopher Walter Benjamin (1892–1940), Alan Clinton thus pays attention to the political elements involved in the painting and its commentary: 'Barnes's method of reading the details of the painting against its historical background reveals how artistic production is a political event in its own right.' The painting 'begins historically, but only to become haunted more and more by the spectres of religion, royalty, and aestheticism'.[36]

Bernard concludes, for her part, that the sheer force of the painting derives from its temporal and symbolical indeterminacy, the suspension of meaning which prevents any referential reading of the work of art.[37] The narrator decides to let the reader decide for himself or herself rather than impose a fixed and stable interpretation on the painting. The narrative strategy of bifocalisation implemented here underlines the subjectivity of viewpoints, and highlights the vanity of trying to enforce a monologic discourse, be it visual or textual, that would reveal a supposedly unique and totalising truth. The fifth chapter, though hybrid in form and genre, thus inscribes reflections about the representation of the past, the knowledge of reality and the interpretation of signs which can apply to the whole novel.

In the last few decades, several theorists of history, among them Hayden White and Dominique La Capra, have pointed to the literary conventions employed by historiography, and several scholars have drawn from White's theories to explain how Barnes emphasises the similarities between fiction and history, stories and History, underlining their discursive and narrative dimension, their fictive and constructed character. Thus, Barnes deliberately mixes imaginary and historical material so as to shatter the certainties of historical knowledge, and redefines history as fabulation: 'We make up a story to cover the facts we don't know or can't accept; we keep a few true facts and spin a new story round them. Our panic and our pain are only eased by soothing fabulation; we call it history' (p. 242). In an interview, the author drew attention to the clinical origin of the term 'fabulation': 'it's a medical term for what you do when a lot of your brain has been destroyed either by a stroke or by alcoholism . . . the human mind can't exist without the full story. So it fabulates and it takes what it thinks it knows, and then it makes a convincing link between the two.'[38] In the fourth chapter, 'The Survivor', doctors argue that Katherine Ferris invented a nuclear catastrophe in order to disavow the breakdown of her relationship with Greg and to avoid confronting her personal pain. According to Steven Connor, who analyses this chapter and its competing stories in detail, 'Kathleen's story of her personal survival is an instance of fabulation in the interests of self-preservation.'[39] Fable and fabulation are cathartic as they attenuate the horror, brutality and arbitrariness of the history of the world.

According to Barnes, the historian needs to mix facts with a pinch of fiction: 'history, if it attempts to be more than a description of documents, a description of artefacts, has to be a sort of literary genre'.[40] Barnes imitates this method by weaving the threads of fiction and history in a book which, right from the first paratext – the title – pretends to be both historical – *A History of the World* – and fictional (*in 10½ Chapters*). As Richard Locke suggests, 'This self-advertising title is a boast that mocks itself by calling attention to its literary and cognitive form.'[41] A few critics nevertheless regretted the predominance of historical facts and the relative fictional deficit, which, according to Marc Porée, prevents the production of a plurality of discursive meanings, specific to the fable.[42] However, Barnes's approach enables him to confront the dramas of history and stare at them, without taking refuge in 'soothing fabulation' (p. 242). Moreover, in an interview, Barnes argued that resorting to authentic events did not deprive him of his status as a fiction writer:

■ even if you're using art history or straight history or legal history or autobiography, the impulse behind it is to tell a story, and what makes each chapter work is that it has a structure and it has a narrative pulse. It leads somewhere. Even if it's taking facts which you've not invented yourself, what you're doing as a fiction writer is imposing a form and a motion on them.[43] □

In this hybrid novel, Barnes crosses ontological boundaries between fiction and history, but the confusion between invention and reality fails to grant credibility and verisimilitude to the fictional world, in contrast to what happens in traditional historical novels. Instead, it throws doubt on the validity of historical facts and raises the question of whether we can ever know the past, a typically postmodernist stance. Several critics have analysed the book through the postmodernist concept of historiographic metafiction, which was also applied to *Flaubert's Parrot* as discussed in Chapter Four of this Guide. As Elisabeth Wesseling suggests, 'Postmodernist writers do not consider it their task to propagate historical knowledge, but to inquire into the very possibility, nature, and use of historical knowledge.'[44] And indeed, to quote Barnes, his novel 'deals with one of the questions that obsessed Braithwaite in [*Flaubert's Parrot*]. And that is: How do we seize the past?'[45] and this question is dealt with self-reflexively, i.e. by including meta-historical comments. Right from the title with its indefinite article and its fraction, the notion of a comprehensive knowledge of the past is denied, as Claudia Kotte remarks: 'The author divides his history into ten chapters and thus conforms to our system of counting, where ten denotes a certain total-ity, completeness and coherence.' This unifying order is, however, under-mined by the addition of a half-chapter through which Barnes 'subverts culturally encoded number systems and alludes to the incomplete nature of his supposedly universal history'.[46]

In 'Parenthesis', the narrator blankly undermines the historians' posi-tivist assumptions of fidelity, objectivity and truth: 'We all know objective truth is not obtainable, that when some event occurs we shall have a multiplicity of subjective truths' (p. 245). As a consequence, the book does not pretend to be 'the' complete, absolute and monologic history of the world but is 'a' partial, subjective and multi-faceted one in which no single discourse or voice achieves outright authority. According to Rubinson, the 'organizing narrative convention' is therefore a 'polarized dispute between interpretive camps'.[47] As Gregory Salyer concludes, 'The bottom line is whose fabulation you choose to believe, which is the same as saying whose history or whose reality you shall believe.'[48]

It should be noted, however, that Barnes does not deny the possibility of valid, authentic historical knowledge. He subverts the notion of objec-tive truth, but then reinstates it in 'Parenthesis' in order to try and make sense of history: 'We all know objective truth is not obtainable . . . . But while we know this, we must still believe that objective truth is obtain-able; or we must believe that it is 99 per cent obtainable; or if we can't believe this we must believe that 43 per cent objective truth is better than 41 per cent' (pp. 245–6). Thus, in the half-chapter, the narrator is coun-termanding what other narrators have been doing in preceding chapters by rehabilitating truth, not as a scientific and absolute truth, but as a goal and a safeguard against the dangers of 'beguiling relativity' (p. 246) and political passivity, thereby approaching Walter Benjamin's views on history as analysed by Gasiorek.[49] Barnes acknowledges this new perspective proposed in 'Parenthesis': 'that part is . . . against part of what the book has already been doing, which is undermining traditional history'.[50] As Pateman explains, this position is paradoxical because it places Barnes in opposition to the philosophers of the postmodern, such as Jean-François Lyotard (1924–98), who deny the very idea of the accessibility of truth.[51] Rubinson concurs by suggesting that Barnes does not assert a 'relativistic postmodern despair about the human capacity to have reliable knowl-edge'.[52] However, this stance also corresponds to the postmodernist strat-egy of inscribing and subverting, installing and deconstructing, except that Barnes does it in the reverse way: he first deconstructs the notion of objective truth and then reinscribes it. As Salyer suggests, 'With this para-dox of subverting objective truth and then reinstalling it, Barnes is right back in the thick of postmodernist thought.'[53]

Still within the postmodernist context, a major issue of interest for critics such as Gregory Salyer, Claudia Kotte and myself is the way in which the problematising of historical discourse in the novel leads the author to highlight the intimate links that connect historical accounts and political power. Official history is usually written from the vantage point of dominant groups (the victors, the colonisers, men . . .), while minorities and subordinate communities are condemned to silence, but Barnes departs from the established versions of history and substitutes apocryphal and heterodox rewritings. Rewriting entails revision and re-vision, as American poet Adrienne Rich (born 1929) suggests: 'Re-vision – the act of looking back, of seeing with fresh eyes, of entering an old text from a new critical direction.'[54] Thus, the book articulates a resistance to the monological and totalitarian aspect of canonised history, and gives voice to a series of marginalised groups (victims, women, even woodworms!) whose narrations have been excluded from legitimate historical discourse. According to Salyer, the regular staging of wood-worms in the book, seen as parasites and despicable creatures, works as 'a reminder of [the] submerged voices of history'.[55] This strategy is typical of postmodernist and post-colonial literature, as the purpose is to 'decen-tre the established authoritative "objective" Western account of historical events', to quote Robert Holton,[56] and to 'wrest historical materials from the androcentric and ethnocentric contexts in which they are embed-ded', to quote Elisabeth Wesseling.[57]

Salyer adds that Barnes's novel 'problematizes more than history – it problematizes the sacred'.[58] In the first chapter, 'The Stowaway', the narrator, who will turn out to be a woodworm, presents a revisionist version of sacred history, and more particularly the episodes of Noah's Ark and the Flood. These biblical events are part of the collective culture and the reader is supposed to know them, as Barnes suggested: 'obviously, you use Genesis because that is something everyone knows, that's an easy point of access, it's the Book'.[59] Claudia Kotte and myself analysed in detail the way in which the insubordinate narrator deconstructs the biblical version by, on the one hand, filling in the deliberate gaps in the official narrative and, on the other hand, openly contradicting several factual aspects of the authorised discourse.[60] A scrupulous comparison between the biblical text and the woodworm's rewriting reveals that the parasite's aim is not only to compensate for the inadequacies and insuffi-ciencies of the official document, but also to question its validity, to correct mistakes and to establish a new truth, which is apocryphal but pretends to be reliable. The perspective is clearly decentred as the narra-tor is a stowaway aboard the Ark, a woodworm, a parasite, who will subvert the language of authority in colloquial and humorous terms, evoking the manner of a stand-up comedian.

According to Alan Clinton, 'the woodworm forms the counterpart to the bookworm, or voice of scholarly authority'.[61] He is thus cheekily subversive when he turns Noah into a quick-tempered, narrow-minded, despotic drunkard, and desacralises the figure of the patriarch by direct attacks, euphemisms or comparisons with more dignified animals. The irreverent woodworm deconstructs canonised history by taking off the poetic varnish which distorts and embellishes people and events, revealing instead that the true story has been erased so as to make the official version more acceptable. To those who cannot stare at the truth, the parasite shows how the concepts of discrimination, of selection, of the separation between the clean and the unclean, the pure and the impure, which will recur in later chapters, find their origins in the Ark and the Bible. He reveals that hybrids or cross-breeds were sacrificed because of a theory about the purity of the species. He gives details of the oppression, the arbitrary dictatorship, the tyranny led by Noah on the Ark, which will find echoes in the history of the world as described in the next chapters through the wars of religion, terrorism, the nuclear war and the Holocaust. Even though the first chapter is full of humour, playfulness and jokes, the undertones are bleak and according to Frank Kermode, suggest 'a witty Post-Modern sadness'.[62]

In the end, as Barnes suggested, 'saying what "really" happened from the point of view of a woodworm is still a very partial truth'.[63] The author's aim is not to replace one truth, one unquestionable myth, one master narrative by another – as the indefinite article of the title makes clear – but to undermine the discourse of authority. As Kotte remarks, 'On the one hand, the title conjures up totalising notions of history, but on the other hand, the use of the indefinite article subverts the implied assumptions of totality and objectivity.'[64] Throughout the book, the competing historical narratives and the chaotic presentation challenge the ideal of universal history and, by telling tales of suffering, oppression and exploitation, undermine any conception of history as a process of constant progress and emancipation. In her attempt to decide whether the events presented in Barnes's book confirm that history follows a single and coherent movement or plot, Claudia Kotte examines in detail three historical patterns, or metanarratives, which are simultaneously proposed and undermined in the novel. Kotte first shows how eschatology, or the apocalyptic vision, according to which history is governed by divine providence and design, is offered as a solution in several chapters but eventually challenged by the tragedy of the Jewish passengers on board the St Louis: 'After the Holocaust, God or any other transcendental principle, which would confer intelligible meaning on existence, can no longer be a legitimating or legitimate authority upon which the course of history can be based.'[65]

Kotte then considers the secular teleology of G. W. F. Hegel (1770–1831), the historical materialism of Karl Marx (1818–83) and the ideas of evolution and of the survival of the fittest derived from Charles Darwin (1809–82), which all view history as rational and intelligible, marked by continuous progress. The narrator of 'Parenthesis' ironically reminds the reader of this vision:

> ■ History is just what historians tell us. There was a pattern, a plan, a movement, expansion, the march of democracy; it is a tapestry, a flow of events, a complex narrative, connected, explicable. One good story leads to another. First it was kings and archbishops with some offstage divine tinkering, then it was the march of ideas and the movement of masses, then little local events which mean something bigger, but all the time it's connections, progress, meaning, this led to this, this happened because of this.   (p. 242) □

The narrator also rages against the illusion of coherent and constant progression created by historical dates (p. 241), an impatience with chronology which certainly explains why the chapters are seemingly arranged at random. Kotte explains that Darwin's theory of the survival of the fittest 'cannot constitute a valid model for the course of human history'[66] as the ones who survive in Barnes's chapters are sometimes the most cunning (the woodworm, Lawrence Beesley), 'the cowards, the panickers, the deceivers' (p. 174) during the *Titanic*'s shipwreck, 'the Worriers' (p. 97) such as Kathleen Ferris, or the ones supposed to be pure and clean according to the Nazis. Kotte also shows that Marx's pattern of history as tragedy followed by farce is confirmed by a few episodes in the novel, but the majority of stories actually present a succession of tragedies without any farcical element in them. *A History of the World in 10½ Chapters* deconstructs the rational, consistent and coherent model for the course of history, and replaces it with a sense of entropy which reflects the mutability, discontinuity, arbitrariness and chaos of history: 'Our current model for the universe is entropy, which at the daily level translates as: things fuck up' (p. 246). As Barnes suggested, 'There is either a God and a plan and it's all comprehensible, or it's all hazard and chaos, with occasional small pieces of progress. Which is what I think.'[67]

It should be noted finally that the linear and teleological model of history is replaced not only by entropy but also perhaps by a view of history as cyclical. The numerous echoes between chapters and the circular movements of boats suggest that history may come full circle. However, as Kotte argues, 'Barnes's *History* stages numerous repetitions of the deluge with crucial variations, which invalidate historical circularity and instead focus on the specificity and singularity of events.' Highlighting 'ruptures, subtle contradictions and inconsistencies, differences and conflicts',[68] rejecting any theory of history as pattern, Barnes displays a postmodernist 'incredulity towards metanarratives' to quote Jean-François Lyotard's famous phrase.[69] Master narratives that would grant meaning and rationality to events no longer exist and are replaced by a variety of stories, a polyphony of voices, a plurality of versions. The celebration of heterogeneity and the rejection of any monologic discourse will be taken up again in Barnes's next novel, *Talking It Over*, and its sequel, *Love, etc*, which juxtapose different voices and contradictory versions, but also probe into the issues of love, infidelity and happiness, already discussed in 'Parenthesis'. The modes and strategies are different, however, and these will be examined in detail in the next chapter.

# CHAPTER SEVEN

# The Polyphony of Love and Truth: *Talking It Over* (1991) and *Love, etc* (2001)

When *A History of the World in 10½ Chapters* was published and reviewers commented upon its formal experimentation, Julian Barnes said: 'My next book is less experimental-looking than *Flaubert's Parrot* and this one.'[1] Published two years later, *Talking It Over* presents a fairly conventional triangular relationship but applies an original narrative technique. It was well received by reviewers and won the Prix Fémina for a foreign novel in France in 1992. The novel contrasts two friends: dull Stuart, an investment banker, and brilliant Oliver, a teacher of English to foreigners. Stuart meets Gillian, a picture restorer, and marries her, but soon afterwards, Oliver falls in love with Gillian, who gets a divorce from Stuart and marries Oliver. Stuart is desperate and leaves for the United States while Gillian and Oliver move to the South of France and have a daughter. Ten years later, in *Love, etc*, Gillian and Oliver have moved back to London and have two daughters, but Oliver has had a nervous breakdown and is jobless. Stuart comes back from America where he has made a fortune, remarried and divorced again, and he decides to help Gillian and Oliver financially by having them go back to the house where he and Gillian lived when they were married, and getting a job for Oliver. It appears, however, that Stuart is also here to win Gillian back. The first novel is funny and witty, especially thanks to Oliver's virtuoso interventions, while the sequel is much more bitter, cruel and dark.

When *Talking it Over* and *Love, etc* were published, many reviewers saw through the deceptive simplicity of plot and applauded the original narrative technique and confessional style. Adapting the convention of the epistolary novel (a novel told in letters), both books are composed of dramatic monologues by the main protagonists but also by a few secondary characters. Each monologue is preceded by the name of the protagonist who intervenes so that, to a certain extent, the novel resembles a play. A few reviewers drew attention to this generic blurring, such as Edward T. Wheeler: 'the form of the book most resembles a television play done in narration and voice-over'.[2] David Holloway, for his part, assimilated the book to a television documentary in which the protagonists would be 'talking heads nattering on and answering questions thrown at them by some off-screen researcher'.[3] John Bayley pointed to the way in which the protagonists talk to the reader, 'as actors in the present-day theatre address the audience'.[4] Richard Todd commented: 'The status of the narrative in fact hovers uneasily between fiction and drama, though a drama from which all stage-directions have been removed.'[5] The technique of juxtaposed monologues had already been developed before, for example by William Faulkner (1897–1962) in *As I Lay Dying* (1930) and by the South African writer André Brink (born 1935) in *A Chain of Voices* (1982) – though in both of these the form was that of the interior monologue rather than the spoken monologue. It was taken up again more recently by Graham Swift in *Out of This World* (1988) and *Last Orders* (1996).

As Michael Levenson suggests, the title of Barnes's first volume is 'a great irony, since talking it over is exactly what these people fail to do. All through Barnes's body of work, in fact, dialogue signally fails to occur.'[6] Ironically, once jilted, Stuart is only 'talking it over with money' (p. 230), while Gillian's assertion that she and Oliver discussed the idea of moving to the South of France – 'We talked it over beforehand' (p. 246) – is forcefully denied by Oliver: 'It was Gill's decision' (p. 246). When Stuart is found spying on Oliver and Gillian from his hotel, Gillian knows she should have 'suggested we talk things over in a sensible manner', but adds: 'But I can't do that' (p. 264), thus signalling the failure of the conversational mode and the solipsism of each character. In the first chapter of *Love, etc*, the three characters go on talking in monologues addressed to the reader but for once they hear what the others say, so that each monologue is a reaction to what has just been said by the others. The whole chapter thus sounds like a mock dialogue until Gillian reminds Oliver and Stuart of the agreed format: 'Look, stop it, you two. Just stop it. This isn't working. . . . If we're getting into this again, we have to play by the rules. No talking among ourselves' (p. 7).

Apart from this first chapter, the reader is therefore the unique – though silent – interlocutor who should listen to the cues rather than read them, as Stuart suggests when referring to Oliver in *Talking It Over*: 'I can't reproduce the way he talks – you'll have to listen to him for yourself' (p. 2). Both books are characterised by the narrative technique of 'skaz', which David Lodge defines as

■ a rather appealing Russian word . . . used to designate a type of first-person narration that has the characteristics of the spoken rather than the written word. In this kind of novel or story, the narrator is a character who refers to himself (or herself) as 'I', and addresses the reader as 'you'. He or she uses vocabulary and syntax characteristic of colloquial speech, and appears to be relating the story spontaneously rather than delivering a carefully constructed and polished written account.[7] □

This method, which, according to John Bayley, 'goes back both to the novel in letters and the dramatic monologue in poetry',[8] was notably employed by J. D. Salinger (born 1919) in *The Catcher in the Rye* (1951), in his creation of the 'voice' of its protagonist, Holden Caulfield, as well as by Kingsley and Martin Amis in some of their first-person novels, and by Barnes himself in the woodworm's tale in *A History of the World in 10½ Chapters*.

Several critics, and more particularly James Buchan[9] and Erica Hateley,[10] compared the novels to *Success* (1978) by Martin Amis. Even if in *Love, etc*, Stuart warns the reader against the temptation of comparison – 'I'm suspicious of people comparing things with other things' (p. 159) – the two main characters of Amis's novel, Terry Service and Gregory Riding, greatly resemble Stuart Hughes and Oliver Russell. Both Terry and Stuart are introverted, unimaginative and pitiful, while Gregory and Oliver are extroverted, pedantic and self-centred. *Success* applies the same narrative technique as Barnes's books, i.e. the protagonists address the silent reader, giving him/her their own version of the same events and competing for his or her sympathy. Barnes and Amis's close friendship until the mid-1990s may explain this complicity between the two books.

The narrative technique of monologues is an efficient device of characterisation as the protagonists are revealed through the way they speak, their idiosyncrasies, their cultural references, their centres of interest. Drawing attention to Barnes's knack for ventriloquy, Mick Imlah remarks that 'Barnes' selection and balance of three dissimilar styles of discourse is shrewdly done.'[11] This plurality of voices and styles corresponds to what Mikhail Bakhtin called 'polyphony'. Each voice becomes readily recognisable thanks to a specific vocabulary, syntax and rhythm, as may be perceived by analysing the introductory words of each protagonist. Stuart starts *Talking It Over* with 'My name is Stuart, and I remember everything' (p. 1) and ends his first monologue with the same sentence: 'I remember everything' (p. 7). In *Love, etc*, he addresses the reader with insistence: 'I remember you. *I* remember *you*' (p. 1). The repetition marks Stuart's self-proclaimed reliability, but also his doggedness. Gillian, reticent and quiet, proves reluctant to engage in a conversation at first and is the least talkative character until she opens up later on. In

*Talking It Over*, she starts with 'I haven't got anything to say' (pp. 7–8), 'What I remember is my business' (p. 8), and in *Love, etc*, she adopts the same defensive and wary tone: 'You may or may not remember me' (p. 3). Finally, Oliver's tone is much more relaxed in *Talking It Over* – 'Hi, I'm Oliver, Oliver Russell. Cigarette?' (p. 8) – and he wittily insists on differentiating himself from Stuart from the start: 'I remember all the *important* things' (p. 9). In *Love, etc*, Oliver once again chooses to differ from Stuart by inverting the original order of the personal pronouns: 'I could tell you remembered *me*' (p. 3). The reader will later understand that memory works differently for each character, each of them providing complementary and contradictory versions of the past, an issue Barnes had already examined in some of his previous novels.

Oliver's voice, though seemingly unreliable, is certainly the most memorable and entertaining as he is characterised by his erudition, flamboyance, wit and a tendency to 'scatter *bons mots* like sunflower seeds' (p. 239), as he says in *Talking It Over*. Mick Imlah called him 'the literary life of the novel'[12] because he very often makes literary but also musical allusions, combined with the use of French, Latin, Italian or German words,[13] all highlighting his pedantry and pretentiousness as well as his wit and cleverness. He enjoys repeating sophisticated or unusual words such as 'steatopygous' or 'crepuscular' and uttering polyglot sentences, such as 'hie me to the vomitorium *pronto!*' (p. 43) in *Talking It Over*, or '*Et tu?* O narcoleptic and steatopygous Stuart, he of the crepuscular understanding and the *Weltanschauung* built of Lego' (p. 12) in *Love, etc*. In the sequel, Oliver sarcastically makes fun of literary conventions when describing a fable as it might be related in various literary genres, among them Realism, Sentimental Romanticism, Surrealism and Postmodernism (pp. 156–7). As John Bayley suggested, 'Oliver is the self-appointed clever one, the word-agile but also rather endearing Lucky Jim who fascinates his friends.'[14] The allusion to the eponymous hero of Kingsley Amis's *Lucky Jim* (1954) is developed later on by Bayley when he compares the atmosphere, the verbal patter and the wisecracks of *Talking It Over*, to those of Kingsley Amis, P. G. Wodehouse, Evelyn Waugh and, more recently, Martin Amis. Several reviewers remarked that Barnes's own voice and verbal tricks could be heard in Oliver's monologues: 'Then we get the unsheathed pen, the unloosed tongue, the darting, lashing, dare-to-say-anything whip of the high-stepping mind,' Michael Levenson comments.[15] In an interview Barnes himself admitted: 'Oliver is of all my characters probably the most self-constructed.'[16] In *Love, etc*, Oliver, suffering from depression, becomes more cynical and his wit is wilting. A few reviewers, such as Elaine Showalter, found his verbal riffs less entertaining in the sequel: 'His clever wordplay has degenerated into irritating campy mannerisms.'[17] This may actually reflect the drifting into middle-age of Oliver, who is supposed to irritate or at least provoke the reader: 'you're meant to have quite sharp reactions to Oliver', Barnes told an interviewer.[18]

The epigraph to *Talking It Over*, which is also appropriate to *Love, etc*, is '*He lies like an eye-witness*'. As Oliver later explains (p. 220), this is a Russian saying quoted by Dmitri Shostakovich (1906–75) in his memoirs, and it warns the reader that what follows will not necessarily be the truth and that he/she should question the reliability of each speaker. As Linda Hutcheon remarks: 'Even an eye-witness account can only offer one limited interpretation of what happened; another could be different.'[19] This will be confirmed in the novel itself as each protagonist gives his or her own different version of the same events, and each competes for the reader's sympathy and interest: 'we had this argument. Oliver and Gillian and me. We each had a different opinion. Let me try and set down the opposing points of view' (p. 3). According to Tim Adams, the three protagonists are 'defence counsels for their own versions of the events that forced them together and apart, slick-talking, misty-eyed lifestyle attorneys appealing to our emotions and plea-bargaining for sympathy and special dispensations'.[20] The reader's role is therefore central as Anthony Quinn suggests, 'We are, indeed, the reader-as-jury, and must piece together a story, from Stuart, Oliver and Gillian as they assume and depart the witness stand, delivering their version of What Happened.'[21] From his/her privileged position, the reader, who is repeatedly addressed as 'you', offered cigarettes and asked to take sides, can compare the contradictory points of view and infer that some or all might lie or distort the truth. For example, in the first chapter of *Talking It Over*, the three characters describe the circumstances of Stuart and Gillian's wedding and the variations in their accounts are amusing but blatant. Stuart nostalgically remembers a 'gentle breeze' (p. 6), which becomes 'too much wind' (p. 11) in Oliver's version. Stuart describes the registrar as 'a dignified man who behaved with the correct degree of formality' (p. 6), whereas Oliver refers contemptuously to 'this perfectly oleaginous and crepuscular little registrar' (p. 11). Stuart's euphemism – 'I said my vows a bit too loud' (p. 6) – is contrasted with Oliver's hyper-bole: 'Stuart bellowed his words' (p. 11).

Gillian's job as a painting restorer seems to offer a metaphor of the reader's constant efforts at uncovering the truth lying beneath layers of subjective versions. When in *Talking It Over* she explains what her work consists in – 'you take off overpaint and discover something underneath' (pp. 58–9) – she actually seems to be telling the reader what he/she should do with the texts at hand. However, Gillian adds that the original picture – or truth – can never be completely deciphered: 'You're bound to go a little bit too far or not quite far enough' (p. 120). Oliver rejoices in this relativity of truth: 'Oh effulgent relativity! *There's no "real" picture under there waiting to be revealed.* What I've always said about life itself. . . . It's just my word against everybody else's!' (p. 120). Mick Imlah remarks, however, that the contradictions between the versions of the various protagonists 'are matters of emphasis or of taste . . . rather than lapses of veracity', as the episode of the wedding confirms, certainly because 'the known presence of two other witnesses in the wings is an effective check on falsification'.[22]

Nevertheless, some passages remain unclear, such as, in both books, the endings which John Bayley categorises as 'aporia',[23] an ancient Greek term which means 'in rhetoric, the expression of doubt, and which has been revived by deconstructionist critics to mean a final, irresolvable impasse in a text. In *Talking It Over*, Gillian stages a quarrel with her husband in the middle of the street to get rid of Stuart, who is spying on them from a hotel room across the street. This fake quarrel, however, arouses fear in Gillian – 'the fear is this: that what I'm showing Stuart turns out to be real' (p. 269) – and incredulity in Oliver – 'surely this isn't real, is it?' (p. 271) – but the novel ends abruptly before the reader is able to decide what will ensue. In an interview, Barnes said: 'I like the kind of novel or work of art or film which implies that it's going on after it ends, which leaves some things unresolved.'[24] The open ending of *Talking It Over* and its unknown consequences, about which readers disagreed, are actually what enabled Barnes to write a sequel. In *Love, etc*, Stuart remarks: 'In life, every ending is just the start of another story' (p. 93), which proves true also for Barnes's novel. The sequel is much darker than the first volume and Stuart's motives are unclear from the start, as William Hutchings remarks: 'is he a benign, almost Dickensian benefactor, willing to let bygones be bygones? Or is he a Machiavellian manipulator seeking revenge?'[25] As Barnes points out, Stuart is a 'damaged survivor' and therefore potentially dangerous: 'as the book proceeds he turns out to be less and less a voice on whom we can rely'.[26] This ambivalence lasts until the end with an ambiguous scene between Stuart and Gillian, from which the reader cannot decide whether they made love or whether Stuart raped Gillian, all the more so as Gillian's version changes from 'He wasn't pulling me towards him: I was the one who moved' (p. 216), to 'Yes, I do consider it to have been rape' (p. 229), to 'When we were making love – no, when he was raping me – no, let's say when we were having sex' (p. 242). As Craig Hamilton explains in his essay, the same word – 'fucking' – pronounced by the same character to refer to the same scene, may yield several meanings – making love, raping, having sex – according to the context; hence the polysemy of the text.[27]

The absence of any authorial or authoritative voice forces readers to make their own judgement on the events described. After having made his presence blatant in 'Parenthesis' in *A History of the World in 10½ Chapters*, Barnes enjoyed hiding in the wings again: 'I found the novel's technique very alluring, with this notion of reducing the authorial presence to the smallest it could possibly be and having no intervention between characters and reader.'[28] Barnes suggested he may have been influenced by the film *Rashômon* (1950) by Akira Kurosawa (born 1910), adapted from a novella (1915) by Ryunosuke Akutagawa (1892–1927), in which contradictory points of view on the same events are juxtaposed without any final truth being revealed about what really happened.[29] The apparent absence of the author allows for a greater involvement of the reader, as Barnes explained: 'Obviously, I'm still behind the scenes and running the show to some extent, but this way of writing allows for a freer range of interactions between reader and character than normal.'[30] The books thus constantly move to and fro, between intimacy with and distance from the readers, who are undoubtedly made aware of the fact that the narrator is manipulating them, guiding their judgements, controlling their reactions, but also know that they have access to all versions. The three protagonists thus repeatedly try to obtain information about the others from the reader, for example in *Talking It Over* when Stuart is beset with doubts: 'Of course, *you* know if they're really fucking, don't you? *You* know. So tell me. Go on, tell me' (p. 163), or when Oliver wonders about Stuart's sentimental life: 'Do you know if he's got a girl?' (p. 251), or when Gillian slyly asks the reader's opinion: 'Just out of interest, do you think Oliver's been faithful to me since we were married?' (p. 268). In *Love, etc*, Barnes pushed the form a step further in the chapter entitled 'Question Time', which is composed of answers made to the reader, except that the reader has to imagine the questions he or she is supposed to have asked (pp. 230–41). The constant breaking of the frame of fiction by a polyphony of voices which address the reader, and the insistence on the elusiveness and fragility of truth, force the reader into an active role.

Apart from the narrative technique of intercutting monologues which create a polyphony of voices, what mainly attracted the attention of critics was Barnes's handling of the themes of love, jealousy and betrayal, which he had already dealt with in his previous novels, notably in *Before She Met Me*, *Flaubert's Parrot* and 'Parenthesis' in *A History of the World in 10½ Chapters*. The title of the sequel, *Love, etc*, should really have been that of the first volume, except that Barnes found out there was already an American novel called *Love, etc* (1979) by Bel Kaufman (born 1911). He reluctantly switched to *Talking It Over* but the French publishers were perfectly happy with the original title, which was retained for the French translation. Ten years later, Barnes silenced his qualms and entitled the sequel *Love, etc*, which proved embarrassing to the French publishers, who named the second volume *Dix ans après* [*Ten Years Later*]. The much cherished title *Love, etc* is actually taken from a reflexive passage in *Talking*

*It Over*. Remembering letters published in newspapers and ending with
'Yours etc.' (p. 138), Oliver invents the expression 'Love, etc.' (p. 139),
which he inscribes at the end of his own letters. He derives from this
formula a theory according to which he divides the world into two
groups: 'those who believe that the purpose, the function, the bass pedal
and principal melody of life is love, and that everything else – *everything
else* – is merely an *etc.*; and those, those unhappy many, who believe
primarily in the *etc.* of life, for whom love, however agreeable, is but a
passing flurry of youth, the pattering prelude to nappy-duty, but not
something as solid, steadfast and reliable as, say, home decoration' (p. 139).
As this essay-like passage appears when Oliver has fallen in love with
Gillian and tries to provoke her separation from Stuart, it seems that this
division corresponds to the split of personality between Oliver and Stuart
themselves.

In an article on *Talking It Over*, Barnes also used a binary opposition
to describe the central theme of the novel as the struggle between obsessive love and reasonable love.[31] The issue of obsession is recurrent in
Barnes's novels as the analysis of *Before She Met Me* and *Flaubert's Parrot*
has demonstrated, and it appears again in *Love, etc* except that it is now
Stuart, rather than Oliver, who is the victim of a persistent obsession with
his first wife and first love, Gillian. In the sequel, the three protagonists
give their respective definitions of love before expatiating upon it, which
reveals much of their personality. According to Stuart, 'First love is the
only love,' while for Oliver, 'As much love as possible is the only love,'
and to Gillian, 'True love is the only love' (p. 171).

Love is certainly the main theme of the two novels and is very often
the subject of short essays, thus echoing 'Parenthesis' in *A History of the
World in 10½ Chapters*. Both Bryan Appleyard and James Wood compared
*Talking It Over* to Ford Madox Ford's *The Good Soldier*, one of Barnes's
favourite novels about a love triangle, to which critics had already
referred in relation to *Flaubert's Parrot*. According to Appleyard, both
novels play with 'the structural drama of emotional exposure',[32] and
Wood points in both to an 'intelligent surgery on the damp but fickle
English heart'.[33] In *Talking It Over* and *Love, etc*, many of the maxims and
reflections on love and passion are uttered by Gillian's mother Mme
Wyatt, a Frenchwoman who very often quotes the French moralist
Chamfort (1740–94), and who is, according to Peter Kemp, 'a prodigy of
sage finesse in matters erotic and emotional'.[34] Oliver also offers discussions, elaborations, aphorisms and epigrams on love, for example when,
in *Talking It Over*, he points to the similarities between love and market
forces through a capitalistic extended metaphor: 'Love too has its buy-
outs, its asset stripping, its junk bonds. Love rises and falls in value like
any currency' (p. 158). Oliver's corroding wit, however, does not last.
According to Michael Levenson, Barnes 'tests love as the antidote to

irony', as 'through the person of Oliver he satirizes satire, ironizes irony, lacerates his wit, until that other value – love – rises in the ashes'.[35] Once Oliver falls in love with Gillian in *Talking It Over*, he becomes prey to passion and finds it hard to control his emotions. This is made clear by the structure of the first volume: each of the first six chapters is marked by a regular alternation of monologues by Stuart, Gillian and Oliver, but from the time Oliver offers Gillian a bunch of flowers and tells her 'I love you' (p. 88), the distribution of speech becomes chaotic and irregular. Craig Hamilton suggests that form imitates content as the narrative disorder reflects the emotional disorder provoked by Oliver's declaration of love.[36] However, the tone is mainly comic and has none of the tragic and pathological undertones of *Before She Met Me*, which staged an unconventional love triangle between husband, wife, and the wife's past or fictitious lovers. The second volume is much crueller, and Barnes's preoccupation with jealousy, betrayal and obsession is stated anew. Elaine Showalter suggests that in the sequel, 'romantic comedy has turned into madness and horror'.[37] The traditional figure of the love triangle can indeed initiate a comedy of manners or comedy of adultery, but may also provoke more tragic outcomes, such as depression, domestic violence or even rape, as the two books demonstrate.

Scholars have been drawn to analyse the love triangle, predominantly in *Talking it Over*, as *Love, etc* was published too recently to have attracted much academic attention as yet. Richard Todd in particular focuses on the performative aspect of Barnes's *Talking It Over* in the domestic arena. Todd argues that this apparently banal domestic situation is deceptive and hides deeper issues, such as the place of women in discourse. He takes as an example the intervention of Stuart's ex-girlfriend Val, a spiteful feminist, who subversively hypothesises Oliver's latent homosexual desire for Stuart. Oliver and Stuart join to gag her (pp. 218–19) and thus expel her from the story, so that 'one particular feminine voice or discourse is effectively silenced'. Todd wonders moreover if Gillian herself, though able to talk, is not 'becoming an object of desire and nothing more, incapable of sustaining the politics of her gender'; Todd asks: 'Does a male discourse of desire ultimately triumph?'[38]

There is no doubt as to Erica Hateley's answer to that question as she argues that the traditional patriarchal model of masculine authority is what predominates in *Talking It Over*. Comparing it to *Success* by Martin Amis, she suggests that the triangulated affairs in both novels 'illustrate the ascribed importance of male homosocial relationships and the subordination of female autonomy to male authoritarianism', reasserting 'traditional patriarchal ideals of feminine silence, passivity and objectification'. Hateley explains that Stuart and Oliver have established a homosocial relationship based on economic exchange, as Stuart very often lends money to Oliver. When Oliver falls in love with Gillian, he proposes an exchange of positions by developing an economic metaphor: 'It's market forces, Stu, that's what you've got to get hold of. And I'm going to take her over' (p. 159). Gillian, who is essentially passive, has thus been 'reduced to an object of competitive ownership', a marketable item.[39] Matthew Pateman agrees with this interpretation and points to 'the complete immersal of the discourse of love into the discourse of commerce'.[40] Pateman recalls in particular the way in which Oliver, before confessing his love for Gillian, hands Stuart an envelope with a quarter of the loan the latter had advanced him, as though buying Gillian. The latter 'is an object, and Stuart and Oliver have to try and arrange some exchange value that will allow the transfer of ownership'.[41] In her essay, Hateley goes on to interpret Gillian's orchestration of violence at the end of *Talking It Over* as a sacrifice on her part in order to placate Stuart and as a sign that she is still 'subordinate to the needs and interests of both Stuart and Oliver'. The love triangle has served to 'confirm that women remain potentially disposable tools for the negotiation of patriarchal power'.[42] This interpretation could certainly also be applied to *Love, etc* in which Stuart, very much at ease in mercantile society, asserts his power by coming back to reclaim Gillian, denying that any exchange has taken place: 'I'm your husband. I've always been your husband. You're my wife' (p. 242).

Merritt Moseley suggests, for his part, that Gillian, for all her reticence and quietness, may be the most cunning of the three and the real manipulator, who seduced Oliver in the first place, as Val herself argues in *Talking It Over*: 'when exactly did she start giving him the come-on without him realising that she was doing it? Because that's her trick. She hasn't been doing it to you, has she?' (p. 188). As Moseley adds, 'if readers "sympathize" with Gillian, Val is right: she *has* worked her trick on them'.[43] In *Love, etc*, Oliver comes to realise he may have been manipulated by Gillian and warns the reader: 'Point is – *question* is – how much has she been manipulating you as well? Think about it' (p. 239). The distribution of power in this triangular relationship turns out to be much more complex than it appears at first reading, and may vary according to the degree of reliability the reader grants each protagonist.

Several reviewers – and many French ones – analysed the love triangle through a comparison with the famous film by French director François Truffaut (1932–84), *Jules et Jim* (1962) – adapted from the novel (1953) by Henri-Pierre Roché (1879–1959) – the echoes of which I have examined in detail.[44] Charles Nicholl, for example, called Barnes's novel 'a kind of spoof yuppie version of *Jules et Jim*'.[45] At the beginning of *Talking It Over*, Stuart draws a parallel between their trio and that of Jules, Jim and Catherine in Truffaut's film: 'there were the three of us. All that summer. The three of us. It was like that French film where they all go bicycling together' (p. 22). A few pages later, Olivier confirms the echo though with irony and sarcasm: '*Jules et Jim*. Oskar Werner, the short, blond, and − dare one say it − quite possibly steatopygous one, Jeanne Moreau, and then the tall, dark, elegant, good-looking one who doubtless had kissable teeth (what was his name?)' (pp. 23–4). The choice of vocabulary leaves no doubt as to the casting since Oliver previously referred to 'the benign, rumpled and somewhat steatopygous figure of my friend Stu' (p. 23) and celebrated his own 'dark, dark hair and kissable ivory teeth' (p. 13) similar to those of the actor Henri Serre. The reference to Truffaut's film so early in the novel creates a horizon of expectation − at least for the reader who knows the film − and foreshadows what may occur between the three characters later on. It is therefore ironic that Stuart should refer to the film, in which the man who plays his part will be betrayed and abandoned by his two friends. Later on, after Gillian has left Stuart for Oliver, it is Oliver who repeats the cinematographic reference in one of the rare passages of the book in which the two male characters actually address each other: 'It was just like old times, wasn't it? That? Just like old times. Remember? *Jules et Jim*.' But Stuart has grown wiser and is now aware of the irony: 'Fuck off, Oliver' (p. 219). A few elements from the plots of the film and novel bear similarities, as well as some of the features of the two male characters, as several reviewers have suggested, but the originality of *Talking It Over* lies in the variations from the film, which, unlike the novel, ends tragically. Barnes knows and appreciates Truffaut's films − he even devoted an essay to his correspondence which is collected in *Something to Declare* (pp. 35–47) − but he insists that the echoes between film and novel should not be overstated: 'I always resist the idea that *Talking It Over* is a homage to or a reworking of *Jules et Jim*. When it comes, it's a sort of necessary joke, it's a passing illusion . . . it was more a sort of wink.'[46]

In 1996, *Talking It Over* was turned into a French film entitled *Love, etc* − the French translation chosen for the title of the first volume − directed by Marion Vernoux and starring Charlotte Gainsbourg, Yvan Attal and Charles Berling. The film was well received and successful. It was difficult to adapt the monologues for the screen without making the film tedious, but the director developed a few strategies which enabled her to retain some of the effects of the dramatic monologues. She used the conventional technique of the voice-over, which helped the characters to comment on what was happening or gave access to their thoughts and feelings. When photos of Gillian and Stuart's marriage are taken, the screen is frozen and each of the three protagonists expresses his/her feelings to the camera one after the other. The silent reader whom the characters address in the novel is embodied in the film by a middle-aged lady and a young man sitting on a bench in a park, whom Oliver talks to and who actually give him their opinion. On the platform of the tube station, Stuart explains his desperate situation to a female passenger, who listens to him without answering. The major difference between novel and film concerns the ending. The novel ends in 1990 when Gillian and Oliver have moved to the South of France (p. 243). Gillian knows Stuart is spying on them from a nearby hotel, which leads her to stage a quarrel. In the film, the three characters meet again a few years later, on 1 January 2000 in Boulogne, as they had planned, to celebrate the beginning of the twenty-first century. Oliver and Gillian have no children yet. Stuart has made a fortune in Russia and his girlfriend Katya is five months pregnant. As Barnes suggested, the novel's ending is sinister and cruel while the film's conclusion, which may appear rather sentimental, is in fact bitter sweet.[47] Barnes also said he was pleased with the film and particularly with the fact that it was unfaithful. He recalls telling Vernoux: 'I hope you have betrayed me.'[48] A few years earlier, analysing the adaptation for the screen of *Doctor Fisher of Geneva* (1980) by Graham Greene, Barnes had written: 'The point is there's no such thing as a "faithful" adaptation of a novel; there are only degrees of infidelity.'[49] He developed the same argument in 'Faithful betrayal', an analysis of the adaptation of Flaubert's *Madame Bovary* by the French director Claude Chabrol (born 1930), included in *Something to Declare* (pp. 269–87). Even though Vernoux changed the conclusion of *Talking It Over* in her film, making it much less ambiguous than that of the book, she did leave a door open for the spectator to imagine the futures of the three protagonists.

The open ending of *Love, etc* also suggests that there may be room for another sequel ten years later, but as Mme Wyatt, the concluding voice of the novel, says: 'Something will happen. Or nothing. . . . So as for me, I will wait. For something to happen. Or for nothing to happen' (p. 250). While waiting for 2011 and a possible third episode of the love triangle, the reader may now turn to a wholly different type of novel, the political fable published in 1992 – *The Porcupine* – which appears as a complete change of direction in Barnes's literary production, as the next chapter will demonstrate.

# CHAPTER EIGHT

# Politics and Fiction: *The Porcupine* (1992)

After addressing the question of the elusiveness of truth through a polyphony of voices entangled in the web of love in *Talking It Over*, Julian Barnes approached the issue of truth again a year later in *The Porcupine* but from a completely different perspective, that of politics and ideology. This brief novel, or novella, takes place in an unnamed country of Eastern Europe in January and February 1991, and deals with the trial of Stoyo Petkanov, a former Communist Party leader, who is opposed to Prosecutor-General Peter Solinsky, a proponent of democracy and capitalism. The trial is relayed on television and a group of students react to the proceedings. Petkanov is eventually convicted but retains his arrogance and honour, while Solinsky is portrayed as inept, and mocked for his shameless ambition and spitefulness. *The Porcupine* is the only novel by Barnes which is dedicated not to Pat Kavanagh but to 'Dimitrina', i.e. Dimitrina Kondeva, his Bulgarian publisher and translator, who helped him with the novel.

Most reviewers celebrated the way Barnes came to terms with the Communist experience – born in 1946, the writer spent his childhood and part of his adult life in the shadow of the Cold War – but some were disconcerted by the choice of a serious realistic novel about politics, adding that they missed Barnes's playfulness and literary experimentation. Comparing it with previous novels, John Bayley remarks that *The Porcupine* 'looks like a complete departure – in style, purpose and manner'.[1] Patrick Parrinder agrees that it is 'a new departure' for Barnes but adds that 'his development has never been predictable, and no one could accuse him of writing the same novel twice'.[2] Robert Brown concurs that 'the novel suggests a clear continuation from neither the celebrated experimental mode of Barnes's earlier work nor the more personal sides of it'.[3] Merritt Moseley, slightly disappointed by the thin novel, observes: 'There is nothing postmodern about it; it is not tricky, or experimental, or dazzling, or even – barring a few wry inventions – particularly witty.'[4] Barnes had probably none of these adjectives in mind when composing *The Porcupine*, which he defined as 'a political novel about . . . the weakness of liberalism confronted by the certainty of a system [Communism] that believes it has all the answers'.[5]

If the country where *The Porcupine* takes place remains unnamed in the novel, Barnes made no secret about its identity in an article published in 1992: 'The novel deals with the trial of a former communist leader somewhere in the Balkans; the only such country where an ex-leader has actually been brought to trial is Bulgaria: ergo . . .'.[6] Moreover, the novel was first published in Bulgarian as *Bodlivo Svinche*, six weeks before its publication in English in the United Kingdom. Barnes's interest in Bulgaria had in fact started a few years before, as he recounts in 'Trademan's Entrance' (1990), a long essay devoted to the situation of Bulgaria. Barnes explains that he spent nine days there in November 1990 in order to promote *Flaubert's Parrot*, published in Bulgarian, and that for months before, he had cut out and collected every reference to Bulgaria in newspapers. His focus on Bulgaria was, paradoxically, due to the West's lack of interest in this state: 'Bulgaria is the forgotten item in the East European unshackling, a country that is doggedly down-page.'[7] Barnes's visit made him aware of the disastrous political and economic situation of the country in the wake of the fall of Communism, and at the dawn of the introduction of a free market economy. In his article, he drew attention to the food shortages, the lack of petrol, the ration coupons, the electricity cuts, the queues, the upsurge of pornography and erotica, and the pollution, and he developed a metaphor to characterise the country: 'If nations were children, this place would be taken into care; the world would be seeking a foster mother for it. Bulgaria was a chubby little country boy on whose flesh Communism and heavy industry decided to stub out their cigarettes; the burns are everywhere.'[8] During his visit, Barnes took many notes, causing his translator to ask if he was writing down all the absurdities about Bulgaria in his notebook. Six months later, drawing inspiration from these notes, he started composing *The Porcupine*.

Matthew Pateman's thesis on Barnes's fiction, and my *Postmodernisme*, give information on the political and legal events on which Barnes based his novel, and on the similarities between fiction and reality, which can be useful to situate the historical context of *The Porcupine*.[9] Bulgaria became a Communist state in 1949, with Todor Zhivkov (1911–98) as head of the Communist Party from 1954 and head of state from 1971. On 10 November 1989, Zhivkov was forced to resign and on 18 January 1990, he was arrested and charged with incitement of ethnic hatred, fraud and gross abuse of power. In February, Zhivkov's health deteriorated and he was placed in a military hospital before being moved to prison in July. When Barnes visited Bulgaria in November 1990, the date of Zhivkov's trial was still uncertain. It eventually began on 25 February 1991 but the ex-leader's ill-health caused postponements and the trial started again only on 23 October 1991. After another series of postponements, on 4 September 1992 Zhivkov was found guilty of the embezzlement of 24 million dollars and sentenced to seven years' imprisonment.

A few examples of the similarities and differences between the authentic Zhivkov and the fictional Petkanov can help the reader distinguish fiction from reality. While Zhivkov was the Communist Party leader in Bulgaria for 35 years, Petkanov was 'party leader and head of state for 33 years' (p. 25). The charges against Petkanov are slightly different from those against Zhivkov: 'deception involving documents . . . abuse of authority in your official capacity . . . mismanagement' (p. 32). Zhivkov's 39-year-old daughter Ludmilla Zhivkova, a Politburo member in charge of culture but suspected of being a political opponent, mysteriously died in 1981 from a brain haemorrhage; Petkanov's 35-year-old daughter Anna Petkanova, Minister of Culture, died of a heart attack on 23 April 1972 despite her previous excellent health (p. 110). Zhivkov's trial, postponed several times because of ill-health, started in February 1991, lasted for 18 months and ended with a sentence of seven years' imprisonment. In *The Porcupine*, Barnes chose to compress time as Petkanov, 'a powerful man' (p. 31), is sentenced to 'Thirty years of internal exile' (p. 134), after a trial which started on 10 January 1991 (p. 29) and lasted for 45 days (p. 116). While Zhivkov would only talk through his lawyers, Petkanov refuses legal representation. As Barnes explained, his intention was to portray not a fragile, sick old man but someone tough and arrogant who continues to believe in Communism, unlike Zhivkov who renounced his Communism, calling it a 'big mistake'.[10] Barnes's hypothesis was the following: 'what if, instead of running away or pretending he had cancer or whatever, what if he decided to defend himself by attacking?'[11] From such a quotation, one may conclude, as most critics did, that the 'Porcupine' of the title is Petkanov, defending himself against his opponent Solinski who, to try and handle him, has to wear 'porcupine gloves' (p. 29).[12]

In his review of the novel, Julian Duplain suggested that reality may have influenced fiction in more oblique ways, as the fictional dictator's first name, Stoyo, may have been inspired by the name of the President of the Supreme Court in Zhivkov's trial, Stefanka Stoyanova.[13] Professor Michael Scammel, for his part, compared *The Porcupine* to Zhivkov's extended interview with a Bulgarian reporter, conducted between December 1990 and February 1991, and remarked: 'Barnes has captured the tone of Zhivkov's voice, and some elements of his personality, with considerable accuracy, including the braggadocio and the slipperiness, the vehemence and the vagueness, and above all the complacent and egocentric conviction in his own rightness.'[14] Scammel nevertheless reproaches Barnes for a series of deviations from the original, for example the fact that contrary to Zhivkov, Petkanov speaks in Marxist–Leninist jargon and contemptuously criticises Gorbachev, 'that weak fool in the Kremlin who looked as if a bird had shat on his head' (p. 79). The reviewer also mentions that the 'sordid shiftiness, the cynical disregard for facts, the blatant readiness to change versions of the past, and the insinuating alternation of bluster with whining, so recognizably present in the real live Zhivkov . . . is lost in Barnes's version of a dictator at bay'.[15] Despite his protestations to the contrary, Scammel seems to look in the novel for a faithful reflection of historical reality. He concedes at first that 'Barnes, of course, cannot be held to account for not portraying the historical Zhivkov,' but then adds: 'But he can be held accountable for historical plausibility, since he intends *The Porcupine* to be a serious comment on contemporary Eastern Europe.'[16]

Such comments suggest that readers may have found it difficult to draw a straight line between fiction and reality, a recurrent ambiguity in Barnes's literary production since *Flaubert's Parrot* and *A History of the World in 10½ Chapters*. The blurring of the frontiers between two heterogeneous worlds is one of the key issues of *The Porcupine* and also of its reception. In September 1992, Barnes travelled back to Sofia in Bulgaria in order to promote his new novel, and the next month, he published a long article in *The Times*, 'How Much is that in Porcupines?', in which he addresses the issue of the 'recurrent problems with the demarcation line between history and fiction'.[17] He first claims that *The Porcupine* is mainly a work of the imagination: 'it is true I had used the rough outline of Todor Zhivkov's trial, borrowed bits of the local topography, listened to Bulgarian friends; but then I had gone off on my own, inventing the characters, making a plot out of a process, and so on'.[18] However, Barnes remembers his anxiety when he was about to meet his Bulgarian readers, who, he surmised, might prefer 'to read the book as history à clef rather than as a novel'. He wondered at that time: 'would they think I had imaginatively transformed their recent history, or merely pillaged and perverted it?'[19] Barnes's apprehensions were partly justified. Even though Bulgarians were friendly and hospitable, they could not help comparing fiction and reality, either highlighting inaccuracies or praising the perfect reflection of the truth: 'opinions rained down on me from "You have told the truth" to "You have falsified history". . . . Some critics, for instance, complained that I had made "my" dictator more intelligent than theirs, as if I were thereby ennobling him.'[20] Another example of such ontological confusion occurred when Zhivkov was given a seven-year sentence and the television newscaster ended his presentation by holding up a copy of *Bodlivo Svinche*, saying: 'Soon you will be able to read what an English writer has to say about the Zhivkov trial.'[21]

The writer's nationality, mentioned by the newsreader, can raise problems. At the official presentation of *The Porcupine* in Bulgaria, the former dissident poet Blaga Dimitrova, who had become vice-president of the country, told Barnes: 'We have become accustomed to foreigners explaining our country to us.'[22] In his 1992 article, Barnes recalls examples in Western literature which portrayed Bulgaria unfavourably, such as the play *Arms and the Man* (1898) by George Bernard Shaw (1856–1950), John Updike's short story 'The Bulgarian Poetess' (1970) about the same Blaga Dimitrova, or the novel *Rates of Exchange* (1983) by Malcolm Bradbury (1932–2000). Some reviewers have referred to the tradition of committed literature by André Malraux (1901–76) or George Orwell (1903–50),[23] and drawn attention to the interest of contemporary Western novelists in recent European politics. D. J. Taylor compares *The Porcupine* to two novels published in the same year: Ian McEwan's *Black Dogs*, about the ideological estrangement of a couple of Communists, and *The Call of the Toad* by German writer Günter Grass (born 1927), about the overthrow of Communism.[24] Michael Scammel, for his part, alludes to American writers such as Philip Roth (born 1933), Saul Bellow (1915–2005) and John Updike, but also to Malcolm Bradbury. Scammel remarks that while those writers 'have filtered their narratives through Western eyes', Barnes has attempted to 'narrate events from the inside' by 'impersonating a native', which, according to the critic, 'marks an uncharacteristic error on Barnes' part'.[25] Bayley shares this opinion when he remarks that Barnes 'seeks to be intimate with people and situations too distant and too alien to be controlled by the creative process'. As a consequence, the characters seem stiff and symbolic as if Barnes thought that 'characters, whether on contemporary television or in the pages of novels, just don't come alive any more'.[26]

Several reviewers, such as Bayley, Stone, Scammel and Parrinder, compared *The Porcupine* to *Darkness at Noon* (1941) by the Hungarian writer Arthur Koestler, who was one of Barnes's close friends. In 1988 Barnes wrote an essay entitled 'Playing Chess with Arthur Koestler', and in 2000, he published in 'The Afterlife of Arthur Koestler' a scathing review of David Cesarani's biography of him. Koestler's well-known novel, which Barnes finds 'impressive',[27] deals with a confrontation between a Communist politician, Rubashov, and his two interrogators, in a reflection of the 1937 Moscow trials. Bayley argues that unlike Petkanov, 'Rubashov lived in the novel as a realized character can and should do.'[28] Scammel, who is working on the official biography of Koestler, also draws a parallel with *Darkness at Noon* and remarks that in contrast to Barnes, Koestler 'had the benefit of having himself been a Communist and been intimate with the Communist mentality'.[29] Such a remark suggests that only an insider could write about Communism and echoes a quote from one of Barnes's short stories, 'One of a Kind' (1982), in which a British narrator shares his personal theory on Romania with Marian Tiriac, an exiled Romanian writer. The narrator asks Tiriac whether there were any dissidents in Romania, which provokes the latter's irritation, 'as if I didn't have the right to an opinion – or even a question – on the subject of his homeland'.[30] Barnes rejects such arguments – 'That way you only end up writing about your own country or experience'[31] – but writing about Bulgaria as a British novelist, he could fear the way in which he would be perceived by the Bulgarians themselves: 'Perhaps I would look like just another western entrepreneur, only this time of the literary sort, snapping up a tasty local story.'[32] As it turned out, Bulgarian readers, including the historical models for the two main protagonists, mainly applauded the novel, which came third in the best-seller lists. Zhivkov asked for a copy to be sent to him in prison, while the first Prosecutor in the dictator's trial, Krasimir Zhekov, greeted Barnes in Bulgaria: 'alarm probably showed on my face when I was introduced at the Union of Bulgarian Composers to a man who said: "I am Peter Solinsky." It was Mr Prosecutor Zhekov, who has so recently vanquished his near-homonym.'[33]

Barnes's 1992 article clearly reveals the porosity of the frontiers between fiction and reality, and the difficulty in maintaining a clear distinction between the two in a novel obviously based on recent historical facts. The confusion is heightened by the fact that many real political figures are alluded to in the novel, thus authenticating the historical and geographical context and establishing a continuity between reality and fiction. An effect of verisimilitude is therefore attained when Petkanov compares his reaction to the fall of Communism with that of his colleagues in the real world: Erich Honecker (1912–94) in East Germany – 'Erich running away to Moscow'; Janos Kadar (1912–89) in Hungary – 'Kadar dead after the betrayal of opening his frontier'; Gustav Husak (1913–91) in Czechoslovakia – 'Husak dead too, eaten up by a cancer'; General Wojciech Jaruzelski (born 1923) in Poland – 'Jaruzelski not up to it, joining the other side'; Nicolae Ceausescu (1918–89) in Romania – 'Ceausescu, at least he went down fighting' (p. 79). Such allusions grant a degree of realism to the novel. According to Linda Hutcheon, 'In many historical novels, the real figures of the past are deployed to validate or authenticate the fictional world by their presence, as if to hide the joins between fiction and history in a formal and ontological sleight of hand.'[34] Fiction and reality belong to two incompatible worlds, i.e. worlds of a different ontology or mode of being, and yet such strategies tend to erase the differences.

While acknowledging the effect of verisimilitude, Bruce Sesto suggests that Barnes's insertion of real-world figures also 'foregrounds the ontological boundaries between fiction and reality',[35] in that the author brings together characters that belong to disparate worlds. Brian McHale explains that 'There is an ontological scandal when a real-world figure is inserted in a fictional situation, where he interacts with purely fictional characters.'[36] The encounter between two heterogeneous worlds is, for example, made obvious when the fictional Petkanov recalls his physical contacts with such a historical figure as Nicolae Ceausescu, who ended up executed: 'Nicolae's body, the very body he'd hugged on many a state occasion, emptied of life. The collar and tie still neat, and an ironic, half-smiling expression on those lips that he, Stoyo Petkanov, had many times kissed at the airport' (p. 76). The violation of boundaries between worlds is reinforced when Petkanov enumerates the titles and medals he received from countries around the world (pp. 116–20), and reads excerpts from statements by historical heads of state who praised his achievements as a political leader (pp. 122–5). These statements supposedly uttered by real-world figures about an imaginary dictator tend to highlight the transgression of the boundaries between fiction and reality, but also to deprive the historical figures of their authenticity, turning them into puppets which have been manipulated by a fictional protagonist.

Such manipulations alert the reader to the fragility of truth in the novel, an issue which is recurrent in Barnes's fiction. In *The Porcupine*, the elusiveness of truth is foregrounded in many ways, first of all ironically through the name of the newspaper '*Truth*' (*Pravda*), 'the mouthpiece of the Socialist (formerly Communist) Party' (p. 40). Having been subjected to a constant evasion or distortion of truth under the Communist leadership of Petkanov, the students have great hopes of a new era: 'It was the end of lies and illusions; now the time had arrived when truth was possible, when maturity began' (p. 20). The day before the trial begins, the four students, Vera, Stefan, Dimiter and Atanas, share their expectations about the proceedings. Dimiter's and Stefan's forceful statements are marked by the anaphora (repetition at the beginning of sentences) of 'I want to know' (p. 24), while Vera is both more cautious and more ambitious: 'I hope we learn the truth' (p. 23). The students belong to these people who, according to Solinsky, 'preferred facts to ideology' and 'wanted to establish small truths before proceeding to the larger ones' (p. 27). Solinski himself offers the media a daring comparison when referring to his 'plan of easing truth like a dandelion leaf from between the teeth of lies' (pp. 37, 107).

Cynical Petkanov is, for his part, suspicious of the retrievability of truth and views the trial in dramatic terms: 'They would stage the trial their way, how it suited them, lying and cheating and fixing evidence, but maybe he'd have a few tricks for them too. He wasn't going to play the part allotted him. He had a different script in mind' (p. 17). The trial is relayed on television and Petkanov is determined to play the part he has chosen himself. Thus, before making his first statement, he asks: 'Which camera am I on?' (p. 33). Later on, the ex-leader will qualify the trial as a 'show' (p. 126) and a 'farce of a trial' (p. 136). Petkanov is in fact right in pinpointing the theatrical dimension of the trial. For instance, Solinski arranges for a female prison officer to be standing behind the former President and 'therefore always in shot when Petkanov was on camera' (p. 31). The narrator explains that 'this little touch of stage management' was meant to suggest that this was just an ordinary case brought to justice. Later on, as the trial runs out of steam, Solinski produces a document – certainly forged – that could condemn the dictator, a new development which is qualified as a '*coup de théâtre*' (p. 127). When his wife hears about this manipulation, she exclaims: 'It's a show trial' (p. 113), and she never stops denigrating her husband, 'disparaging his performance, calling him a TV lawyer' (p. 127). Reviewers emphasised the theatrical aspect of the novel, for example Robert Stone, who argued that *The Porcupine* 'might work better as a play',[37] or Maureen Howard, who remarked: 'What should play as grand inquisition, or at least as pure melodrama, becomes serious farce.'[38]

As might be expected, Petkanov denies the truth of the accusations (p. 126), a claim which happens to be partly justified. Indeed, Solinski finds it hard to obtain straightforward evidence as the truth balks at being unveiled: 'Little was written down; what had been written down was mostly destroyed; and those who had destroyed it suffered reliable attacks of memory loss' (p. 38). In order to prove that Petkanov ordered the elimination of political opponents when he was head of state, Solinski produces a memorandum supposedly signed by Petkanov, authorising 'the use of all necessary means against slanderers, saboteurs and anti-state criminals' (p. 94). The authenticity of the document is, however, questionable, as Lieutenant-General Ganin discloses it to Solinski only when the trial seems to have come to a dead end after the public humiliation of the Prosecutor-General: Petkanov has just ruthlessly revealed to the public that Solinski, when going to Turin as part of a trade delegation in the 1970s, spent the money given him by the Communist Party on a shiny Italian suit and a prostitute. Moreover, the statement ends not with a signature but with initials, as Petkanov remarks: 'I do not call that a signature. I call it a set of initials, quite probably forged' (p. 109). Solinski's wife bluntly accuses her inept husband of 'inventing fake evidence' (p. 112). Solinski's own arguments do not sound convincing: 'If Petkanov hadn't signed that memorandum, he must have signed something like it. We are only putting into concrete form an order he must have given over the telephone' (p. 113). His conclusion discredits his earlier accusation: 'The document is true, even if it is a forgery. Even if it isn't true, it is necessary' (p. 113). Solinski has failed in that he has resorted to the very strategy which constitutes his first charge against Petkanov: 'deception involving documents' (p. 39). As Moseley remarks, 'The end justifies the means,' and the need for a conviction of Petkanov is more important than the truth or forgery of a document.[39] Pateman concludes: 'In order for justice to be done, documents are forged and are given the status of truths: fakes, forgeries and lies are the platforms for a justice that is supposed to be condemning fakes, forgeries, and lies.'[40] Politics triumphs over justice, and both sides evade the truth. In that respect, as Richard Brown suggests, *The Porcupine* develops a theme which was already central to Barnes's previous novels: an 'attempt to evaluate competing claims to the truth in a postmodern cultural environment where all unitary claims are to be questioned'.[41]

The distortion of truth is presented in the novel as an inheritance of the closed Communist system of thought, especially in the way language is used. As British novelist Nick Hornby (born 1958) suggests, '*The Porcupine* is as much about the inadequacy of language as it is about political turmoil.'[42] Solinski identifies the clichéd and ideological characteristics of the former dictator's language: the 'cheap analogies . . . the parables, the exhortations, the made-to-measure moralities, the scraps of peasant wisdom' (p. 68), 'bureaucratic distortions of the language' (p. 91). The totalitarian and imprisoning ideology is thus reflected in a sterilised, stilted and uniform language which still prevails. For instance, Ganin goes on calling Solinski 'Comrade': 'It would take a while for the old forms of address to die away' (p. 50). Solinski himself cannot answer a simple question by 'yes' or 'no' but has to resort to periphrases such as 'If you think it appropriate' (p. 51). People hesitate to use straightforward words and to stare at the truth, for example when referring to the fall of the Communist regime: 'instead of Revolution, people here spoke only of the Changes' (p. 42). The students witnessing Petkanov's trial on television are well aware of this political corruption of language: 'he corrupted even the words that come out of our mouths' (p. 133), thus echoing the very words one of the students had uttered previously to describe Petkanov's constant evasion of truth: 'All that's coming out of his mouth is lies and hypocrisy' (p. 71).

Barnes explains in an interview that even everyday language has been poisoned by the Communist regime so that it becomes necessary to invent a new language.[43] That entails using direct words rather than periphrases, as Solinski, 'eager for fresh rhetoric' (p. 37), is aware: 'he must practise saying *Yes* and *No* and *That's stupid* and *Go away*' (p. 51). This new language, which still has to be found, is symbolised at the beginning of the novel by the demonstration by women who, instead of shouting slogans against the food shortages, produce a cacophony by banging kitchen implements against each other. As Hornby remarks, 'immediately we are thrust into a world where words have failed'.[44] The women's distrust of words is blatant: 'They spoke without words, they argued, bellowed, demanded and reasoned without words, they pleaded and wept without words' (p. 6). Later on, in the course of another demonstration, a student organisation – the Devinsky Commando – chooses to resort not to the women's wordless language but to ironic language. Chanting slogans such as 'THANK YOU FOR THE PRICE RISES', 'THANK YOU FOR THE FOOD SHORTAGES' or 'GIVE US IDEOLOGY NOT BREAD' (pp. 46–7), the students reveal the inadequacy of language and use irony – one of Barnes's favourite tools – as a political strategy of destabilisation, 'a subtle weapon against totalitarianism' to quote Moseley.[45] As Barnes once suggested, the political situation 'would be intolerable without a sense of irony'.[46]

The replenishment of language is echoed in the novel by a multiplicity of points of view, which counteracts the unique perspective formerly imposed by the Communist regime and reflects 'a refusal to impose one dominating system', according to Matthew Pateman.[47] The technique of free indirect discourse, which mixes direct and indirect styles – as, for example, in 'he must practise saying *Yes* and *No*' (p. 51) – is a means of portraying the consciousness of characters. It gives access to the thoughts and speech of the two main protagonists through their interior monologues but also to those of secondary characters. The students' sardonic comments are conveyed either in free indirect discourse or in direct speech while they watch the trial on television. The transcription of their stringent reactions, in square brackets and in italics, typographically highlights the opposition of conflicting views and, according to Pateman, disrupts the stability of the narrative voice 'who appears to provide an absolute and authoritative account' of the trial.[48] Many reviewers have suggested that they acted as a Greek chorus. The students' perspective is interesting as, like the Devinsky commando, they both condemn Communism and are suspicious of the new capitalist regime. Petkanov's trial marks the failure of the Communist regime, based on a dictatorship which provoked political oppression and economic ruin, but it does not legitimate the free market economy, which entails shortages, corruption and misery.

While Solinski argues that the new liberal regime gives people freedom and truth, the old dictator sarcastically counters: 'You give women the freedom to . . . tell you this truth – that there is no fucking sausage in the shops. And you call this progress?' (p. 105). Both Communism and capitalism are undermined in the novel, and the two main protagonists gradually come to resemble each other. As Michiko Kakutani observes in her review of the novel, the initials of Stoyo Petkanov and Peter Solinski are the same though reversed, and the two men 'are, in fact, alter egos of one another'.[49] Scammel remarks, for his part, that by portraying Solinski as 'a turncoat' – he left the Communist Party for the Greens at the most

propitious period – and 'a vacillating wimp', Barnes weighs the scales in
favour of Petkanov, privileging his 'utopian ideals, however twisted, and
power politics, however unscrupulous, over Solinski's democratic doubts
and tortured moralism'.[50] Many reviewers found Petkanov much more
impressive and compelling than his dull opponent, but one could argue
that both sides are treated with scepticism. Faced with 'the breaking wave
of history' (p. 103), *The Porcupine*, like *A History of the World in 10½
Chapters*, conveys an equal suspicion of the master narratives of
Communism and capitalism, or an 'incredulity towards metanarratives',
to repeat Jean-François Lyotard's quote.[51]

Once again echoing *A History of the World in 10½ Chapters*, *The
Porcupine* opposes the apparent lack of progress and emancipation with
the suggestion of a circularity of history through the character of Stefan's
grandmother, who believes that Communism is not dead and that 'the
whole glorious cycle of revolution' will start again (p. 55) The term 'revolution', which Bulgarians are reluctant to use, etymologically suggests
both a categorical transformation and the idea of return. The return to
Communism is what Stefan's grandmother wishes and the novel ends
with a vision of her standing in front of the Mausoleum of the First
Leader and holding a small framed print of Lenin, oblivious to the insults
thrown at her. As Pateman remarks, this vision – 'an old woman stood'
(p. 138) – echoes that of Petkanov in the first sentence of the novel –
'The old man stood' (p. 1) – granting a 'pleasing circularity to the narrative'. The very last words – 'she remained silent' (p. 138) – also recall the
wordless demonstration of women in the first chapter, thus disrupting
'this easy symmetry'[52] and calling into question the cyclical theory of
history. According to Moseley, the closure of the novel with a vignette of
Stefan's grandmother suggests that 'Barnes sees no progress in the movement from communism to a freer society.'[53]

Like other novels by Barnes, *The Porcupine* is characterised by an open
ending, emblematic of the uncertainty of the political and economic
future of Eastern countries at the end of the twentieth century. Such a
keen interest in recent and current politics appears as an exception in
Barnes's fictional production, but emerges more visibly in some of the
essays that he wrote and collected in *Letters from London* (1995). As
many reviewers praised Barnes for his ideas and his essayistic style, it
seems appropriate to open a parenthesis in the next chapter in order to
examine his three volumes of essays.

# PARENTHESIS

## The Brilliant Essayist: *Letters from London* (1995), *Something to Declare* (2002), *The Pedant in the Kitchen* (2003)

In *A History of the World in 10½ Chapters*, the half-chapter is a 'Parenthesis' which consists of an essay on love and history, in which the author seems to step in from the wings and speak in his own name without the mediation of a narrator. In this Guide in 10½ chapters, our half-chapter or parenthesis will temporarily move away from Julian Barnes's fiction and focus instead on his production as a brilliant essayist. Barnes's talent in that respect is visible not only in the three volumes of essays, in the many uncollected essays published in newspapers and magazines, and in various introductions or prefaces, but also within the novels themselves, which are marked by a recognisable essayistic quality. Critics constantly refer to this characteristic feature of Barnes's prose – he was called 'a novelist of ideas' by John Walsh[1] and James Wood,[2] and was sometimes criticised for scattering too many ideas in his fiction: 'Some people don't like finding ideas in a novel. . . . They react as if they've found a toothpick in a sandwich. I probably come across personally to some interviewers as aloof and ideas-ridden.'[3] While Mark Lawson agrees that 'Barnes has certainly used the essayist's techniques more than most novelists – the urbane dissertation, the sardonic commentary', he suggests that a 'favourite way of slighting the novels of Julian Barnes has been to mutter that he is essentially an essayist'.[4] This is what several critics have done, such as Henry Hitchings – 'Barnes the novelist has often resembled an essayist manqué'[5] – or Jason Cowley – 'Above all, you read him as an essayist'[6] – or James Wood, who argues that Barnes 'is a brilliant essayist inside whom a novelist is struggling to get out'.[7] The latter also remarks: 'To say that Julian Barnes is more of an essayist than a novelist is merely to note that his journalism is indistinguishable – in tone, style, and world-making power – from his fiction. In a sense, all his fiction is a Letter From London.'[8] Barnes himself would disagree with this interpretation as he perceives an essential difference between the two aspects of his literary production: 'Isn't it the case in journalism that you are saying things are understandable, reduceable, whereas the propulsion of the novelist is to say things are less comprehensible, more chaotic, more anarchic than we like to believe them to be? You could crudely say that a novel asks questions and journalism tries to give answers – not to the same questions of course.'[9]

*Letters from London, 1990–1995* was Barnes's first collection of essays. All of them originally appeared in the American magazine *The New Yorker* between 1990 and 1994, when Barnes was the magazine's London correspondent. In the preface to the book, Barnes draws attention to the 'technical challenge' of the job, as he was to address American readers who were not familiar with the customs and events of Britain, which led to a fruitful process of 're-examining the supposedly familiar': 'I was, in effect, to be a foreign correspondent in my own country' (p. x). Whereas Barnes's predecessor, the novelist Mollie Panter-Downes (1906–97), had been the *New Yorker*'s London correspondent for nearly half a century, Barnes decided to stop after five years, when the idea of a book grew: 'While it's stimulating to be made to go out and look at one's own country, that does drain other energies.'[10] The 15 articles, 'a mixture of political analysis, commentary on the arts, and contemporary history' according to Merritt Moseley,[11] are witty and insightful reports on late Thatcherite and post-Thatcherite England. They deal with very varied subjects, such as the downfall of Margaret Thatcher (born 1925), the arrival of John Major (born 1943), the sudden explosion of mazes in Britain, the relationship between the Royal Family and the press, the Channel Tunnel or the fall of Lloyd's, 'a model of narration and selection, one of the best accounts of the affair that social historians of the future will have', according to Henry Porter.[12] The volume ends with a very detailed and sometimes incongruous and highly humorous index. Hazel K. Bell takes a few examples to show 'how cleverly – and selectively – Barnes has contrived his index entries from passages of text'.[13] For instance, in one essay, Barnes refers to the absence from a fund-raising event of a fellow-novelist who was 'unavoidably unable to make it', which the author glosses as: 'he had unavoidably gone skiing' (p. 293), adding that he is not permitted to name the culprit. However, in the index, the entry for 'McEwan, Ian' bears one unique reference: 'unavoidably goes skiing' (p. 349).

The pieces, which David Buckley calls 'political essays as literary products',[14] combine affection and despair for Britain, the British and their follies, and may already announce the satirical vein of *England, England*.

The volume was praised by a majority of reviewers, both in England and in the United States, who celebrated Barnes as an acute political observer and commentator. Margaret Thatcher, 'the great she-elephant' (p. 5), 'domineering, mean-spirited, divisive, unheeding' (p. 251), is a recurring figure in the volume, and Ian Buruma finds that Barnes 'catches her presence, her *ton*, very nicely'.[15] A Labour supporter who even campaigned alongside actress Glenda Jackson (born 1936) in the 1992 general election (pp. 110–45), Barnes is, according to Moseley, 'wry and devastating on British politics', even though the prevailing tone of his pieces is 'urbane, ironic, knowing, often understated'.[16] Buckley insisted also on 'the slight detachment' and 'the calmness of contemplation' of the author, which prevents him from giving in to outright caricature: 'on the whole this is a reassuring voice'.[17] Jeremy Paxman applauded Barnes as 'a master practitioner of . . . the extended essay. He seduces you with a low-key anecdote, goes on to engage with subject matter that is by turns profound, silly and provocative and emerges at the end with a series of conclusions which have been buried on the way, so that you are scarcely aware of having picked them up.'[18] Patrick Cockburn argued that the articles, 'very much letters from the metropolis', retained 'their crispness and immediacy', 'their freshness partly because they are extremely well written, but also because they are modest and very detailed'. He added: 'They are far superior to the usual run of journalistic pieces reconstituted into instant history.'[19] Moseley also insisted on the acuity of Barnes's style, which makes his descriptions 'come alive' and turns colourless politicians into interesting characters, 'a tribute to his novelistic power'.[20]

In the hilarious letter devoted to the Royal Family, Barnes adopts at one point the narrative strategy of the list or guide, frequently used in his fiction, and proposes a 'thumbnail guide to the current fortunes and popularity of the Royal Family' (p. 154). Each family member is referred to in italics and the style of the gloss that follows recalls that of 'Braithwaite's Dictionary of Accepted Ideas' in *Flaubert's Parrot* (pp. 182–9), with a succession of short nominal or adjectival sentences, the ellipsis of pronouns and an ironical and mischievous tone. For example, Elizabeth II is presented as '*The Queen*. Popular, respected, thought to be "good at her job". Suspected of having a secret sense of humour' (p. 154). Barnes also gives a masterly account of the Garry Kasparov–Nigel Short chess match of 1993 – which recalls his earlier essay 'Playing Chess with Arthur Koestler' (1988) – even though jokingly warning his readers in advance: 'Sceptics maintain that live chess is as much fun as watching paint dry. Ultra-sceptics reply: Unfair to paint' (p. 258). Several critics drew attention to Barnes's passionate letter about the *fatwa* or death sentence against Salman Rushdie for the publication of *The Satanic Verses* in 1989. Moseley argues that Barnes 'writes movingly of the plight of Rushdie, defends free thought, and denounces various members of the

British government and the British intelligentsia for their cowardice and moral fence-straddling'.[21] Patrick Cockburn notes that in this article, Barnes's 'deep distaste' towards the political and social atmosphere of Britain 'turns into disgust'.[22] Barnes repeatedly denounces the attitude of the British government from 1989 to 1993, which he variously describes as 'inactivity and glacial indifference' (p. 294), 'conciliatory passivity' (p. 296), 'torpor' (p. 300), 'apathy' (p. 301), 'Torpid pragmatism laced with a little upside-down racism' (p. 302) and 'active indifference' (p. 303). Barnes's distaste for some 'despicable' (p. 321) aspects of his own country also emerges in 'Froggy! Froggy! Froggy!' in which he examines an example of Anglo-French collaboration, the Channel Tunnel, to which he would devote another essay a few years later, 'European Solutions to Travel' (1997). Barnes presents himself as 'an English Francophile' (p. 320) and as such, finds it hard to 'explain the chauvinism, aggression and contempt' (p. 320) of Britain's popular press, marked by its Francophobia. Barnes starts his essay by recalling a scene from Flaubert's *Bouvard and Pécuchet* in which Pécuchet explains to his friend that if there were an earthquake beneath the English Channel, the two land-masses of France and Britain would be united, which leads Bouvard to 'run away in terror' at the notion of 'the British coming any nearer' (p. 312). Eight years later, Barnes would take the same example in the preface to his next collection of essays, *Something to Declare*, to allude to the reluctance to bring France and Britain closer: 'some of my compatriots still exhibit a Bouvardian alarm at having the French as neighbours' (p. xv).

Having considered his own country for the benefit of American readers, Barnes subsequently collected, in *Something to Declare*, 17 essays and reviews written from 1982 to 2000, in which he shares his passion for France with a British readership. In *Flaubert's Parrot*, the narrator, driving off the boat at Newhaven, imagines answering the customs officer's question 'Have you anything to declare?' with 'Yes, I'd like to declare a small case of French flu, a dangerous fondness for Flaubert, a childish delight in French road-signs, and a love of the light as you look north' (pp. 115–16). The 2002 collection of essays serves as a developed account of that first declaration. While *Letters from London* dealt mainly with contemporary and political subjects, *Something to Declare*, dedicated to his now deceased parents who were French teachers, is more concerned with culture and the late nineteenth century. According to Hilary Spurling, the essays are 'an expansive, astute and increasingly magisterial salute to French sophistication in all departments, from cinema to cycling, singing and writing above all'.[23] As Barnes explains in his preface – 'a neat and funny essay in its own right' according to Gillian Tindall[24] – the France he likes is 'provincial, villagey, under-populated' (p. xiii), and the 'cultural period [he is] constantly drawn back to is roughly 1850–1925, from the culmination of Realism to the fission of

Modernism' (p. xiv). The first half of the book is therefore devoted to such famous Frenchmen as the poets Charles Baudelaire and Stéphane Mallarmé (1842–98), the film director François Truffaut, the writer Boris Vian (1920–59), the singers Jacques Brel (1929–78) and Georges Brassens (1921–81), the painters Gustave Courbet (1819–77), Edouard Manet (1832–83), Edgar Degas (1834–1917), Pierre Bonnard (1867–1947) and Henri Matisse (1869–1954). Barnes also includes his preface to *A Motor-Flight Through France* (1908) by American writer Edith Wharton (1862–1937) about her trip through France with Henry James (1843–1916) in 1907. According to Anne Haverty, 'This is Barnes at his best, drily humorous, empathic, his nostalgia self-aware, his metaphors original and acute.'[25] In March 2004, Julian Barnes and Hermione Lee actually followed the tracks of Henry James and Edith Wharton, driving round France for a two-part series for BBC Radio 4.[26]

Even though Barnes recalls in his preface Kingsley Amis's complaint about him: 'I wish he'd *shut up* about Flaubert' (p. xiv), the second half of the book is composed of nine remarkable pieces all devoted to Gustave Flaubert, be they reviews of Flaubert's *Carnets de Travail*, of his correspondence, of biographies and works of critical analysis, or a thought-provoking essay about the film-adaptations of *Madame Bovary* by Jean Renoir (1894–1979) in 1933, Vincente Minnelli (1913–86) in 1949 and Claude Chabrol in 1991, or an insightful analysis of a secondary character in *Madame Bovary*, Justin. As Barnes remarks, 'Not Shutting Up about Flaubert . . . remains a necessary pleasure' (p. xiv). Like *Letters from London*, *Something to Declare* ends with a precise, original, 'delightful and intriguing' index.[27] Thus, the entry for 'cows' reads: 'as intelligent as village girls, 128; Flaubert wants to hug one, 240; bad pianist makes them flee, 240' (p. 309). Flaubert's long entry comprises expected items such as his works, 'realism', 'epilepsy', but also 'resemblance to James Mason?', 'erotic bifurcation' and 'rain in his head?', and ends logically with 'perfection' (pp. 311–12). In a public meeting, Barnes referred to the 'pleasure of indexing' and added: 'Everything to me is a narrative. Even when I write an index, I try to put narratives in it.'[28] In April 2005, the Society of Indexers asked Barnes to become their next President, an offer he declined, however.

This new collection confirmed Barnes's attachment to France, which had emerged through most of his fiction, the pieces on Flaubert providing a most useful complement to *Flaubert's Parrot*. If, as Hilary Spurling remarks, *Something to Declare* 'inevitably recycles material familiar from the *Parrot*' (quotations, attitudes, motifs and anecdotes), the main differences are of point of view – 'Where Braithwaite posed as an amateur, Barnes writes as a professional' – and of tone: 'his tone here is weightier, more measured – in short, more Flaubertian'. She judges his response to Flaubert 'passionate': 'at once cagey and confessional, reverent and surgically probing'.[29] Henry Hitchings finds Barnes Flaubert's 'arch-apologist – a more subtle translator than his accredited translators, a more sensitive biographer than the tin-eared pedants who have botched his biography'.[30] Claire Messud agrees and notes that 'Barnes has been made not simply an English spokesman for things French but, more particularly, *the* critical voice on Flaubert,' and she finds him 'sharp about the authors he is reviewing', especially with biographers, which leads her to wish 'for Barnes's biography of Flaubert instead of his dismissal of Lottman's'. She admits regretting that 'Barnes himself makes only rare appearances'[31] apart from the autobiographical preface and the second essay, 'Spending Their Deaths of Holiday', in which Barnes recalls his youthful experience as a teacher in Rennes. Alain de Botton analyses Barnes's habits as an essayist, one of which consists in 'a colloquialism or blokeishness in the authorial voice' even when dealing with 'high-art subjects'.[32] For example, Flaubert and George Sand (1804–76) are prone to 'brief bouts of Old Fartery' (p. 221), while Gustave Courbet, who painted *The Origin of the World* in 1866, 'a splayed female nude, from breast to mid-thigh', is said to be an 'in-your-face-realist' (p. 120). De Botton moves on to another recurring trait of Barnes's writing: 'its biting intelligence. By biting, I mean that he is always on the look out for sentimentality, pretension, self-delusion and propaganda in his subjects.' Finally, de Botton remarks on Barnes's 'concern with pessimists. Barnes loves nothing better than a great grump.'[33]

Some critics have accused Barnes of sentimental idealism and nostalgia in his portrayal of France, but Barnes acknowledges his partiality in the preface: 'Is my view of France partial? Certainly. Knowing a second country means choosing what you want from it, finding antitheses to your normal, English, urban life' (p. xiii). In an interview in 1996, Barnes had said: 'You need another country on which to project, perhaps, your romanticism and idealism.'[34] In the final short story of *Cross Channel*, 'Tunnel', the elderly protagonist, who is an alter ego of Barnes, holds the same view: 'Judgments on other countries are seldom fair or precise: the gravitational pull is towards either scorn or sentimentality. The first no longer interested him. As for sentimentality, that was sometimes the charge against him for his view of the French. If accused, he would always plead guilty, claiming in mitigation that this is what other countries are for' (p. 207). Claire Messud therefore interprets *Something to Declare* as 'a vision, like any good piece of fiction, more vivid and pithy than the reality'.[35] Cowley notes that there is no mention of the 'cynical' and 'disastrous' examples of French foreign policy in recent years, nor of the 'disgrace' of the Vichy collaboration or of the war of independence in Algeria, and he concludes that Barnes's idealised France is 'a product of wilful fantasy'.[36]

Barnes's passion for France also entails praise for Mediterranean food through the figure of Elizabeth David (1924–92), 'the doyenne of food writers' (p. 52), evoked in an essay dating back to 1998 and reproduced in *Something to Declare* (pp. 49–62). Barnes complains there about her 'laconic', 'impressionistic' instructions in her recipes: 'Many of us cook with a kind of anxious pedantry, convinced that if the exact wording, and the exact spirit behind that wording, isn't followed, then our guests will throw up first their hands and then their stomachs' (p. 57). The author, renamed 'the Anxious Pedant' (pp. 58, 59), will confirm this qualification in an interview in 2002 – 'As a cook, I would describe myself as an anxious pedant'[37] – and will become 'The Pedant in the Kitchen' in 2003 in his collection of 17 pieces on reading and using cookery books, which had been published weekly in the *Guardian* from March to June 2003. The collection is dedicated to 'She For Whom', meaning 'She For Whom the Pedant Cooks' (p. 9), that is Barnes's wife, Pat Kavanagh. A 'self-taught, anxious, page-scowling domestic cook' (p. 7), he finds himself reluctant to deviate from recipes, and struggles with the exact meaning of 'lump', 'slug', 'gout' or 'cup' (p. 19). Critics mainly welcomed this amusing collection with enthusiasm. Jane Jakeman described the book as 'an elegantly written commentary which records Barnes's various engagements with culinary instructions', adding that the book is 'a witty sampler of culinary experiences rather than an objective survey'. She then explains that Barnes's preference goes neither for 'the restaurateurs who have recently rushed into print', nor for celebrity chefs, but for 'writers who were not primarily professional chefs, such as Édouard de Pomiane and Elizabeth David'.[38] Judy Rumbold was less convinced by the appropriateness of Barnes's precision and accuracy, pointing instead to his fretfulness, 'fastidiousness' and 'uptight, starched-pinny approach'.[39] The volume recalls an earlier short story, 'Appetite' (2000), that was to be included in *The Lemon Table* (2004), in which a woman reads recipes to her elderly husband who is suffering from Alzheimer's disease, to calm him down. The protagonist's favourite books, '*The Joy of Cooking, The Constance Spry Recipe Book, Margaret Costa's Four Seasons Cookery*' (p. 161), are also alluded to in *The Pedant in the Kitchen* (pp. 30–1) as being 'in regular use' or 'occasional service' (p. 32). Both Barnes (p. 13) and his invented character hate 'the modern celebrity chefs' and 'the TV cooks' (p. 161). However, while Barnes admires Elizabeth David, the fictional heroine finds her 'no use' to appease her husband (p. 161). Like the author who wonders 'Is a "cup" a rough-and-ready generic term or a precise American measure?' (p. 19), the protagonist of the short story hates the imprecision of recipes: 'he doesn't like the way Americans give measures in cups, any fool knows how the size of a cup can vary' (p. 166).

Barnes's attention to detail and fondness for precision are made obvious in his collections of essays, whose subjects vary from the political to the cultural to the culinary. After offering his ironic perspective on Britain in *Letters from London* and before collecting the essays which would subjectively attempt to capture the essence of Frenchness in *Something to Declare*, Barnes published *England, England*, a novel that was to list the Fifty Quintessences of Englishness and present a disquieting future view of England, which will be examined in the next chapter.

# CHAPTER NINE

# The Simulacrum of National Identity: *England, England* (1998)

In 1998, six years after *The Porcupine*, Julian Barnes published his next novel, *England, England*. Even though the two books are very different in content and form, Barnes remarked that both belonged to the genre of the 'political novel'.[1] In the interval between these two novels, in 1995, Barnes published *Letters from London*, in which the essay entitled 'Fake!' may have foreshadowed the central theme of *England, England*: 'The British are good at tradition; they're also good at the invention of tradition' (p. 27). In its structure, the new novel echoes *Metroland* and *Staring at the Sun* in that it is divided into three parts in chronological order. The first one, 'England' (23 pages), focuses on Martha Cochrane as a teenager, fond of jigsaws, suspicious of religion and of the mechanisms of memory. The second part, 'England, England' (210 pages), is set in the near future and presents a fantasy: media mogul Sir Jack Pitman and his associates (amongst them a cynical and sceptical Martha approaching middle age) turn the Isle of Wight into a gigantic theme park called England, England, in which one finds replicas of England's best known historical buildings, sites and figures. The Island Project is a great success while the mainland suffers a vertiginous decline. The third part, 'Anglia' (25 pages), takes place decades later when Martha, now an old and wiser woman, has gone back to the former England, which has reverted to a pre-industrial era. The novel plays the satirical public story of Sir Jack's megalomaniac venture against the private story of Martha's development from teenager to elderly lady. As Matthew Pateman suggests, the focus on 'a woman looking back on her life', who is supposed to 'represent simplicity, honesty, and truth', may remind the reader of the narration of Jean Serjeant's life in *Staring at the Sun*.[2]

A highly original, witty and ambitious novel, *England, England* appeared on the shortlist for the Booker Prize in 1998 when the prize was awarded to Ian McEwan's *Amsterdam*. Barnes, whose attachment to France had been reflected in his previous novels and essays, takes the opposite course in *England, England* by focusing on the issue of Englishness, a subject which was recurrently explored in late twentieth-century British fiction, for example by Peter Ackroyd in *English Music* (1992). According to Barnes, *England, England* is 'an "idea of England" novel',[3] as well as 'a letter to my own country at the turn of the millennium', a phrase which echoes the title of his collection of essays *Letters from London*.[4] Critics variously referred to the novel as a 'satirical comedy',[5] a 'corrosive critique of what may be thought to be England',[6] or 'a cartoonish romp whose real concern is seriousness',[7] and they thoroughly applauded Barnes's mastery of satire, irony and parody. Satire is the term that appears most frequently in analyses of the novel, and yet it is one which Barnes feels awkward with: 'the purpose of satire or the real function of satire is to console the dispossessed, is to mock the mighty for the consolation of the weak and the poor . . . but I don't see myself . . . as actually writing satire'. The writer adds that his novel 'is farcical rather than satirical',[8] and he thus prefers to refer to it as a 'semi-farce'.[9] The farcical element is mostly due to the character of the megalomaniac newspaper tycoon Sir Jack Pitman, who, as the author and several reviewers have suggested, is reminiscent of British publishing magnate Robert Maxwell (1923–91) and Australian media mogul Rupert Murdoch (born 1931), both of whom are referred to in Barnes's essay 'Fake!' in *Letters from London* (pp. 30, 38). Anthony Thwaite and Richard Eder remark that the 'publishing megabeast' may also have traces of the fictional Lord Copper in *Scoop* by Evelyn Waugh,[10] while Peter Childs argues that the 'surname suggests Englishness and Britain's decrepit mining industry'.[11]

Though unique in Barnes's production, *England, England* addresses some of the key issues developed in his previous novels, in particular the evasiveness of truth, the construction of history and the elusive nature of memory. To quote Barnes, the book is about 'the idea of England, authenticity, the search for truth, the invention of tradition, and the way in which we forget our own history'.[12] The first words of the novel sound familiar in their echoing of the opening of *Talking It Over* and *Love, etc* as Martha Cochrane highlights from the start the fallibility of her memory: ' "What's your first memory?" someone would ask. / And she would reply, "I don't remember" ' (p. 3). Martha insists moreover that there exists no pure, no 'true', no 'unprocessed' memory (p. 5), and that as the original event drifts further back into the past, mediations tend to proliferate: 'A memory now of a memory a bit earlier of a memory before that of a memory way back when' (p. 3). This accumulation of genitives emphasises the inevitable transformation, distortion and gradual disappearance of original facts. Martha's awareness of 'the impurity and corruption of the memory system' (p. 7) leads her to draw a parallel with national memory: 'It was like a country remembering its history: the past was never just the past, it was what made the present able to live with itself' (p. 6). Dr Max, the Official Historian on the Island, also compares the mechanisms of individual and collective memory: 'people remembered history in the same conceited yet evanescent fashion as they recalled their own childhood' (p. 82).

In their incompleteness, both history and memory resemble the jigsaw of the counties of England which is partly reproduced on the cover of the original Jonathan Cape hardback edition, and whose pieces Martha would try to assemble as a girl. Pateman suggests that the jigsaw 'is a handy metaphor for the idea of a country being constructed, arbitrarily divided into administrative centres, historically open to change'.[13] As a child, Martha could never complete her jigsaw until her father gave her the last piece he had teasingly hidden: 'Staffordshire had been found, and her jigsaw, her England, and her heart had been made whole again' (p. 6). The term 'whole' sounds ironic for when Martha's father deserts the family, supposedly to go and find the missing county of Nottinghamshire, neither the jigsaw, nor England, nor Martha's heart can be made whole again: there is no 'way of filling the exact, unique, fretsaw-cut hole within her' (p. 24). This apparently innocent image in the first part of the novel provides a metaphor for the essence of history and memory, whose wholeness is a mere illusion. The malleability of history and the unreliability of collective and individual memory are what enable the creators of the theme park on the Isle of Wight to rewrite, simplify and caricature national history so as to meet the expectations of tourists.

The extravagant idea for the Island Project, which was praised by many reviewers for its originality and its fictional potential, coincidentally echoes a scheme imagined by architect Clough Williams-Ellis (1883–1978) at the beginning of his book on the National Trust, *On Trust for the Nation* (1947); Barnes, however, had never heard of this.[14] Ian Sansom refers to the architect's imagining 'that by some miracle, all the lands and buildings possessed by the National Trust were to be uprooted and set adrift and then, by some further sorcery, reassembled into one fabulous island . . . the pith and pick of England close-packed into a compass smaller than that of the Isle of Wight'.[15] In *England, England*, the 'Quality Leisure' (p. 58) park is situated on the Isle of Wight so that tourists, instead of traipsing all over England to visit historical sites, can see all the replicas in one location. Asked why he chose the Isle of Wight, Barnes seriously answered that it was 'one of the first places in Great Britain to be perverted by becoming a tourist destination',[16] but he also humorously remarked: 'it has a superb stretch of flat downland which I thought the developers would love to use as an airport . . .'.[17]

The name of the venture sounds both patriotic and ironic as the doubling of 'England' seems to grant a doubled value to the fake country while the original England has been erased from the history of the world. The ambitious design of Sir Jack, 'a patriot at heart' (p. 30) – 'We must sell our past to other nations as their future' (p. 40) – aims at re-establishing the conquering dynamism of the British Empire, which the poet William Ernest Henley (1849–1903) had celebrated in the poem 'Pro Rege Nostro', included in the volume entitled *England, my England* (1888). In these patriotic lines, Henley glorified the imperial surge of England and its political and economic supremacy: 'They call you proud and hard, / England, my England: / You with worlds to watch and ward, / England, my own!'[18] The poet's exultation found an echo some thirty years later in a short story by D. H. Lawrence (1885–1930), 'England, my England' (1922), in which the robustness and patriotism of the Marshalls, representing 'the old England of hamlets and yeomen', is opposed to the frailty and political indifference of their son-in-law.[19] A few years later, Scottish writer A. G. MacDonell (1895–1941) adopted a comic and sparkling tone in his novel *England, their England* (1933), a witty and amusing satire, mocking the foibles of educated Englishmen and some of the specific features of England. During the Second World War, in 1941, George Orwell wrote an essay entitled 'England, Your England', where he purports 'to try and determine what England *is*, before guessing what part England *can play* in the huge events that are happening'.[20]

The title of Barnes's novel thus resonates with patriotic intertextual echoes, but, as in MacDonell's book, the glorified consideration of national history and Englishness is tainted with irony. As Vera Nünning suggests, the satirised 'patriotic view of history' is 'exemplified by the peculiar way history is taught at Martha's school'.[21] Miss Mason makes her pupils cling 'to a scrap of rhythm' (p. 12) and sing wholeheartedly 'the chants of history' (p. 11) learnt by rhyming rote, dates calling for actions or actions calling for dates, 'making history not a dogged progress but a series of vivid and competing moments' (p. 12). She would also appeal to the pupils' sense of imagination by telling them 'tales of chivalry and glory, plague and famine, tyranny and democracy' (p. 11) that supposedly make up the history of England. In her essay, Nünning analyses the way in which '*England, England* explores, parodies, and deconstructs those "invented traditions" known as "Englishness" ' and argues that Barnes self-consciously explores 'the question of how established versions of Englishness have come to be invented and upheld'.[22] The Official Historian becomes aware of it when he is asked to find out 'how much History people already know' (p. 71) and realises that they know very little about the origins of their own nation. Dr Max concludes with a paradox: 'that patriotism's most eager bedfellow was ignorance, not knowledge' (p. 82). As Nünning remarks, 'Any attempt at forging a national identity therefore has to reckon with elusive memories, lack of knowledge, and highly distorted patriotic views of history.'[23]

Patriotism may seem to be an uneasy position to hold at the dawn of the new millennium, when the British Empire no longer exists and England is declining. As one of the characters prosaically indicates, 'We're in the third millennium and your tits have dropped' (p. 37). Sir Jack solves the problem by evacuating the present, capitalising instead on England's past and glorious history. The Island Project which he invents has been called a utopia by Patrick Parrinder,[24] i.e. an imaginary world that is supposed to be perfect, but Richard Eder and Valentine Cunningham more pointedly referred to it as 'a trendy dystopia'[25] and a 'merry dystopia',[26] i.e. an imaginary world which is supposed to be perfect but seems, in some respects, to be worse than our own. The blatantly regressive venture is based on a 'nostalgic desire to replicate the past' and 'recuperate past glories', to quote James J. Miracky, who offers a comparative analysis of *England, England* and the science-fiction novel *Jurassic Park* (1990) by Michael Crichton (born 1942) in which a theme park populated by genetically developed dinosaurs goes awry.[27] In *England, England*, a survey conducted by the Concept Developer lists the Fifty Quintessences of Englishness, or characteristics people around the world associate with the word 'England', an eclectic mix including the Royal Family, Big Ben, Robin Hood, Manchester United Football Club, but also less favourable items such as the class system, snobbery, hypocrisy, whingeing, emotional frigidity and not washing (pp. 83–5). The design team carefully prunes the list so as to retain only the glorifying items of the past, and to make the experience palatable for worldwide tourists. As Peter Childs remarks, 'The focus of the items is on pre-1960 if not Olde England. It is England in aspic, disabled by its past, backward- rather than forward-looking, assembling a populist past for consumer entertainment.'[28]

Nünning shares this view, suggesting that 'Barnes exposes the one-sidedness that characterizes many contemporary versions of Englishness, which overwhelmingly locate "true" Englishness in the past.' She adds that the tourists visiting the Island Project 'prefer and demand an idealized version of Englishness that is adjusted to the tastes of the present',[29] thus calling for short cuts and bowdlerisations in the history of England: 'Here, on the Island, they had learnt how to deal with history, how to sling it carelessly on your back and stride out across the downland with the breeze in your face. Travel light: it was true for nations as well as for hikers' (p. 203). Sir Jack Pitman and his Co-ordinating Committee marvel at the success of the theme park which has eventually replaced mainland England or Old England, and propagate negative views of the original land, where 'people were burdened by yesterday, and the day before, and the day before that. . . . By history' (p. 203). England, which has been dispossessed of all its historical characteristics and most of its population, is redefined as 'a nation fatigued by its own history' (p. 253).

According to *The Times of London*, the newspaper published from Ryde on the Isle of Wight, 'Old England had lost its history, and therefore – since memory is identity – had lost all sense of itself' (p. 251). In an interview, Barnes remarked that *England, England* was 'about the creation of false truths about a country, and these coarse icons that are made to stand in for real things'. He added:

■ After I had written it, I came across a wonderful quotation from [Ernest] Renan [1823–92]: 'Getting its history wrong is part of being a nation.' It would have made a perfect epigraph for the book. Getting its history wrong is also part of creating a nation. You have to build up those myths of liberation, myths of fighting the oppressor, myths of bravery. Often they have a certain percentage of truth in them, so they're easy myths to build up. But then being a nation as well as becoming a nation also depends on the continuation of those myths.[30] □

In the artificial England, England, all unflattering traits of Englishness are discarded, and all the major historical figures and episodes are caricatured and simplified, to be adapted to a contemporary and family audience, hence what Martha calls 'the repositioning of myths for modern times' (p. 148). For example, the life story of Nell Gwynn, the seventeenth-century orange seller who became Charles II's mistress 'at a relatively tender age' (p. 94), referred to herself as a 'Protestant whore' (p. 94) and was the mother of two bastard sons by the King, needs to be transformed: 'Perhaps a *little* massaging, to bring her into line with third millennium family values' (p. 93). To conceal the background of adultery, paedophilia and 'three-in-a-bed' sex (p. 94), Martha brightly suggests a rewriting of Gwynn's history: 'We could make her older, . . . lose the children, lose the other mistresses, and lose the social and religious background' (p. 94). Later on, Martha reflects: 'her essence, like her juice, had been concentrated, and she remained a version of what she had once been, or at least what Visitors . . . expected her to have been' (p. 186). The myth of Robin Hood is also deemed 'politically incorrect', to quote Nünning,[31] as the fact that, just like history, it is 'male-dominated' (p. 148) may not appeal to feminist and homosexual visitors. As Barnes remarks, Dr Max, who 'is probably gay' and 'very provocative and waspish',[32] does not want the minorities to be forgotten. Hence, he reminds his colleagues that within the band of outlaws was a woman, Maid Marian, that the name 'Robin' is 'sexually ambiguous' and that 'Hood' 'denotes a garment which is ambisexual' (p. 148). The Hood myth is therefore rewritten, depoliticised and adapted to the spirit of the new century and to the tourists' expectations: 'It was a primal myth, repositioned after considerable debate. Band personnel had been realigned with great sensitivity; offensive elements in the scenario – old-fashioned attitudes to wildlife, over-consumption of red meat – had been expunged or attenuated' (pp. 221–2). According to Barnes, the simplification process described in the fictional world of *England, England* is also at work in the real world: 'increasingly countries are caricaturing themselves and are using a very air-brushed version of certain aspects of their own history. It's not new, but it's certainly being done more extremely and with more commercial efficiency now than before.'[33] Even though Pitman denies it – 'We are not talking Disneyland' (p. 59) – the marketing venture on the Isle of Wight amounts to the packaging of history.

By foregrounding the construction of national history, *England, England* problematises issues relating to the art of representation, the simulacrum, and the relationship between the replica and the original, a theme Barnes had already approached in *Flaubert's Parrot* through the figure of the stuffed parrot, and in *A History of the World in 10½ Chapters* through Géricault's painting *The Raft of the Medusa*. Right from the start in *England, England*, Sir Jack Pitman asks a central question: 'What is real?' (p. 31), and warns his employees: 'I could have you replaced with substitutes, with . . . simulacra' (p. 31). In a compelling essay, James J. Miracky provides an examination of *England, England* as both a reflection on and a parody of the postmodern theories of French philosopher Jean Baudrillard (born 1929) about reality and the simulacrum, as expounded in *Simulacra and Simulation* (1981).[34] For Baudrillard, simulation consists in the reproduction of the same symptoms, signs or images as the real, thus blurring the distinction between the authentic and the copy. Miracky reminds us that Baudrillard defines a first-order simulation as 'a representation of the real', a second-order simulation as 'a blurring of the boundaries between reality and representation', and a third-order simulation – which he calls 'hyperreality' – as the situation where the replica is given precedence over the real.[35] In *England, England*, the French intellectual who delivers a lecture to the Project's Co-ordinating Committee celebrates the 'hyperreal' or third order of simulation: 'nowadays we prefer the replica to the original. We prefer the reproduction of the work of art to the work of art itself' (p. 53). Baudrillard's name is mentioned at the beginning of the lecture (p. 54) and his theory of the simulacrum forms the basis of the speech, but it is another French philosopher and sociologist, Guy Debord (1931–94), author of *The Society of the Spectacle* (1967), who, though never named, is directly quoted: ' "All that was once directly lived", he wrote, "has become mere representation" ' (p. 54);[36] 'He understood, this old thinker, that we live in the world of the spectacle. . . . Once there was only the world, directly lived. Now there is the representation – let me fracture that word, the re-presentation – of the world' (p. 55). Miracky notes that while Baudrillard laments the predominance of hyperreality and scorns the replica, the French intellectual openly celebrates it: 'We must demand the replica' (p. 55). Through the caricatured figure of the academic, Barnes mischievously mocks the jargon and abstract doctrines of French intellectuals in what Pateman views as 'a reasonable pastiche of a sort of postmodern theory'.[37] As Miracky remarks, 'Barnes satirizes both the world of hyperreality and that of critical theory, in effect creating a parody of a parody.'[38]

When the venture is implemented, even though one of the members of the design team insists on 'keeping reality and illusion separate' (p. 111), little by little, the boundaries between the authentic and the simulacra become blurred. The replica island becomes '*the thing itself*' (p. 59), and any access to the original past is deemed impossible: 'The world began to forget that "England" had ever meant anything except England, England, a false memory which the Island worked to reinforce' (p. 253). As Parrinder suggests, the supposedly authentic past might be a fantasy, while the replica might seem truthful: 'what if our ideas of national history and national identity are also extrapolations, in the sense of being the products of a deliberate backward projection coloured by unconscious wish-fulfilment? A theme park or scale model could then be no less authentic than the supposed archaeological–historical "reality" of the nation's past.'[39]

The actors hired to represent historical or mythical figures on the Isle of Wight are never known by their own names but always by those of their roles, thus confusing their fictional and real identities, which corresponds to Baudrillard's second order of simulation: 'within a few months of Independence, certain members of Backdrop could no longer be addressed as Pitco employees, only as the characters they were paid to inhabit' (p. 198). The authentic King of the United Kingdom believes he is meeting the real Queen Victoria even though she is a fake one: 'Gave a chap quite a turn to shake hands with his own great-however-many-times-granny' (p. 164). In 'Traffic Jam at Buckingham Palace' in *Letters from London*, Barnes had already drawn attention to the impossibility of distinguishing myth from reality in relation to the Royal Family. After presenting a 'colourful dramatis personae' of members of the Royal Family which makes the latter look like a 'supersoap', Barnes added: 'But the Royals are not played by actors; they merely (however hammily at times) play themselves' (p. 156). The author concluded by pointing to the shattering of any sense of identity: 'you do not exist: you are what others decide that you are, you are only what you seem to be. And therefore you depend for your existential reality on the whole mythmaking, knee-bending, lie-telling business of promotion and packaging' (p. 157).

In *England, England*, the actors eventually forget that they are playing a role and, as Miracky suggests, instead of 'improving on the original, the replicas move back toward reality'.[40] In the course of what Michael Wood refers to as 'reality crises, clashes between the simulacrum and desire, or vertiginous excesses of identification',[41] order starts to break down and the actors identify so completely with their role models that they become the original. Thus, threshers and shepherds choose to live like authentic threshers and shepherds, therefore without modern facilities (p. 198); the members of the Battle of Britain squadron decide to sleep on the runway in case of a surprise attack (p. 198); smugglers start smuggling for real (pp. 199–200); Robin Hood and his band turn into genuine outlaws (pp. 223–5). The actor who plays Samuel Johnson (1709–84) thinks he now is the real lexicographer, essayist, poet and critic, even though Martha tries to remind him he is only playing a part: 'We want you to *be* "Dr Johnson", don't you understand?' (p. 211). The quotation marks highlight the difference between the replica ("Dr Johnson") and the original (Dr Johnson), but the actor, who has appropriated the melancholy and supposed lack of civility of his namesake, has definitely discarded the inverted commas: 'turning "Dr Johnson" into Dr Johnson . . . peeling off the protective quotation marks' (p. 217). The actors prefer their roles or their hyperreality to their real selves, which leads Parrinder to compare *England, England*'s Island Project to the Wessex Project in the science-fiction novel *A Dream of Wessex* (1977) by Christopher Priest (born 1943). The Wessex Project enables a group of volunteers, in a state of controlled hypnosis, to experience life in the year 2137. This future life is unreal, but the participants, just like the actors of the Island Project who become addicted to their roles, enjoy more fulfilling lives there than in the present: 'The simulacrum replaces reality because it is more addictive than reality.'[42]

Miracky remarks that while Barnes satirically portrays a world in which hyperreality (or the simulacrum) triumphs, thus 'validating postmodern theory', he also sometimes 'incorporates elements that reach for an authentic human experience of the real, ultimately leaving the novel positioned somewhere between homage and parody of the dominance of the "hyperreal" '. Thus, the romantic relationship between Martha and Paul Harrison is presented as 'a possible antidote to the hyperreal world of the project' as it is 'described using the language of the real',[43] for example, when Paul naively tells Martha: 'I just think you're . . . real. And you make me feel real' (p. 135). Barnes intended the contrast between the public story and the private one, the latter being a 'search for some sort of inner truth about life and love',[44] and he admits that the hardest thing was 'getting the balance and also the point of adhesion between the personal intimate life realistically treated, and the large, semi-farcical story of the island'. He adds: 'When I wasn't sure whether it was working or not, I simply extracted from the draft of the book all the sections dealing with Martha's personal life, and then rewrote them as a sort of individual story.'[45] However, as Dr Max tells Martha, such personal authenticity is also an illusion: 'Most people, in my opinion, steal much of what they are. . . . You're just as constructed' (pp. 133–4). John Carey notes: 'Words, gestures, ideas, are largely mimicry,' and he shows how Paul and Martha have been 'constructing their sexuality out of replicas and imitations'.[46] Paul discovered 'girls in magazines' (p. 98) and, rather than having sex with real girls, found it 'much easier to be alone with magazine women' (p. 99). Martha, while making love, prefers concentrating on her dream of an ideal man to thinking of her real partner: 'The reality of that dream. Another might be there and helping, his own contingent presence adding to a supposedly shared reality. But you detached yourself from his reality' (p. 50). Eventually Martha and Paul's love affair fails, foregrounding the illusion of any authentic human love, and Martha is expelled from the Island. Miracky points to the 'apparent victory of the hyperreal' in the second part of the novel.[47]

The third part takes place in a Wessex village in what is now called Anglia and which, as Barnes stated, is 'the result of Old England collapsing and going back to a pre-industrial, agricultural, pre-technology England'.[48] This last section has been variously interpreted by critics and readers. Barnes remarked: 'that third part tends to be a bit misread by people as being what I personally approve of, or it's the book's answer to the questions raised previously. And I don't think it's the answer at all.' Just as in several of Barnes's novels, the conclusion is 'meant to be rather opaque and rather ambiguous'.[49] Parrinder argues that the Wessex village in Anglia represents 'utopia as retrotopia',[50] by which he means the nostalgic re-creation of a pre-industrial world. Even though the narrator remarks: 'The village was neither idyllic nor dystopic' (p. 256), and Martha herself is portrayed as being bored and lonely, a few critics have considered Anglia favourably. For instance, Valentine Cunningham remarks that Anglia 'proves a kind of paradise'.[51] Nünning argues contrarily that the setting 'is a curious amalgam of dystopian fiction and a regression to an idyllic, rural England'. She points to the 'negative sides of village life', such as 'prying and xenophobia',[52] which are exposed in the third part.

According to Barnes, the last part is 'about the question of to what extent a country can begin again, and what that beginning again means'.[53] All the inhabitants of Anglia have changed their names, professions and location in an attempt to start anew, which recalls the actors' personality slippage and confusion of identity in the second part. Miracky remarks that Barnes 'explores the possibility of an alternative, purer reality', and 'presents Anglia as a potential site of renewal or "real"-ization of England's traditions'.[54] However, echoing the Official Historian who had warned: 'There is no authentic moment of beginning, of purity. . . . There is no prime moment' (p. 132), Barnes suggests: 'there's no such thing as a clean slate, you always start with little bits of remembered or rediscovered stuff'.[55] He refers to the way the school-master Mullin referees Cornish wrestling 'with an open encyclopaedia in hand' (p. 264), or the terrible mixture of tunes that the band plays at the annual village Fête which is revived – 'or perhaps, since records were inexact', instituted by the schoolmaster (p. 246). The Fête is a success and becomes part of the village's customs: 'The Fête was established; already it seemed to have its history' (p. 266). Nünning remarks that 'the inven-tion of another tradition has been accomplished',[56] and Parrinder concurs: 'Once again, a dead or dying culture has been reanimated or, perhaps, simply invented,' so that the bucolic village 'is just as artificial as the Island Project'.[57] Barnes also remarks that the location is 'a completely fake village. It's a bogus village reinventing itself.'[58] Thus, Jez Harris, 'formerly Jack Oshinsky, junior legal expert with an American electronics firm' (pp. 242–3), likes to 'play the yokel' (p. 243) and invent 'folklore' and 'fabulation' (p. 244) for anthropologists, travel writers or linguistic theoreticians disguised as tourists. Cunningham is therefore wrong in judging Anglia as 'some sort of genuine old England',[59] and Nünning draws attention to this misreading of the third part as 'an ideal-ized version of authentic rural Englishness'.[60] Miracky also highlights the 'unreality of the village's return to its roots' and argues that 'in presenting the reconstructed, preindustrial Anglia as an equally artificial alternative to "England, England," Barnes is also critiquing the nostalgia of a strand of postmodern theory' which tends to regard traditional rural societies as an emblem of authenticity.[61] Miracky concludes that the unique authen-tic moment of the novel occurs in the second part during a conversation between Martha and the replica Dr Johnson, who is suffering from acute depression. Even though the man is a fake, Martha realises that 'his pain was authentic' (p. 218).

Though unique and highly original, *England, England* appears consis-tent with Barnes's literary production in that it addresses issues which have been approached in previous novels, such as the elusiveness of truth, the vagaries of love, the construction of history or the relationship between reality and fiction. If some central themes recur from one book to the next, many critics have noticed, however, that each novel by Barnes is a new experimentation with form. Until now, this Guide has sought to show the way in which Barnes reinvents the genre of the novel through formal experimentation, generic destabilisation and original combinations. Barnes's achievement is also remarkable in his short stories, which call for a different narrative approach whose distinctive qualities will be analysed in the next chapter.

# CHAPTER TEN

# In Search of Lost Time: *Cross Channel* (1996) and *The Lemon Table* (2004)

Julian Barnes once admitted: 'A story is harder than a novel to write, [there is] less room for manoeuvre,'[1] and yet his achievement as a short story writer is as impressive as his accomplishment as a novelist. *Cross Channel* is a series of ten short stories, ranging across several centuries and presenting the British in France, which were composed between 1990 and 1995, while *The Lemon Table* comprises eleven short stories about the theme of ageing and the fear of death, which had been published independently in magazines from 1996 to 2003. Examining Barnes's collected short stories thus entails looking back on 14 years of literary creation. To these two volumes, one should also add a few short stories which have remained separate. 'A Self-Possessed Woman' (1975) was Barnes's first publication as part of *The Times Anthology of Ghost Stories*. Along with twelve other short stories, it had been selected from several thousand entries in a ghost story competition organised in the spring of 1975 by Jonathan Cape in conjunction with *The Times* newspaper. The judges of the competition were the novelists Kingsley Amis and Patricia Highsmith (1921–95), the actor Christopher Lee (born 1922), John Higgins of *The Times* and Tom Maschler, the editorial director of Cape. In a hilarious piece published in the *Guardian*, Barnes recalls meeting Tom Maschler at a literary party a few weeks before the publication of the anthology. The name of 'Julian Barnes' meant nothing to Maschler and so he asked the author for the title of his short story, at which point Barnes's mind went blank: 'So there we were: a publisher who didn't recognize one of his writers' names, and a writer who couldn't remember the title of his own – his only – work. Welcome to the literary life.'[2] A few years later, between two thrillers, Dan Kavanagh published 'The 50p Santa. A Duffy Detective Story' (1985–6). In 'On the Terrace' (1981), Barnes drew from an authentic anecdote to depict a waiter who threw customers' mean tips into the nearby lake. Barnes also portrayed writers and actors in 'The Writer who Liked Hollywood' (1982) about a case of adultery, 'One of a Kind' (1982) – a conversation between two writers about a Romanian novelist and ironist – and 'Hamlet in the Wild West' (1994) about the performance of Shakespeare's play in Missouri. 'Trespass' (2003) focuses on a couple of young ramblers, Geoff and Lynn, and follows their brief love relationship from beginning to end.

When *Cross Channel* was published, many critics compared the form to that of *A History of the World in 10½ Chapters*, and Barnes had to insist on the autonomy of each story: 'I'm fighting that terrible phrase "linked short stories".'[3] Even though each collection broadly focuses on a common theme, it is approached differently in each piece, in terms of both plot and form, and the short stories all stand individually. The reader may observe, however, that some of the themes developed in the stories recall issues that have been examined in previous novels. *Cross Channel* thus refers back to *Flaubert's Parrot*, in which the middle chapter was entitled 'Cross Channel'. In the novel, Braithwaite makes several journeys by boat from Newhaven to Dieppe and back, and the book testifies to Barnes's attachment to France, French culture, and Gustave Flaubert in particular. In *Cross Channel* as in Barnes's first novel, *Metroland*, the author also asserts his francophilia by portraying English people in France, delighting in the intricacies of the language and celebrating French artists. Referring to 'Hermitage', one of the more subtle pieces of the volume, about two Englishwomen who buy a house and vineyard near Bordeaux in the 1890s, Michael Wood notes: 'The very language here is a love song to a certain France, and also a tribute to the way in which another country can become your own.'[4]

In *Cross Channel*, the figure of Flaubert, who had already featured in *Flaubert's Parrot* and in many essays later collected in *Something to Declare*, appears obliquely in the short story entitled 'Junction'. The piece focuses on the construction of the '82 miles of the Paris and Rouen Railway' (p. 25) by English navvies at the beginning of the 1840s, a venture which had already been alluded to in 'The Train-spotter's Guide to Flaubert' in *Flaubert's Parrot*: 'The Paris to Rouen railway – built by the English – opened on May 9th, 1843' (p. 125), and in the essay 'Froggy! Froggy! Froggy!': '150 years ago it was British engineers and British navvies who laid out the first elements of the French rail network' (*Letters from London*, p. 316). In *Flaubert's Parrot*, Braithwaite had remarked that he could 'imagine village priests delivering sermons on the Devil's invention and being mocked for it' (p. 125). This is precisely what is staged in 'Junction' as the 'curé of Pavilly' calls the English navvies 'the devil's army' (p. 26) and delivers sermons on 'the new follies of the modern age' (p. 34). As James Wood suggests, the short story 'generates a collision between the opposition of scientific triumphalism (the railway) and religious obscurantism'.[5] Though introducing fictional characters, such as the medical student, the priest and his audience, as well as the navvies, 'Junction' also features real people, among them Dr Achille, who is none other than Flaubert's brother, Achille-Cléophas Flaubert; the story is based on authentic facts and places, which implies that Barnes had to maintain a balance between historical events and the creation of his own fictional text:' "Junction" . . . involved a lot of research. The danger with research is that you put too much in; that you get bullied by the original text. You're striving for a prose whose sweat is of the nineteenth century, and you're tempted to use someone else's nineteenth-century prose.'[6]

Barnes had already come to terms with the difficulties inherent in the combination of historical events or figures and fiction in *Flaubert's Parrot*, *A History of the World in 10½ Chapters* and *The Porcupine*, and this hybrid mixture recurs in all the stories of *Cross Channel* either because Barnes presents real people or because he situates his fictional creation against a background of historical events in France. As James Wood suggested, 'his fiction is addicted to fact', and the critic calls Barnes 'an English empiricist . . . for whom facts, real ones and faked ones, are all pieces of information'.[7] Adrian Kempton shares the same view: 'Each of these pieces is full of fascinating facts and is testimony to Barnes's encyclopaedic approach to the presentation of culture', and the critic praises Barnes's gift for the 'imaginative re-creation of significant historical moments'.[8] For example, 'Dragons' deals with the persecutions suffered by French Protestants before and after 1685, the year of the Revocation of the Edict of Nantes (which, in 1598, had established the legal toleration of Calvinism in Roman Catholic France); the 'dragons' (dragoons) were the soldiers who were placed in the households of Protestants in order to convert them to Catholicism. The piece uses this historical basis but relates the dreadful fictional story of the family of Pierre Chaigne, who has to put up with the abuse imposed by Irish 'dragons' who themselves had suffered from the horrors inflicted on Ireland by Oliver Cromwell (1599–1658). As Merritt Moseley suggests, Barnes's 'interest in heresy and religious deviation' recalls the chapter entitled 'The Wars of Religion' in *A History of the World in 10½ Chapters.*[9] Gerald Mangan praised the story for its 'undemonstrative lyricism' which 'allows the deeper human issues to emerge without strain'; he adds that 'its understatements serve to intensify the horror of the events, while drawing out all the ironies of religiously inspired slaughter'.[10] 'Melon' also mixes historical facts and fiction in its three parts, corresponding to three periods: 1774, when Hamilton Lindsay makes a journey through peaceful France; 1789, when an English–French cricket match, in which the protagonist was to take part, is cancelled because of the French Revolution; and 1801, when

General Hamilton is being kept prisoner in France by 'Buonaparte' and is suffering from nostalgia and melancholy, bordering on madness. As Michael Wood remarks, Hamilton's 'lyrical memory' makes him remember France 'as if it were the past itself'.[11]

Nostalgia for the past and an interest in the mechanisms of memory appear in both collections, which focus on the fear of amnesia on a personal and collective level. *Cross Channel* in particular is, according to Michael Wood, 'like a gloss on Braithwaite's question' in *Flaubert's Parrot*: 'How do we seize the foreign past?' (p. 100), and the British protagonists in France 'become the unseizable foreign past, even as they themselves encounter it'.[12] The short story entitled 'Evermore', 'the most powerful story in this volume' according to Kakutani,[13] has been praised by critics for its reflections on memory and oblivion. It was reprinted independently as an artist's book, with individual hand-coloured prints by British painter Howard Hodgkin (born 1932).[14] James Wood compared 'Evermore' to a short story by Rudyard Kipling (1865–1936) entitled 'The Gardener' (1929). In 'Evermore', Miss Moss, a lexicographer (Barnes himself worked as a lexicographer for the *Oxford English Dictionary Supplement* from 1969 to 1972), goes to France each year to visit not only the graveyard of her brother, killed during the First World War, but also all the military cemeteries. In 'The Gardener', Helen Turrell goes to France to visit the graveyard of her nephew, also killed in the First World War, and meets Mrs Scarsworth, who has been visiting the graveyard of her lover and other victims for nine years. Both short stories focus on the need to preserve the memory of the past and to try and postpone oblivion. Wood concedes that 'Evermore' is 'a touching story' but regrets that it 'over-supplies', being too explicit and too literal. He values the passages in which Barnes produces 'something that discovers grief, rather than something that tells us about grief', and therefore hates it when Miss Moss is 'asking herself the kinds of rhetorical questions, perfectly expressed, that only characters in stories ask themselves' or when the writer himself directly addresses the reader.[15]

Despite Wood's reservations, 'Evermore' is a 'deeply touching account of grief' as well as a 'horrifying prediction' of the inevitable obliteration of history, according to Teresa Waugh.[16] Miss Moss wishes that memory could be transferred to the next generation so as to prevent the erasure of the past: 'She wondered if those too young to have original knowledge could be given memory, could have it grafted on' (p. 100), but she fears this may fail: 'What if memory-grafting did not work . . .?' (p. 110). Mourning the victims of the First World War, she resents the way history works, one tragedy replacing and erasing the previous one: 'She hated Hitler's war for diminishing the memory of the Great War' (p. 105). The monuments commemorating the Second World War in France tend to blur the memory of the First: 'an insulting modern date: 1943, 1944,

1945. They blocked the view, these deaths and these dates; they demanded attention by their recency. She refused, she refused' (p. 105). While perpetuating the memory of the past, Miss Moss also projects into the future and foretells how the First World War will be erased from the landscape itself: 'it would be time to plough up the cemeteries, to put them back to good agricultural use' (p. 110). The landscape would then appear amnesic and ahistorical: 'the great forgetting could begin, the fading into the landscape' (p. 110), 'history, gross history, daily history, would forget' (p. 111).

If the last paragraph of 'Evermore' is entirely composed of questions, as though Miss Moss, in 1965, still had hopes about the preservation of collective memory – 'Might there be one last fiery glow of remembering?' (p. 111) – Barnes was much more pessimistic when he referred to this short story in 1998: ' "Evermore" is about the fear that things will be forgotten, but history will be forgotten just as people will be forgotten.'[17] In the last short story of the volume, 'Tunnel', which takes place in 2015, the main protagonist, who is an alter ego of the author, suggests that Miss Moss's fears were well-founded: 'there was a proposal before the European Parliament to rationalise the First World War cemeteries' (p. 209). His conclusion is hopeless: 'What history mainly did was eliminate, delete . . . inescapably, they would delete the graveyards' (p. 209). In 2015, that is 50 years after Miss Moss's visits to the cemeteries and 100 years after the First World War, the narrator of 'Tunnel' asserts that his grandfather's dreadful experience in the trenches in France is irremediably lost: 'No act of will could recreate that putteed and perhaps mustachioed figure of 1915. He was gone beyond memory, and no plump little French cake dipped in tea would release those distant truths' (p. 206) – an allusion to the famous French writer Marcel Proust (1871–1922), whose narrator remembered the past by tasting a 'madeleine', a 'little French cake dipped in tea'. If collective memory is deficient, so is individual memory as the elderly protagonist of 'Tunnel' suggests: 'He remembered ... no, that verb, he increasingly found, was often inexact. He seemed to remember, or he retrospectively imagined, or he reconstructed' (p. 197). And yet, he later remarks that his profession as a writer consists of preserving these memories – though partial and distorted – selecting them and passing them on to his readers: 'What was he, finally, but a gatherer and sifter of memories: his memories, history's memories? Also, a grafter of memories, passing them on to other people' (p. 210). Michiko Kakutani explains that the writer–protagonist's lapses of memory are precisely what gives birth to imagination: 'There are holes in his memories, as well as distortions, elisions and conflations, and out of these slips, the old man spins a series of stories embroidered with imaginative speculation, stories that are meant to illuminate the process of fiction-making itself.'[18]

In *Cross Channel* and more systematically in *The Lemon Table*, the attention to the past and the issue of individual and collective memory are often associated with old age and the fear of death. How one feels about ageing is nicely put by the main protagonist of 'Hygiene': 'Were you as young as you felt, or as old as you looked?' (p. 71). A few reviewers suggested that it might be premature for Barnes, who was 58 years old in 2004, to ponder on these subjects but, according to Thomas Mallon, 'he may be ideally positioned for the subject matter, just close enough to be agitated by its looming personal relevance and still far enough away for it to require the imaginative feats he performs in this compact book'.[19] Thus, *The Lemon Table* presents elderly people who remember or assess their past life as they see death approaching. Sometimes their versions are contradictory, as in the case of 'The Things You Know', in which two widows meeting for a monthly breakfast have conflicting memories of one another's late husband but keep silent about the terrible things they know, so as not to shatter the idealised vision each has created for herself and not to ruin their precarious friendship. Kakutani calls it a 'fable about the illusions people construct around their own pasts'.[20] In 'A Short History of Hairdressing', the main protagonist, Gregory, assesses his own life through the shifting attitudes he held while having haircuts as an anxious boy, a contemptuous young adult and a resigned older man. In 'Appetite', a retired dentist suffering from Alzheimer's disease sputters abusive obscenities at his wife, who is trying to calm him down and bring back memories by reading recipe books. The episodes he remembers are often 'more vivid than a normal memory. It's like storytelling, the way he invents it' (p. 167), but the inventions turn into reality: 'He invents it, but I know it's true, because I now remember it' (p. 167). If illness is not a topic Barnes examines thoroughly in these pieces, one should note that in 2002 he translated into English *La Doulou* (the Provençal word for 'la douleur', i.e. pain), the collection of notes by Alphonse Daudet about his excruciating sufferings because of syphilis.

    The last short story of *The Lemon Table*, 'The Silence', is written in the first person by an octogenarian composer who, approaching death, reflects upon mortality, and, though unnamed, is the fictional embodiment of Jean Sibelius (1865–1957), Finland's greatest composer. His wish in the first sentence – 'a longing to see the cranes' (p. 203) – echoes that of an earlier protagonist – a composer who dies without having heard his last piece – in the opening sentence of 'Interference', the first short story in *Cross Channel*: 'He longed for death' (p. 3). Both composers paradoxically relish silence; in 'Interference', the British composer Leonard Verity, who is based on Frederick Delius (1862–1934), 'lived alone with his art, in silence and in freedom' (p. 8), while the composer of the later short story asserts: 'I do not choose silence. Silence chooses me' (p. 212). In 'The Silence', the composer dines and discusses death with others at the 'lemon table' – so called because 'Among the Chinese, the lemon is the symbol of death' (p. 206) – where 'it is permissible – indeed, obligatory – to talk about death' (p. 206). Most characters in *The Lemon Table* talk about death, or, to quote Kakutani, 'about the pains and humiliations of growing old, about the mistakes and regrets they can no longer do anything about. These are people afflicted by nostalgia and haunted by their youthful failures to seize the day.'[21] Robert MacFarlane suggests that speech in the stories is a way of deferring death for the characters, who are 'working unconsciously to the same logic as Scheherazade; so long as they can keep talking, they won't have to start dying'.[22]

The implicit reference to authentic artists in 'The Silence' and 'Interference' finds an amusing echo in 'Experiment', published in *Cross Channel*, which involved real writers in a situation in which it was difficult for the reader to decide whether the encounter was real or invented. As is often the case with Barnes, according to James Wood, 'It is hard to tell if he is feeding us true or false information. And this is the point.'[23] The short story focuses on Uncle Freddy, a facetious character who may recall Uncle Arthur in *Metroland* and Uncle Leslie in *Staring at the Sun*. The narrator, the main protagonist's nephew, relates the encounter in Paris between fictitious Uncle Freddy and real Surrealist French writers such as André Breton (1896–1966), Jacques Prévert (1900–77), Raymond Queneau (1903–76) or Louis Aragon (1897–1982) in March 1928, and he refers to an authentic text by its original title *Recherches sur la sexualité, janvier 1928 – août 1932*. A few of the quotations by Breton and Aragon, translated into English, are indeed authentic and can be found in the original text, but the narrator also reproduces an appendix to the book which consists of the transcription of a session including Surrealist members and a mysterious T.F. who is supposed to be Uncle Freddy, about the latter's sexual life. The narrator gives 'the transcript in full' (p. 49) because Uncle Freddy's own versions of the session and of his time in Paris were often contradictory, full of 'self-inflicted incompatibilities' (p. 47), and the narrator never trusted his word. The elusiveness of truth in this case is furthered by the fact that the appendix does not exist in the real book and Barnes himself admitted he had invented the Englishman. Moseley considers 'Experiment' to be 'Barnes's finest short story. It is witty, oblique, and sophisticated. In many ways it recapitulates themes and motifs from the novels. Without postmodern play it raises the old question of truth and its verifiability.'[24]

A similar game of hide-and-seek recurs in two other short stories in *Cross Channel* which feature writers: 'Gnossienne', in which the narrator, though named Clements, might be an alter ego of Barnes; and 'Tunnel', in which the character of the writer might be a projection of Barnes in the future, as he suggested himself: 'It's a version of a future biography.'[25] In 'Tunnel', the main protagonist, aged 69 in 2015, was born in the same year as Barnes (1946) and lives in the same area, 'north London' (p. 191). His name remains secret but may echo the double identity of Barnes–Kavanagh – 'He read his name – two words plus an initial' (p. 192) – and his face looks familiar: 'Gaunt, long-faced' (p. 192). The protagonist remembers his past, more particularly 'half a century ago, when he had taught as an *assistant* in Rennes' (p. 204), a hint at Barnes's own past as he taught English at a Catholic school in Rennes in France in 1966–7. The fictional character also draws attention to 'the green stud he now wore in his buttonhole' (p. 209), reminiscent of Barnes's own decorations in France as Chevalier of the Order of Arts and Letters in 1988, promoted Officer in 1995, and finally Commander in 2004. The protagonist's profession is kept secret until the last sentence when he is revealed to be the author of *Cross Channel*: 'the elderly Englishman, when he returned home, began to write the stories you have just read' (p. 211). The numerous allusions to details from previous short stories seem to confirm the identity of the main character, who has been pulling the strings of the volume all along.

If the writer–protagonist bears a fictional name in 'Gnossienne' and remains unnamed in 'Tunnel', on the other hand, in 'Knowing French' from *The Lemon Table*, a lively elderly lady, Sylvia Winstanley, writes letters from 1986 to 1989 to 'Julian Barnes', whose 'Flaubert's Parrot' (p. 139) she has borrowed from the public library. Whereas Barnes was portraying himself as an older man in 'Tunnel', in 'Knowing French', he moves back some 20 years earlier. In this epistolary short story, Sylvia identifies the narrator of *Flaubert's Parrot*, retired doctor Geoffrey Braithwaite, with its author, and addresses her first letter to 'Dr Barnes' (p. 139). The reader is never given access to Barnes's part of the correspondence (his letters were supposedly ruined when the refrigerator Sylvia used for storage was defrosted upon her death) but one can infer that the writer partly corrected her mistake as she addresses him as 'Mr Barnes' in her second letter, though she still seems to confuse narrator and author. It is only later that she admits he must invent things: 'Of course you make things up in your stories' (p 155). The reference to *Flaubert's Parrot*, published 20 years before *The Lemon Table*, is certainly no coincidence in a volume which, according to Robert MacFarlane, has many affinities with the early book: 'the ageing narrator, the wry gentleness, the curative powers of hypothesis'.[26] 'Knowing French' is full of humour thanks to the alertness, intelligence and wit of Sylvia Winstanley and to Barnes's self-mockery. Stephanie Merritt finds the story 'warm, puckish and affectionate'[27] while Peter Conradi argues that the elderly lady 'springs from the page with vividness'.[28]

This funny and lively short story, which brings a fictitious character and a real author into contact may remind the reader of an uncollected piece, 'Hamlet in the Wild West' (1994), in which Shakespeare's famous play is performed by a theatre company in Missouri. When, in the play, Laertes is about to strike Hamlet with his sword, 'a cowboy in the audience rose to his feet and shot Laertes dead. Whereupon the cowboy sitting next to him got up, loudly protested that his friend had plugged the wrong villain, and shot Claudius dead.'[29] The two cowboys have confused fiction and reality, but when they are brought to a trial, the partial judge firmly re-establishes the demarcation line between the two worlds so as to spare the murderers: 'Claudius and Laertes being figments of the imagination, they could not be murdered except by other figments of the imagination' (p. 103).

Together with 'Knowing French', 'Vigilance' is certainly the funniest short story in *The Lemon Table*, dealing with a grumpy classical music fan who can no longer stand the coughing, sneezing and munching of the audience ruining the concerts he attends, and becomes more and more intolerant and violent as the story proceeds. Beneath that comic surface, however, the reader discovers that his intolerance is related to the end of his sexual relationship with Andrew, his partner of 20 years. As MacFarlane suggests, 'displacement is at work – the narrator's anger is a sublimated version of his sadness'.[30]

Sadness and frustration also inhabit 'The Revival', originally published in 1996 and later collected in *The Lemon Table*, which is devoted to Ivan Turgenev (1818–83). Barnes has often referred to his attachment to Russian literature, which he studied at Magdalen College, Oxford, and to Turgenev in particular, who was a close friend of Flaubert's. In *Flaubert's Parrot* (p. 35), Braithwaite and Ed Winterton want to buy the same copy of Turgenev's *Literary Reminiscences* (1852), and in 'Two Moles', included in *Something to Declare* (pp. 209–14), Barnes gives a brief account of the correspondence between Flaubert and Turgenev. 'The Revival' relates the platonic passion of 60-year-old Turgenev for an actress who is 35 years younger than him, and the exploration of love and its relation to happiness echoes previous novels by Barnes. In *Flaubert's Parrot*, Braithwaite had established a direct though naive correspondence between love and happiness – 'I loved her; we were happy . . . . She didn't love me; we were unhappy' (pp. 191, 193) – which Stuart had repeated in *Talking It Over*: 'I love Gillian. I'm happy, yes I'm happy' (p. 47). In the 'Parenthesis' of *A History of the World in 10½ Chapters*, the narrator repeats the same words but contradicts the previous protagonists: 'Love makes you happy? No. Love makes the person you love happy? No. Love makes everything all right? Indeed no. I used to believe this, of course' (p. 231). In 'The Revival', Yvan Turgenev also rejects the equation between love and happiness: 'Love might or might not provoke kindness, gratify vanity, and clear the skin, but it did not lead to happiness' (p. 87). Despite this awareness, Turgenev falls in love with the actress who plays Verochka in the play he himself wrote, and the frail frontier between fiction and reality is shattered as Turgenev actually falls in love not with the real person but with his own creation, the fictitious Verochka: 'Who needs the interference of the real person, the real *her* beneath the sunlight, the lamplight, the heart-light?' (p. 89). If Stuart in *Love, etc* declared that 'First love is the only love' (p. 171), Turgenev values all the more 'his last love' (p. 89), 'his last journey, the last journey of the heart' (p. 91), as 'it was a love predicated upon renunciation, whose excitements were called if-only and what-might-have-been' (p. 90). In *Something to Declare*, Barnes reminds his readers of Turgenev's precocious choice of renunciation: 'Turgenev asserted that after the age of forty, the basis of life is renunciation' (p. 211).

Turgenev's passion for the young actress is presented in a very subtle and touching way, with ample space for the narrator's imagination as no document has survived on what actually happened between the two protagonists in the train compartment they were sharing during the 30 miles from Mtsensk to Oryol on 28 May 1880. The narrator therefore juxtaposes differing versions, for which he gives various interpretations: 'He did not dare to kiss her lips: renunciation. Or he tried to kiss her lips and she turned her face away: shame, humiliation. The banality, too, at his age. Or he kissed her and she kissed him back as ardently: surprise, and leaping fear. We do not know: his diary was later burned, her letters have not survived. All we have are his subsequent letters, whose gauge of reliability is that they date this May journey to the month of June' (p. 91). Such blatant uncertainty echoes the equally dubious affair between Flaubert and the English governess, Juliet Herbert, as related in *Flaubert's Parrot*, where the narrator emphatically confesses his ignorance: 'we know nothing. Not a single letter to or from her has survived. We know almost nothing about her family. We do not even know what she looked like. No description of her survives, and none of Flaubert's friends thought to mention her after his death' (p. 40). It is precisely this irretrievability of the past and of truth which makes the two love affairs a source of inspiration for the artist. As the protagonist of 'The Silence' suggests, 'one may express the truth in more than one way' (p. 212). In 'The Revival', the narrator keeps asking rhetorical questions on what actually happened and what the two protagonists felt, while Turgenev himself wonders what might have occurred if he had abducted the young actress on that day, or imagines other journeys with her in the past or in the future. He takes refuge in the 'if-only' (p. 91), in dream journeys, and his fantasies are safely 'in the past conditional' (p. 95), which does not, however, preclude pain. Michiko Kakutani praises 'The Revival', which she considers as 'a melancholy parable about unfulfilled dreams and emotional risks not taken', and places it among the best tales of the volume, 'beautifully wrought elegies for lost youth, lost promises and lost loves'.[31]

'The Story of Mats Israelson', likewise a 'tale of yearning and missed connections' according to Kakutani,[32] provides another example of the 'voluptuousness of renunciation' (p. 92) and 'the impossibility of love' (p. 93) at a time – the end of the nineteenth century – when 'they knew more about desire . . . they knew more about despair . . . they knew more about memory . . . they knew more about love' (p. 92). The scene takes place in a rural town in Sweden and deals with the frustrated love between Barbro Lindwall, the pharmacist's wife, and Anders Bodén, manager of a sawmill. In 1898, they meet every fortnight on the steamboat that goes up the lake, and talk, which provokes gossip in the neighbourhood. However, when Mrs Lindwall makes an implicit proposal to Bodén by telling him 'I would like to visit Falun' (p. 32), the latter fails to answer 'I shall take you there' (p. 34). Like Turgenev, Bodén spends the rest of his life dwelling on 'the moment that had nearly happened, that could have happened' (p. 35) and thinking in the past conditional, while Barbro Lindwall falls victim to the if-only – 'if only he could have read my heart' (p. 36) – and is gnawed by 'the constant, silent, secret pain' (p. 36); 23 years later, Bodén asks her to come and visit him in hospital at Falun where he is dying of cancer. His aim is to declare his love for her but he miserably fails, vexing her instead. Mrs Lindwall leaves and both protagonists are left with a devastating pain grown out of their inability to express their feelings.

In 'Bark', which takes place in nineteenth-century France, elderly Jean-Étienne Delacour refuses to comply with the demand of his friend Lagrange, to 'renounce' (p. 132) Jeanne, a young maid working at the baths, with whom he has sexual intercourse in exchange for money as 'a matter of hygiene' (p. 132), but for whom he has come to feel a 'surprising love' (p. 134). As in 'The Story of Mats Israelson' however, Delacour never reveals his genuine love for Jeanne, believing instead that love is 'a private matter': 'he also felt that, were he to express what he felt, it [love] might depart, or become complicated in a way he did not desire' (p. 134). In 'Hygiene', the main protagonist, Major Jacko Jackson, though happily married, has visited a prostitute, Babs, once a year for 22 years, also supposedly as a 'matter of hygiene' (p. 72), but as years go by a different type of relationship develops between the two. As MacFarlane suggests, 'Jacko's brassoed military language, we discover, is the defence mechanism of a depressed and insecure man.'[33] On his last visit, when he finds out that Babs is dead and was actually called Nora, his world cracks as the fantasy that kept him going is shattered and he is forced to face his physical and sexual decline as well as his own mortality. As MacFarlane explains, 'Jacko's obsession with sexual performance is in fact a displacement for his much larger fear of death.'[34]

Several short stories in *The Lemon Table* thus deal with the theme of love from the perspective of elderly people, suggesting that love and sex do not belong only to the young. Love is usually remembered nostalgically, having been lived to the full or renounced, but in 'The Fruit Cage' it is lived in the present. The narrator's father, aged 81, decides to leave his 80-year-old wife to go and live with his neighbour Elsie, who is in her mid-sixties. His son is shocked to hear that the relationship is 'physical' (p. 189), but also reflects on why he did not ask about love: 'Would I have been less squeamish if my father had said, "No, son, it isn't physical at all, it's just that I've fallen in love." The question I'd asked, which had seemed hard enough at the time, was actually the easier one' (p. 190). The narrator becomes aware of 'one of the great conspiracies of youth', according to which 'we want – need – to see old age as a time of serenity' (p. 190), and realises that his 'father was declining to play the game' (p. 191). Barnes remarks that *The Lemon Table* is 'against serenity. It's against the notion that things calm down when we get older, when philosophy is supposed to kick in – that the body, the heart and sexual desire develop and age in the same way. They don't, they develop with great disjunctions.'[35] Stephanie Merritt draws a parallel with Mme Wyatt in *Love, etc*, who, in her old age, insists that 'the memory of desire burns just as fiercely in the years when you are sagely supposed to have left it behind'.[36] What Mme Wyatt asserts in *Love, etc* – 'I shall always feel the pain and the wound of the things that I had and that I still want and that will never come again' (p. 223) – echoes the feelings of many protagonists of *The Lemon Table*.

The working title for this second volume of short stories was *Rage and Age*, a homage to the famous poem by Dylan Thomas (1914–53) to his dying father – 'Do not go gentle into that good night' (1951) – in which the poet implored him to 'Rage, rage against the dying of the light.' Barnes said he dropped the original title 'because it gave too much away', but MacFarlane suggests that the first title 'was too misleading', countering that 'although there is plenty of peevishness, bafflement, resignation, ennui, regret and – most destructively – indifference, very little raging occurs'.[37] Kakutani argues contrarily that 'most of Mr Barnes's people are going to go out raging against the dying of the light', referring to the hero of 'The Fruit Cage' but also to the elderly lady of 'Knowing French' who 'pluckily resists giving up'.[38] Merritt concurs, emphasising the protagonists' refusal 'to relinquish the pleasures and passions of the younger self' despite their awareness of a declining vigour.[39] Barnes thus wards off a sentimental and melancholy view of the elderly, and *The Lemon Table* is remarkable for its wit, irony and wry sense of humour. The stylistic and narrative variety of the tales suggests that Barnes does not suffer from the decline in creativity undergone by some of his protagonists. At the beginning of 2004, he started working on a new novel, *Arthur & George*, which was completed within the year and published in July 2005, a novel which confirms that Barnes's creativity is not waning.

# CONCLUSION

# Endings and New Beginnings:
# *Arthur & George* (2005)

Some twenty years after the tremendous success of *Flaubert's Parrot*, which celebrated a French author, Julian Barnes has chosen to devote his tenth novel to the figure of the British writer who is famous for his creation of Sherlock Holmes, Sir Arthur Conan Doyle, and to link him with another, lesser-known real-life figure, the Birmingham solicitor George Edalji (1877–1953), who was wrongly convicted of horse mutilation and whose name Doyle helped to clear. While the title of his 1984 book included the author's surname, the title of the 2005 novel, composed of two Christian names, proves more enigmatic. Divided into four parts, *Arthur & George* logically starts with 'Beginnings' (46 pages), which relates the two boys' separate childhoods and early adulthoods at the end of the nineteenth century. The narration alternates between two periods as George was born 18 years after Arthur, and between a comparatively static and a peripatetic way of life as George remained in Wyrley in England throughout his childhood and studied in Birmingham, while Arthur moved from Edinburgh to England to Austria and back to Edinburgh, before qualifying as a doctor, sailing in the Arctic and near the west coast of Africa, and settling in London. As in *Talking It Over* and *Love, etc*, where each monologue is preceded by the first name of the protagonist who intervenes, so, in *Arthur & George*, each narration, focusing on one or the other protagonist and presenting the events from his perspective, is preceded by his first name. The narration thus moves from one point of view to the other, which brings variety, and occasionally presents the point of view of a secondary character.

The first page of the novel, devoted to Arthur, encourages the reader to expect a detective story, reminiscent of those by Dan Kavanagh, as the boy is confronted with a 'white, waxen thing', in other words, a corpse (p. 3). Yet the reader's expectations are quickly frustrated as the corpse turns out to be that of his grandmother and will only be incidental in the narrative. The episode is, however, crucial in terms of memory – 'What he saw there became his first memory' (p. 3) – which contrasts with the first line devoted to George – 'George does not have a first memory' (p. 3). This echoes *England, England*, which begins with a question – 'What's your first memory?' (p. 3) – as well as *Talking It Over* and *Love, etc*, which both start with the issue of what one remembers. The first page of *Arthur & George* might thus remind the reader of Barnes's previous novels and of their specific qualities: the genre of the Kavanagh novels, the narrative alternation of the Gillian–Oliver–Stuart books, the issue of memory and the related difficulty of defining Englishness in *England, England*. The alternate narration of Arthur's and George's early lives emphasises, more-over, the dichotomy between truth and fiction, as George, the unimagi-native son of a Parsee Vicar and a Scottish mother, 'is expected to tell the truth' (p. 4), while fiction appeals much more to Arthur than the truth of the Bible: 'his imagination preferred the different, parallel version he was taught at home' (p. 4). While George and his family become the inno-cent victims of a series of vicious anonymous letters and hoaxes, the future creator of Sherlock Holmes views his life in terms of stories and narratives: 'Arthur could see the beginning of the story – where he was now – and its happy end; only the middle was for the moment lacking' (p. 5).

The middle comes with the second part, 'Beginning with an Ending' (160 pages), in which the 'ending' refers to the end of the persecutions against George, who becomes a solicitor and the author of *Railway Law for the 'Man in the Train'* (1901). The 'ending' also echoes the method of composition of Conan Doyle, who always conceives the conclusion of his stories first: 'How can you make sense of the beginning unless you know the ending?' (p. 54); 'Beginning with an ending. You cannot know which path to travel unless you first know the destination' (p. 267). Though Arthur and George have never met, the two Christian names are brought together for the first time but in reverse order – 'George & Arthur' (p. 72) – just before the first horse mutilation is related by the narrator, without any reference to the two protagonists. This is followed by a 90-page narration of the sentencing of innocent George in 1903 to seven years of penal servitude for horse mutilation, of which he served three before being freed in 1906, and a 45-page narration going back in time to 1897 to Arthur's platonic relationship with Jean Leckie despite his marriage to Louisa – 'Touie' – Hawkins. The chronology is thus disrupted, which is confirmed, for example, by the fact that George in prison in 1904 is being lent 'a tattered cheap edition of *The Hound of the Baskervilles*', which he finds 'excellent' (p. 119). It is only 65 pages later, in the part devoted to Arthur, that the narrator implicitly alludes to the composition of this book and the resuscitation of Sherlock Holmes, who is despatched 'in the footprints of an enormous hound' (p. 184). The second part ends in 1906 with the death of Arthur's wife and his receiving a letter from George Edalji, the two parallel narrations thus coinciding temporally for the first time.

The third part, 'Ending with a Beginning' (115 pages), starts with the replication of the title of the novel – 'Arthur & George' (p. 209) – and is concerned with Doyle's own investigation of Edalji's case, in 1906–7, until George is given a free pardon and declared innocent of the horse mutilation but still guilty of writing anonymous letters back in 1903. The last part, 'Endings' (35 pages), moves forward to Arthur's death in 1930, celebrated by a memorial meeting of spiritualists at the Albert Hall, which George attends. Doyle's interest in spiritualism is regularly referred to in the novel and one may recall that Barnes's first short story, 'A Self-Possessed Woman' (1975), portrayed a medium, Mrs Beesley, who received the spirits of dead writers. In *Arthur & George*, the focus on a criminal case and on Doyle's own investigation might remind the reader that Barnes himself studied law at university and passed the bar exams in 1974, but chose at that time the career of a freelance journalist rather than that of a barrister: 'I was getting more pleasure out of doing a round-up of four novels for a provincial paper than I was out of preparing what I might say defending some criminal.'[1]

Just like *Flaubert's Parrot*, *A History of the World in 10½ Chapters*, *The Porcupine* and *Cross Channel*, Barnes's new novel mixes reality and imagination so that the book is part history, part biography and part fiction. After the Author's Note, signed J. B. and dated 'January 2005', which gives a few indications as to the later lives of the main protagonists apart from Doyle, one sentence draws attention to the historical basis of the novel: 'Apart from Jean's letter to Arthur, all letters quoted, whether signed or anonymous are authentic; as are quotations from newspapers, government reports, proceedings in Parliament, and the writings of Sir Arthur Conan Doyle' (p. 360). Details of Conan Doyle's involvement in the Edalji case can indeed be found in Doyle's *Memories and Adventures* (1924)[2] – George himself keeps rereading the pages devoted to it (p. 335) – as well as in *The Story of Mr George Edalji* (1985)[3] which contains Doyle's first article, published in two parts in the *Daily Telegraph* on 11 and 12 January 1907, his three-part letter published in the same newspaper on 23, 24 and 27 May 1907, and the full text of his 'Statement of the Case against Royden Sharp' – the man he believed was the prime suspect – which he presented to the Home Office in 1907. Barnes actually went to the Newspaper Library in London, but also to Birmingham, to do research on the case. Apart from the Edalji case, the details from Doyle's life also testify to research on the part of the author, even though the biography is only partial as Barnes focuses on specific periods and aspects of Sir Arthur's life and hardly considers his work as a writer. The result is a hybrid of fiction and biography, a now popular sub-genre, for example recently employed by three British writers who devoted novels to episodes in the life of Henry James: *Felony* (2002) by Emma Tennant (born 1937), *The Master* (2004) by Colm Tóibín (born 1955), and *Author, Author* (2004) by David Lodge. In *Arthur & George*, Barnes uses his licence as a novelist to try and imagine what the two protagonists were thinking or feeling, or to invent conversations, and the passages devoted to George Edalji certainly bear the mark of his imagination more strongly than some other sections.

Even though Doyle's activities as a writer are only mentioned in passing, the novel draws much from the genre of detective fiction as the reader follows Edalji's trial and Doyle's later investigation with acute attention. Many implicit and explicit references to Sherlock Holmes confirm the detective drive and the appeal to suspense. When Arthur starts investigating the case, he himself impersonates Holmes, while his secretary, Wood, plays the role of Dr Watson. The frontier between Sir Arthur as investigator and defender of an innocent victim, and Conan Doyle as writer, becomes blurred, and a series of metafictional remarks are inserted, comparing Arthur's investigation of a real case to the composition of a novel: 'It was like starting a book: you had the story but not all of it, most of the characters but not all of them, some but not all of the causal links. You had your beginning, and you had your ending' (p. 237). Reading Doyle's articles about the case in the *Daily Telegraph*, George feels like 'a character in a novel' (p. 297), partly because he believes Arthur has fictionalised some aspects of his personality: 'This was all true, and yet untrue; flattering, yet unflattering; believable, yet unbelievable' (p. 298). Yet, when Arthur asks Captain Anson to tell him what, in his opinion, really happened on 17 August 1903, Anson laughs and declines to provide a satisfying answer: 'That I'm afraid, is a question from detective fiction. It is what your readers beg, and what you so winningly provide. *Tell us what really happened*' (p. 272). Anson openly mocks Doyle's investigation and impersonation of Holmes: 'Doyle wondered if he would ever cease being punished for having invented Sherlock Holmes. Corrected, advised, lectured, patronized' (p. 273). Later on, when Arthur eventually seems to have solved the case and found the real culprit, he regrets the lack of coincidence between his real investigation and the fictional method: ' "It's not meant to happen like this," said Arthur. "I should know. I've written it enough times. It's not meant to happen by following simple steps. It's meant to seem utterly insoluble right up until the end. And then you unravel the knot with one glorious piece of deduction, something entirely logical yet quite astounding, and then you feel a great sense of triumph" ' (p. 293). Still, George is dissatisfied with Arthur's 'Statement of the Case against Royden Sharp' (p. 304) as all of his evidence is 'circumstantial, and much of it hearsay' (p. 304), and

Arthur had the horse lancet – the instrument of the mutilations and main piece of evidence – stolen from Sharp's household. George resents Arthur's confusion of reality and fictional creation: 'it was all, George decided, the fault of Sherlock Holmes. Sir Arthur had been too influenced by his own creation' (p. 305).

Later, when George reads the account of his case in Doyle's autobiography, *Memories and Adventures*, he is again struck by Arthur's relative unreliability: 'George knew from taking witness statements how the retelling of events always smoothed the edges of stories, rendered the speaker more self-important, made everything more certain than it had seemed at the time' (p. 336). The instability of the boundaries between truth and fiction is made blatant.

If issues related to the search for truth and its irretrievability are familiar to readers of Barnes's fiction, *Arthur & George* introduces a new topic which had not been dealt with by the author before: racial prejudice. Several passages are therefore devoted to the ambiguity of what being English means. As a young adult, Doyle chooses Englishness because he is fascinated by the world of chivalry: 'Irish by ancestry, Scottish by birth, instructed in the faith of Rome by Dutch Jesuits, Arthur became English' (p. 23). Later on, he defines himself and George as 'unofficial Englishmen' (p. 217), a categorisation which George, 'a freeborn Englishman' (p. 91), disputes: 'How is he less than a full Englishman? He is one by birth, by citizenship, by education, by religion, by profession . . . he has no other land. He cannot go back two generations. He can hardly return to India, a place he has never visited and has little desire to' (p. 217). If George always refused to consider racial prejudice as a motive for the persecutions against him, Captain Anson suggests, for his part, that 'it is the mixing of blood that is partly the cause of all this' (p. 275) and refers to the commingling of Parsee and Scottish blood as a 'sudden and deplorable miscegenation' (p. 275). After the publication of the Report of the Gladstone Committee, which fails to grant compensation to George for his three years in prison, one of the questions asked in Parliament is: 'Is Edalji being thus treated because he is not an Englishman?' (p. 314) – though he in fact is an Englishman – but no answer is returned. Several references in the novel suggest a parallel with the Dreyfus case in France, which Barnes referred to in 'Holy Hysteria' (2003), his review of *The Anti-Semitic Moment: A Tour of France in 1898* by Pierre Birnbaum. It was actually through Birnbaum's book that Barnes learned about the Edalji case and decided to try and find out more; he was therefore not so much interested in Conan Doyle as in a miscarriage of justice which incidentally involved Doyle. Alfred Dreyfus (1859–1935), an Alsatian Jewish officer, was falsely accused of giving information to the German military attaché in Paris and convicted in 1894. Many people tried to prove Dreyfus's innocence, including the novelist Emile Zola, who published in 1898 an open letter entitled 'J'accuse', attacking the army and bringing the matter to public attention. Dreyfus was tried again in 1899 and again found guilty. It was only in 1906 that he was vindicated by a civilian court and re-admitted to the army. The affair provoked a prolonged political crisis and revealed the prevalence of anti-Semitism in France. The closeness of dates with the Edalji affair explains why Doyle wants to 'make the Edalji Case into as big a stir as they did with Dreyfus over there in France' (p. 242). Although the stir was not as big and George later 'dwindled into a footnote in legal history' (p. 332), it is partially as a result of the Edalji case that the Court of Criminal Appeal was established in 1907 as a way to try and correct other miscarriages of justice.

Barnes's tenth novel is a remarkable achievement which confirms that the author is constantly looking for new topics and original ways of dealing with narrative. In an interview in 1998, Barnes said: 'You don't want to go to the grave having not tried out every prose facility and faculty you've got.'[4] The diversity of his literary production to date clearly demonstrates that the author never stops experimenting with form, style and subject matter. He has the knack of surprising his readers with each new book: publishing a conventional novel after a dazzling experimental one, offering a political fable and then a satirical farce, translating a nineteenth-century book from the French, writing essays about cooking. . . . In 1996, Barnes had defined writing as 'a furious activity within a close formal structure with rules', adding mischievously: 'but I like breaking rules'.[5] One can hardly foretell what Barnes might write next but there is no doubt that he will catch his readers unawares, and delight, thrill and enchant them. The half-chapter or 'Parenthesis' of this Guide suggests that Barnes's production is far from being complete and that there still remains room for future novels, short stories and essays, room for new beginnings.

# Notes

INTRODUCTION

1 Andrew Billen, 'Two Aspects of a Writer', *Observer Magazine* (7 July 1991), p. 27.
2 In Steven Poole, 'Why Don't we Make it All Up?' *Independent on Sunday*, 447 (30 August 1998), Culture, p. 10.
3 Peter Childs, 'Julian Barnes: "A Mixture of Genres" ', in *Contemporary Novelists: British Fiction since 1970* (Basingstoke: Palgrave Macmillan, 2005), p. 86.
4 A. S. Byatt, 'People in Paper Houses', in Malcolm Bradbury (ed.), *The Contemporary English Novel* (London: Edward Arnold, 1979), p. 34.
5 In Amanda Smith, 'Julian Barnes', *Publishers Weekly*, 236:8 (3 November 1989), p. 73.
6 Julian Barnes, 'When Flaubert Took Wing', *Guardian* (5 March 2005), p. 30.
7 Barnes, 'When Flaubert Took Wing' (2005), p. 30.
8 In Simon Banner, 'Word Painter's Brush with the Future', *The Times* (20 September 1986), p. 10.

CHAPTER ONE

1 Andrew Billen, 'Two Aspects of a Writer', *Observer Magazine* (7 July 1991), p. 27.
2 In Ronald Hayman, 'Julian Barnes in Interview', *Books and Bookmen*, 25.8:296 (May 1980), p. 36.
3 Billen (1991), p. 27.
4 M. Moseley, *Understanding Julian Barnes* (Columbia, SC: University of Carolina Press, 1997), p. 18.
5 Julian Barnes, 'Out of Place', *Architectural Digest*, 54:5 (May 1997), p. 38.
6 In Mira Stout, 'Chameleon Novelist', *New York Times* (22 November 1992), Section 6, p. 29.
7 In Hayman (1980), p. 36.
8 In Stout (1992), p. 29.
9 In Hayman (1980), p. 36.
10 Frank Kermode, 'Obsessed with Obsession', *New York Review of Books*, 32:7 (25 April 1985), p. 15.
11 Edward Blishen, 'Growing Up', *Times Educational Supplement*, 3334 (2 May 1980), p. 22.
12 David Williams, 'Paperbacks of the Month: Fiction', *The Times*, 60995 (1 August 1981), p. 9.
13 Paul Bailey, 'Settling for Suburbia', *Times Literary Supplement*, 4018 (28 March 1980), p. 345.
14 Bernard Levin, 'Metroland: Thanks for the Memory', *Sunday Times*, 8128 (6 April 1980), p. 42.
15 Williams (1981), p. 9.
16 David Leon Higdon, ' "Unconfessed Confessions": the Narrators of Graham Swift and Julian Barnes', in James Acheson (ed.), *The British and Irish Novel since 1960* (Basingstoke: Macmillan, 1991), p. 176.

17 Matthew Pateman, 'Julian Barnes and the Popularity of Ethics', in Steven Earnshaw (ed.), *Postmodern Surroundings*, Postmodern Studies, 9 (Amsterdam and Atlanta, GA: Rodopi Press, 1994), p. 183.

18 Moseley (1997), p. 25.

19 In Hayman (1980), p. 36.

20 In Rudolf Freiburg, ' "Novels come out of life, not out of theory": an Interview with Julian Barnes', in Rudolf Freiburg and Jan Schnitker (eds), *'Do you consider yourself a postmodern author?'* Interviews with Contemporary English Writers (Reihe: Erlanger Studien zur Anglistik und Amerikanistik, vol. 1, 1999), p. 50.

21 Tom Paulin, 'National Myths', *Encounter*, 54:6 (June 1980), p. 63.

22 Levin (1980), p. 42.

23 In Freiburg (1999), p. 49.

24 In Freiburg (1999), p. 62.

25 Higdon (1991), p. 177.

26 Moseley (1997), p. 29.

27 Jay Parini, 'Two Clever Lads from London', *New York Times Book Review*, 92 (3 May 1987), p. 26.

28 Higdon (1991), p. 177.

29 Moseley (1997), p. 29.

30 Michael Church, 'New Books. Fiction', *The Times*, 60586 (27 March 1980), p. 11.

31 Moseley (1997), pp. 19, 30.

32 William Boyd, 'Late Sex', *London Magazine*, 20:7 (October 1980), p. 96.

33 Richard Todd, 'Domestic Performance: Julian Barnes and the Love Triangle', in *Consuming Fictions: The Booker Prize and Fiction in Britain Today* (London: Bloomsbury, 1996), p. 265.

34 Bailey (1980), p. 345.

35 Williams (1981), p. 9.

36 Bailey (1980), p. 345.

37 Moseley (1997), p. 21.

38 Levin (1980), p. 42.

39 Hayman (1980), p. 36.

40 Nicholas Shrimpton, 'Bourgeois v. Bohemian', *New Statesman*, 99:2558 (28 March 1980), p. 483.

41 Richard Brown, 'Julian Barnes', in Neil Schlager and Josh Lauer (eds.), *Contemporary Novelists*, 7th edn (1996; updated by Tobias Wachinger, New York: St James Press, 2001), p. 68.

42 Vanessa Guignery, *Postmodernisme et effets de brouillage dans la fiction de Julian Barnes* [*Postmodernism and Modes of Blurring in the Fiction of Julian Barnes*] (Villeneuve d'Ascq: Presses Universitaires du Septentrion, 2001), pp. 119–20, 159.

43 Matthew Pateman, *Julian Barnes* (Tavistock: Northcote House, Writers and their Work, 2002), p. 8.

44 Pateman (2002), p. 5.

45 Todd (1996), p. 266.

46 Renaud Matignon, 'Les Terrains vagues de la mémoire', *Figaro Littéraire* (30 March 1995), p. 1.

47 Vanessa Guignery, 'Excentricité et interlinguisme dans *Metroland* et *Talking It Over* de Julian Barnes' [Excentricity and interlinguism in Julian Barnes's *Metroland* and *Talking It Over*]', *Études britanniques contemporaines*, 15 (December 1998), pp. 13–24; Guignery, *Postmodernisme* (2001), pp. 232–3, 242–3, 245, 250–1.

48 Frank Goodman, 'Growing up in Metroland', *Northamptonshire Evening Telegraph* (24 April 1980).

49 Moseley (1997), p. 30.

50 Elizabeth Kastor, 'Julian Barnes' Big Questions', *Washington Post, Book World*, 111 (18 May 1987), p. 9.

51 David Gritten, 'Definite Traces of Intelligent Life', *Electronic Telegraph*, 1184 (22 August 1998).

52 Julian Barnes, 'You Ask the Questions: Julian Barnes', *Independent* (16 January 2002), p. 8.

CHAPTER TWO

1 Nicholas Wroe, 'Literature's Mister Cool', *Guardian* (29 July 2000), pp. 6–7.

2 David Leon Higdon, ' "Unconfessed Confessions": the Narrators of Graham Swift and Julian Barnes', in James Acheson (ed.), *The British and Irish Novel since 1960* (Basingstoke: Macmillan, 1991), p. 176.

3 Richard Brown, 'Julian Barnes', in Neil Schlager and Josh Lauer (eds) *Contemporary Novelists*, 7th edn (1996; updated by Tobias Wachinger, New York: St James Press, 2001), p. 68.

4 Bill Greenwell, 'Flashback', *New Statesman*, 103:2665 (16 April 1982), p. 19.

5 Matthew Pateman, *Julian Barnes* (Tavistock: Northcote House, Writers and their Work, 2002), p. 15.

6 Anthony Thwaite, 'A Course in Creativity', *Observer* (18 April 1982), p. 31.

7 Greenwell (1982), p. 19.

8 Thwaite (1982), p. 31.

9 Mark Abley, 'Watching Green-Eyed', *Times Literary Supplement*, 4125 (23 April 1982), p. 456.

10 Isabel Raphael, 'Fiction', *The Times*, 61208 (15 April 1982), p. 8.

11 Greenwell (1982), p. 19.

12 Richard Todd, 'Domestic Performance: Julian Barnes and the Love Triangle', in *Consuming Fictions: The Booker Prize and Fiction in Britain Today* (London: Bloomsbury, 1996), p. 267.

13 Merritt Moseley, *Understanding Julian Barnes* (Columbia, SC: University of Carolina Press, 1997), p. 65.

14 Philip Larkin, 'To Julian Barnes – 20 April 1982', in Anthony Thwaite (ed.), *Selected Letters of Philip Larkin, 1940–1985* (London: Faber & Faber, 1992), p. 667.

15 Gary Krist, 'She Oughtn't to have Been in Pictures', *New York Times Book Review*, 91 (28 December 1986), p. 12.

16 John Mellors, 'Bull's Balls', *London Magazine*, 22:1–2 (April–May 1982), pp. 133, 134.

17 Abley (1982), p. 456.

18 Raphael (1982), p. 8.

19 Greenwell (1982), p. 19.

20 Todd (1996), p. 269.

21 Elizabeth Kastor, 'Julian Barnes' Big Questions', *Washington Post, Book World*, 111 (18 May 1987), p. 9.

22 Larkin (1992), p. 667.

23 Michiko Kakutani, 'Books of the Times', *New York Times*, 142 (17 December 1986), p. C26.

24 Thwaite (1982), p. 31.

25 Frank Kermode, 'Obsessed with Obsession', *New York Review of Books*, 32:7 (25 April 1985), p. 15.

26 Krist (1986), p. 12.

27 Moseley (1997), pp. 54, 55.

28 In Amanda Smith, 'Julian Barnes', *Publishers Weekly*, 236:8 (3 November 1989), p. 74.

29 Jérôme Garcin, 'Julian Barnes, période scato . . . [scato period . . .]', *Événement du jeudi* (11–17 April 1991), p. 113.

30 Moseley (1997), p. 55.

31 William Shakespeare, *Othello* (Act III, scene 3, line 168).

32 Higdon (1991), p. 178.

33 Shakespeare, *Othello* (Act III, scene 4, lines 161–2).

34  Abley (1982), p. 456.
35  Nicholas Shrimpton, 'Fiction – The Crocodile File', *Sunday Times*, 8233 (18 April 1982), p. 40.
36  David Montrose, 'Julian Barnes', in D. L. Kirkpatrick (ed.), *Contemporary Novelists*, 4th edn (London: St James Press, 1986), p. 69.
37  Julian Barnes, 'Remembrance of Things Past', *Observer* (24 July 1983), p. 22.
38  Patrick McGrath, 'Julian Barnes', *Bomb*, 21 (Fall 1987), p. 21.
39  Higdon (1991), p. 178.
40  Barnes, 'Remembrance' (1983), p. 22.
41  In Shusha Guppy, 'Julian Barnes: the Art of Fiction, no. 165', *Paris Review* (www.parisreview.com/viewinterview.php/prmMID/562) 157 (Winter 2000).
42  In Rudolf Freiburg and Jan Schnitker (eds), '*Do you consider yourself postmodern author?*' *Interviews with Contemporary English writers* (Reihe: Erlanger Studien zur Anglistic und Amerikanistic, vol. 1, 1999), p. 55.
43  In Freiburg (1999), p. 55.
44  Moseley (1997), p. 67.
45  Pateman (2002), p. 14.
46  Greenwell (1982), p. 19.
47  Pateman (2002), p. 21.
48  Frédéric Monneyron, 'Lien, liage et déliages de la jalousie dans *Before She Met Me* de Julian Barnes [Bond, bonding and unbonding of jealousy in Julian Barnes's *Before She Met Me*]', in *L'Écriture de la jalousie* (Grenoble: Editions Littéraires et Linguistiques de l'Université de Grenoble, 1997), pp. 137–51.
49  Monneyron (1997), pp. 146–8.
50  Mark K. Millington and Alison S. Sinclair, 'The Honourable Cuckold: Models of Masculine Defence', *Comparative Literature Studies*, 29:1 (1992), p. 15.
51  Millington and Sinclair (1992), p. 15.
52  Pateman (2002), pp. 15–21; Vanessa Guignery, *Postmodernisme et effets de brouillage dans la fiction de Julian Barnes* [*Postmodernism and Modes of Blurring in the Fiction of Julian Barnes*] (Villeneuve d'Ascq: Presses Universitaires du Septentrion, 2001), pp. 520–1.
53  Pateman (2002), p. 19.
54  Mellors (1982), p. 133.
55  Brian McHale, *Postmodernist Fiction* (New York and London: Methuen, 1987), p. 16.
56  Pateman (2002), p. 20.
57  Pateman (2002), p. 20.
58  Moseley (1997), p. 64.
59  Bruce Sesto, *Language, History, and Metanarrative in the Fiction of Julian Barnes*, vol. 3 (New York: Peter Lang, 2001), p. 26.
60  Nicole Zand, 'Barnes et son double [Barnes and his double]', *Le Monde* (29 March 1991), p. 24.
61  Thwaite (1982), p. 31.
62  Moseley (1997), p. 54.

CHAPTER THREE

1  In Amanda Smith, 'Julian Barnes', *Publishers Weekley*, 236:8 (3 November 1989), p. 73.
2  Simon Banner, 'World Painter's Brush with the Future', *The Times* (20 September 1986), p. 10.
3  In Ronald Hayman, 'Julian Barnes in Interview', *Books and Bookmen*, 25.8: 296 (May 1980), p. 37.
4  In Smith (1989), p. 73.
5  In Smith (1989), p. 74.
6  Alan Clinton, 'Faking Gestures: a Brief Guide to Art, Literature, and Politics', in Philippe

Romanski and Aïssatou Sy-Wonyu (eds), *Trompe(-)l'œil. Imitation et falsification* (Rouen: Publications de l'Université de Rouen, 2002), p. 373.

7   In Hayman (1980), p. 37.

8   In Philip Marchand, 'English Novelist Re-creates God in His Own Image', *Toronto Star* (17 October 1989), p. E1.

9   In David Sexton, 'Still Parroting On about God', *Sunday Telegraph*, 1463 (11 June 1989), p. 42.

10  David Streitfeld, 'Fancy Dan', *Washington Post, Book World*, 111:22 (27 December 1987), p. 15.

11  In Smith (1989), p. 74.

12  In *Contemporary Authors*, Literature Resource Center, on CD-Rom (Detroit, MI: Gale Group, 2001).

13  Martha Duffy, 'Pleasures of Merely Circulating', *Time* (8 April 1985), p. 56.

14  *London Review of Books*, 9:18 (15 October 1987), p. 1.

15  'In Brief', *Times Literary Supplement*, 4415 (13 November 1987), p. 1250.

16  David Montrose, 'Julian Barnes', in D. L. Kirkpatrick (ed.), *Contemporary Novelists*, 4th edn (London: St James Press, 1986), p. 69.

17  Richard Brown, 'Julian Barnes', in Neil Schlager and Josh Lauer (eds), *Contemporary Novelists*, 7th edn (New York: St James Press, 1996; updated by Tobias Wachinger, 2001), p. 78.

18  Julian Barnes, 'My team', *Observer on Sunday* (5 August 2001), p. 61.

19  François Rivière, 'Barnes et son double [Barnes and his double]', *Libération* (23 May 1991), p. 29.

20  Montrose (1986), p. 70.

21  Lidia Vianu, 'Giving Up Criticism is Much Easier than Giving Up Alcohol or Tobacco', *România Literara* (13–19 December 2000).

22  Nicole Zand, 'Barnes et son double [Barnes and his double]', *Le Monde* (29 March 1991), p. 24.

23  In Hayman (1980), p. 37.

24  Merritt Moseley, *Understanding Julian Barnes* (Columbia, SC: University of Carolina Press, 1997), p. 39.

25  Moseley (1997), pp. 5–6.

26  Alexander Stuart, 'A Talk with Julian Barnes', *Los Angeles Times Book Review* (15 October 1989), p. 15.

27  Mark Lawson, 'A Short History of Julian Barnes', *Independent Magazine* (13 July 1991), p. 36.

28  Brown (1996), p. 78.

29  Charles Moritz, 'Julian Barnes', in *Current Biography Yearbook 1988* (New York: H. W. Wilson, 1988), p. 41.

30  In Hayman (1980), p. 37.

31  Rivière (1991), p. 29.

32  Moseley (1997), p. 38.

33  Simon O'Hagan, 'Interview: Julian Barnes – "I May Not Like it Much, but I Still Live Here" ', *Independent on Sunday* (1 December 2002), p. 10.

34  Raymond Chandler, 'The Simple Art of Murder' (1945), in *The Simple Art of Murder* (London: Hamish Hamilton, 1950), p. 333.

35  Moseley (1997), p. 38.

36  Moseley (1997), p. 37.

37  Moseley (1997), p. 37.

38  Moseley (1997), p. 49.

39  Moseley (1997), p. 51.

40  Moseley (1997), p. 53.

41  Jérôme Garcin, 'Julian Barnes, période scato . . . [scato period]', *Événement du jeudi* (11–17 April 1991), p. 113.

42  Kate Kellaway, 'The Grand Fromage Matures', *Observer* (7 January 1996), p. R7.
43  In Christopher Hawtree, 'Novel Escape', *The Times*, 65475 (13 January 1996), p. 19.
44  Lawson (1991), p. 35.
45  David Streitfeld, 'Barnes's Albatross', *Washington Post, Book World*, 17 (22 October 1989), p. X15.
46  Lawson (1991), p. 36.

CHAPTER FOUR

1  Nadine O'Regan, 'Cool, Clean Man of Letters', *Sunday Business Post* (29 June 2003).
2  In Vanessa Guignery and François Gallix, 'Julian Barnes at the Sorbonne, 14th November 2001', *Études britanniques contemporaines*, 21 (December 2001), p. 112.
3  The episode and its implications are related by Barnes in 'The Follies of Writer Worship', *New York Times Book Review*, 90 (17 February 1985), pp. 1, 16, 17. Extracts from Barnes's notebooks relating the episode are included in Julian Barnes, 'When Flaubert Took Wing', *Guardian* (5 March 2005), p. 30; Guignery and Gallix (2001), pp. 112–14; Vanessa Guignery, 'Julian Barnes in Conversation', in Antoine Capet et al. (eds), 'Flaubert's Parrot' *de Julian Barnes* 'Un symbole du logos?' (Rouen: Publications de l'Université de Rouen, 2002), pp. 120–3.
4  Gérard Genette, *Paratexts: Thresholds of Interpretation*, trans. Jane E. Lewin (1987; Cambridge: Cambridge University Press, 1997).
5  All references are to the Picador edition of the 2001 reprinting, containing 229 pages.
6  Peter Brooks, 'Obsessed with the Hermit of Croisset', *New York Times Book Review*, 90 (10 March 1985), p. 7.
7  David Montrose, 'Julian Barnes', in D. L. Kirkpatrick (ed.), *Contemporary Novelists*, 4th edn (London: St James Press, 1986), p. 69.
8  Laurent Milesi, '(Double) Dealing with *Flaubert's Parrot*(s)', *QWERTY*, 11 (October 2001), p. 190.
9  Philip Larkin, 'To Julian Barnes – 25 October 1984', in Anthony Thwaite (ed.), *Selected Letters of Philip Larkin, 1940–1985* (London: Faber & Faber, 1992), p. 721.
10  David Lodge, 'The Home Front', *New York Review of Books*, 34:8 (7 May 1987), p. 10.
11  In Guignery, 'Julian Barnes in Conversation' (2002), p. 120.
12  In Rudolf Freiburg and Jan Schnitker (eds), '*Do you consider yourself a postmodern author?*' *Interviews with Contemporary English Writers* (Reihe: Erlanger Studien zur Anglistik und Amerikanistic, vol. 1, 1999), p. 59.
13  In Guignery, 'Julian Barnes in Conversation', (2002), p. 123.
14  Andrzej Gasiorek, *Post-War British Fiction: Realism and After* (London: Edward Arnold, 1995), p. 159. This interpretation of *Flaubert's Parrot* as an 'intellectual whodunnit' has also been developed by Vanessa Guignery in 'Sur la piste des perroquets: les figures de la quête dans *Flaubert's Parrot* de Julian Barnes [On the track of parrots: figures of the quest in Julian Barnes's *Flaubert's Parrot*]', in Capet et al. (2002), pp. 29–45.
15  In Freiburg (1999), p. 59.
16  James Fenton, 'A Novelist with an Experiment: Discuss', *The Times*, 61953 (4 October 1984), p. 13.
17  Ramón Suárez, 'Notas acerca de un loro famoso [Notes about a famous parrot]', *Revista Chilena de Literatura*, 29 (April 1987), p. 155.
18  In Hermione Lee, 'In Conversation', Institute of Contemporary Art, London (16 October 1984).
19  In Michael Ignatieff, 'Julian Barnes in 10½ Chapters', BBC2 (14 November 1994).
20  Barnes, 'When Flaubert Took Wing' (2005), p. 30.
21  Patti White, 'Stuffed Parrots', in *Gatsby's Party: The System and the List in Contemporary Narrative* (West Lafayette, IN: Purdue University Press, 1992), p. 113.
22  William Bell, 'Not Altogether a Tomb: Julian Barnes: *Flaubert's Parrot*', in David Ellis (ed.), *Imitating Art: Essays in Biography* (London: Pluto Press, 1993), p. 160.

23  Catherine Bernard, '*Flaubert's Parrot*: le reliquaire mélancolique [the melancholy reliquary]', *Études anglaises*, 54:4 (2001), pp. 453–64.
24  White (1992), p. 123.
25  Frank Kermode, 'Obsessed with Obession', *New York Review of Books*, 32:7 (25 April 1985), p. 15.
26  Tania Shepherd, 'Towards a Description of Atypical Narratives: Study of the Underlying Organisation of *Flaubert's Parrot*', *Language and Discourse*, 5 (1997), p. 72.
27  Vanessa Guignery, 'Flaubert's Parrot' *de Julian Barnes* (Paris: Nathan Université/Armand Colin, 2001).
28  James B. Scott, 'Parrot as Paradigms: Infinite Deferral of Meaning in *Flaubert's Parrot*', *ARIEL*, 21.3 (July 1990), p. 64.
29  White (1992), p. 114.
30  In Freiburg (1999), p. 59.
31  David Coward, 'The Rare Creature's Human Sounds', *Times Literary Supplement*, 4253 (5 October 1984), p. 1117.
32  John Updike, 'A Pair of Parrots', *New Yorker*, 61 (22 July 1985), p. 87.
33  Julian Barnes, *Le Perroquet de Flaubert*, trans. Jean Guiloineau (Paris: Stock, Bibliothèque Cosmopolite, 1986), p. 211.
34  Scott (1990), p. 65.
35  Bell (1993), p. 151.
36  Neil Brooks, 'Interred Textuality: *The Good Soldier* and *Flaubert's Parrot*', *Critique: Studies in Contemporary Fiction*, 41:1 (Fall 1999), p. 46.
37  Scott (1990), pp. 57, 58.
38  Alison Lee, *Realism and Power: Postmodern British Fiction* (London: Routledge, 1990), p. 39.
39  Merritt Moseley, *Understanding Julian Barnes* (Columbia, SC: University of Carolina Press, 1997), p. 87.
40  In Guignery, 'Julian Barnes in Conversation' (2002), p. 126.
41  Linda Hutcheon, *A Poetics of Postmodernism. History, Theory, Fiction* (New York and London: Routledge, 1988), p. 5.
42  Elisabeth Wesseling, *Writing History as a Prophet: Postmodernist Innovations of the Historical Novel* (Amsterdam and Philadelphia: John Benjamins, 1991), p. 89.
43  Gasiorek (1995), p. 158.
44  Lee (1990), p. 38.
45  Linda Hutcheon, *The Politics of Postmodernism* (London: Routledge, 1989), p. 114.
46  Bell (1993), p. 158.
47  Bell (1993), p. 159.
48  In Guignery, 'Julian Barnes in Conversation' (2002), p. 125.
49  In Guignery and Gallix (2001), p. 115.
50  Philip Larkin, 'To Julian Barnes – 27 September 1985', in Thwaite (1992), p. 751.
51  Bell (1993), p. 161.
52  Bell (1993), pp. 167, 171.
53  Neil Brooks, 'The Silence of the Parrots: Repetition and Interpretation in *Flaubert's Parrot*', *QWERTY*, 11 (October 2001), p. 161.
54  Brooks (1999), p. 48.
55  Brooks (1999), p. 49.
56  In Guignery and Gallix (2001), pp. 120–1.
57  Erica Hateley, '*Flaubert's Parrot* as Modernist Quest', *QWERTY*, 11 (October 2001), p. 177.
58  Hateley (2001), p. 179.
59  Hateley (2001), p. 181.
60  David Leon Higdon, ' "Unconfessed Confessions": the Narrators of Graham Swift and Julian Barnes', in James Acheson (ed.), *The British and Irish Novel since 1960* (Basingstoke: Macmillan, 1991), p. 181.

61  Lee (1990), p. 55.
62  Higdon (1991), p. 174.
63  Brooks (1999), p. 47.
64  Vanessa Guignery, ' "My wife . . . died": une mort en pointillé dans *Flaubert's Parrot* de Julian Barnes [death by suggestion in Julian Barnes's *Flaubert's Parrot*]', *Études britanniques contemporaines*, 17 (December 1999), pp. 57–68.
65  Higdon (1991), p. 180.
66  Vanessa Guignery, 'Le Narrataire ou le lecteur de l'autre côté du miroir dans *Flaubert's Parrot* de Julian Barnes [The narratee or the reader through the looking-glass in Julian Barnes's *Flaubert's Parrot*]', *QWERTY*, 11 (Otober 2001), pp. 167–76.
67  Tomasz Dobrogoszcz, 'Getting to the Truth: the Narrator of Julian Barnes's *Flaubert's Parrot*', *Folia Litteraria Anglica*, 3:7 (1999), p. 36.
68  Gasiorek (1995), p. 161.
69  Gasiorek (1995), p. 161.
70  Georgia Johnston, 'Textualizing Ellen: the Patriarchal "I" of *Flaubert's Parrot*', *Philological Papers*, 46 (2000), p. 65.
71  Johnston (2000), p. 68.
72  Coward (1984), p. 1117.
73  Gasiorek (1995), p. 160.
74  Higdon (1991), p. 180.
75  Brooks (2001), p. 159.
76  Terence Rafferty, 'Watching the Detectives', *Nation*, 241:1 (6/13 July 1985), p. 22.
77  Scott (1990), p. 61.
78  Coward (1984), p. 1117.

CHAPTER FIVE

 1  Patrick McGrath, 'Julian Barnes', *Bomb*, 21 (Fall 1987), p. 23.
 2  Ann Hulbert, 'The Meaning of Meaning', *New Republic*, 196:19 (11 May 1987), p. 39.
 3  Christopher Lehmann-Haupt, 'Books of the Times', *New York Times*, 134 (28 February 1985), p. C20.
 4  Simon Banner, 'World Painter's Brush with the Futrue', *The Times* (20 September 1986), p. 10.
 5  Alison Hennegan, 'Aerobatics', *New Statesman*, 112:2897 (3 October 1986), p. 39.
 6  Mira Stout, 'Chameleon Novelist', *New York Times* (22 November 1992), p. 69.
 7  Mark Lawson, 'The Genre-Bender Gets it Wrong', *Sunday Times*, 8460 (28 September 1986), p. 53.
 8  Hulbert (1987), p. 38.
 9  Merritt Moseley, *Understanding Julian Barnes* (Columbia, SC: University of Carolina Press, 1997), p. 92.
10  David Lodge, 'The Home Front', *New York Review of Books*, 34:8 (7 May 1987), p. 10.
11  Andrew Billen, 'Two Aspects of a Writer', *Observer Magazine* (7 July 1991), p. 27.
12  Carlos Fuentes, 'The Enchanting Blue Yonder', *New York Times Book Review*, 92 (12 April 1987), pp. 43, 3.
13  Hennegan (1986), p. 38.
14  Matthew Pateman, *Julian Barnes* (Tavistock: Northcote House, Writers and their Work, 2002), p. 34.
15  Hennegan (1986), p. 39.
16  Hulbert (1987), p. 38.
17  Fuentes (1987), p. 3.
18  Banner (1986), p. 10.
19  D. J. R. Bruckner, 'Planned Parenthood and the Novel', *New York Times Book Review*, 92 (12 April 1987), p. 3.

20  Hennegan (1986), p. 38.
21  In Elizabeth Kastor, 'Julian Barnes' Big Questions', *Washington Post, Book World*, 111 (18 May 1987), p. 9.
22  Lodge (1987), p. 10.
23  Kastor (1987), p. 9.
24  Banner (1986), p. 10.
25  Kastor (1987), p. 9.
26  Hulbert (1987), p. 38.
27  Fuentes (1987), p. 43.
28  McGrath (1987), p. 21.
29  Moseley (1997), p. 99.
30  Richard Pédot, 'Voyage au centre de la métaphore [Journey to the centre of the metaphor]: *Staring at the Sun* de Julian Barnes', *Études britanniques contemporaines*, 15 (December 1998), p. 117.
31  Vanessa Guignery, *Julian Barnes. L'art du mélange* [*The art of mixing*]. Bordeaux: Presses Universitaires de Bordeaux, 2001), pp. 15–16.
32  Pédot (1998), p. 117.
33  Pateman (2002), p. 38.
34  Pateman (2002), p. 39.
35  In Michael Ignatieff, 'Julian Barnes in 10½ Chapters', BBC2 (14 November 1994).
36  Hulbert (1987), p. 38.
37  Fuentes (1987), p. 3.
38  In Nadine O'Regan, 'Cool, Clean Man of Letters', *Sunday Business Post* (http://archives.tcm.ie/businesspost/2003/06/29/story382420037.asp), 29 June 2003.
39  Moseley (1997), p. 98.

CHAPTER SIX

1  In Alexander Stuart, 'A Talk with Julian Barnes', *Los Angeles Times Book Review* (15 October 1989), p. 15.
2  David Sexton, 'Still Parroting On about God', *Sunday Telegraph*, 1463 (11 June 1989), p. 42.
3  D. J. Taylor, 'A Newfangled and Funny Romp', *Spectator*, 262 (24 June 1989), p. 40.
4  In Mark Lawson, 'A Short History of Julian Barnes', *Independent Magazine* (13 July 1991), p. 36.
5  Robert Nixon, 'Brief Encounters', *Village Voice Literary Supplement*, 80 (7 November 1989), p.S5.
6  Merle Rubin, 'From Nebulae to Noah's Ark', *Christian Science Monitor*, 82 (10 January 1990), p. 13.
7  Robert Irwin, 'Tick-Tock, Tick-Tock', *Listener*, 121:3119 (22 June 1989), p. 26.
8  Bruce Cook, 'The World's History and Then Some in 10½ Chapters', *Los Angeles Daily News* (7 November 1989), p. L10.
9  Merritt Moseley, *Understanding Julian Barnes* (Columbia, SC: University of Carolina Press, 1997), p. 108.
10  Kate Saunders, 'From Flaubert's Parrot to Noah's Woodworm', *Sunday Times*, 8601 (18 June 1989), p.G8.
11  Joyce Carol Oates, 'But Noah was Not a Nice Man', *New York Times Book Review*, 94 (1 October 1989), p. 12.
12  Salman Rushdie, *Imaginary Homelands: Essays and Criticism, 1981–1991* (London: Granta Books, 1991), p. 241.
13  In Saunders (1989), p. G8.
14  In Stuart (1989), p. 15.
15  In Michael Ignatieff, 'Julian Barnes in 10½ Chapters', BBC2 (14 November 1994).

16  Claudia Kotte, 'Random Patterns? Orderly Disorder in Julian Barnes's *A History of the World in 10½ Chapters*', *Arbeiten aus Anglistik und Amerikanistik*, 22:1 (1997), p. 109; 'The Moral Negotiation of Truth in Julian Barnes's *A History of the World in 10½ Chapters*', in *Ethical Dimensions in British Historiographic Metafiction: Julian Barnes, Graham Swift, Penelope Lively* (Trier: Wissenschaftlicher Verlag Trier, 2001), pp. 77–80.

17  Brian Finney, 'A Worm's Eye View of History: Julian Barnes's *A History of the World in 10½ Chapters*', *Papers on Language and Literature*, 39:1 (Winter 2003), p. 62.

18  Richard Locke, 'Flood of Forms', *New Republic*, 201:23 (4 December 1989), p. 42.

19  Moseley (1997), p. 115.

20  Oates (1989), p. 12.

21  Lionel Kelly, 'The Ocean, The Harbour, The City: Julian Barnes's *A History of the World in 10½ Chapters*', *Études britanniques contemporaines*, 2 (June 1993), pp. 1–10.

22  Kotte (2001), p. 75.

23  In Ignatieff, BBC2 (1994).

24  In Stuart (1989), p. 15.

25  Matthew Pateman, *Julian Barnes* (Tavistock: Northcote House, Writers and their Work, 2002), pp. 41–53.

26  Isabelle Raucq-Hoorickx, 'Julian Barnes's *History of the World in 10½ Chapters*: a Levinasian Deconstructionist Point of View', *Le Langage et l'homme*, 26:1 (March 1991), p. 49.

27  Rushdie (1991), pp. 242–43.

28  Jonathan Coe, 'A Reader-Friendly Kind of God', *Guardian* (23 June 1989), p. 27.

29  Moseley (1997), p. 123.

30  María Lozano, ' "How You Cuddle in the Dark Governs How You See the History of the World": a Note on Some Obsessions in Recent British Fiction', in Susana Onega (ed.), *Telling Histories: Narrativizing History, Historicizing Literature* (Amsterdam/Atlanta: Rodopi–Costerus New Series, 96, 1995), p. 128.

31  Liliane Louvel, 'L'effet-Méduse ou la drôle "d'histoire" de Julian Barnes [The Medusa effect or Julian Barnes's odd "history"]', in Claudine Verley (ed.), *L'Entre-deux, Cahiers forell*, 6 (March 1996), p. 226.

32  Catherine Bernard, '*A History of the World in 10½ Chapters* de Julian Barnes et *Le Radeau de la Méduse*: L'image comme métaphore incongrue [*A History of the World* and *The Raft of the Medusa*: the image as an incongruous metaphor]', in Jean-Pierre Guillerm (ed.), *Récits/tableaux* (Lille: Presses Universitaires de Lille, 1994), p. 246.

33  Louvel (1996), p. 226.

34  Vanessa Guignery, *Postmodernisme et effets de brouillage dans la fiction de Julian Barnes [Postmodernism and modes of blurring in the fiction of Julian Barnes]* (Villeneuve d'Ascq: Presses Universitaires du Septentrion, 2001), pp. 216–18.

35  Gregory J. Rubinson, 'History's Genres: Julian Barnes's *A History of the World in 10½ Chapters*', *Modern Language Studies*, 30:2 (2000), p. 171.

36  Alan Clinton, 'Faking Gestures: a Brief Guide to Art, Literature, and Politics', in Philippe Romanski and Aïssatou Sy-Wonyu (eds), *Trompe(-)l'œil: Imitation et falsification* (Rouen: Publications de l'Université de Rouen, 2002), pp. 364–5.

37  Bernard (1994), p. 251.

38  In Vanessa Guignery, 'History in question(s): An Interview with Julian Barnes', *Sources*, 8 'History in Question(s)' (2000), p. 64.

39  Steven Connor, *The English Novel in History: 1950–1995* (London: Routledge, 1996), p. 233.

40  In Guignery, 'History in Question(s)' (2000), p. 63.

41  Locke (1989), p. 42.

42  Marc Porée, 'Des choses cachées depuis la fondation de l'Arche [Hidden facts since the foundation of the Ark]', *Critique*, 522 (November 1990), p. 906.

43  In Amanda Smith, 'Julian Barnes', *Publishers Weekly*, 236:8 (3 November 1989), p. 73.

44  Elisabeth Wesseling, *Writing History as a Prophet: Postmodernist Innovations of the Historical Novel* (Amsterdam and Philadelphia: John Benjamins, 1991), p. 73.

45  Cook (1989), p. L10.
46  Kotte (1997), p. 109.
47  Rubinson (2000), p. 167.
48  Gregory Salyer, 'One Good Story Leads to Another: Julian Barnes's *A History of the World in 10½ Chapters*', *Literature and Theology*, 5.2 (June 1991), p. 226.
49  Andrzej Gasiorek, *Post-war British Fiction: Realism and After* (London: Edward Arnold, 1995), pp. 164–5.
50  In Guignery, 'History in question(s)', (2000) p. 65.
51  Matthew Pateman, 'Julian Barnes and the Popularity of Ethics', in Steven Earnshaw (ed.), Postmodern Surroundings, *Postmodern Studies*, 9 (Amsterdam and Atlanta, GA: Rodopi Press, 1994), pp. 186–7.
52  Rubinson (2000), p. 174.
53  Salyer (1991), p. 228.
54  Adrienne Rich, *On Lies, Secrets, and Silence* (New York: W. W. Norton, 1979), p. 12.
55  Salyer (1991), p. 224.
56  Robert Holton, *Jarring Witnesses. Modern Fiction and the Representation of History* (New York: Harvester Wheatsheaf, 1994), p. 240.
57  Wesseling (1991), p. 181.
58  Salyer (1991), p. 221.
59  In Guignery, 'History in question(s)' (2000), p. 68.
60  Vanessa Guignery, ' "Re-vision" et révision de l'histoire sacrée dans le premier chapitre de *A History of the World in 10½ Chapters* de Julian Barnes [Re-vision and revision of sacred history in the first chapter of *A History of the World*]', *Alizés*, 20 (July 2001), pp. 67–86; Kotte (2001), pp. 83–7.
61  Clinton (2002), p. 368.
62  Frank Kermode, 'Stowaway Woodworm', *London Review of Books*, 11:12 (22 June 1989), p. 20.
63  In Guignery, 'History in question(s)' (2000), p. 66.
64  Kotte (2001), p. 74.
65  Kotte (1997), pp. 114–15.
66  Kotte (1997), p. 118.
67  In Saunders (1989), p. G8.
68  Kotte (1997), pp. 122, 123.
69  Jean-François Lyotard, *The Postmodern Condition: A Report on Knowledge*, trans. Geoff Bennington and Brian Massumi (1979; Minneapolis: University of Minnesota Press, 1984), p. xxiv.

CHAPTER SEVEN

1  Bruce Cook, 'The World's History and Then Some in 10½ Chapters', *Los Angeles Daily News* (7 November 1989), p. L10.
2  Edward T. Wheeler, 'Breaking the Frame, Again', *Commonweal*, 119:9 (8 May 1992), p. 23.
3  David Holloway, 'Parroting on about Gillian and Oliver and Stuart', *Weekend Telegraph* (13 July 1991), p. XX.
4  John Bayley, 'Getting to Know You', *New York Review of Books*, 38:20 (5 December 1991), p. 26.
5  Richard Todd, 'Domestic Performance: Julian Barnes and the Love Triangle', in *Consuming Fictions: The Booker Prize and Fiction in Britain Today* (London: Bloomsbury, 1996), p. 275.
6  Michael Levenson, 'Flaubert's Parrot', *New Republic*, 205:25 (16 December 1991), p. 43.
7  David Lodge, *The Art of Fiction* (Harmondsworth: Penguin Books, 1992), p. 18.
8  Bayley (1991), p. 26.

144  NOTES

9 James Buchan, 'An Unsuccessful Likeness', *Spectator*, 266 (20 July 1991), pp. 25–6.
10 Erica Hateley, 'Erotic Triangles in Amis and Barnes: Negotiations of Patriarchal Power', *Lateral* (http://www.julianbarnes.com/sr/erotic-triangles.html), 3 (2001).
11 Mick Imlah, 'Giving the Authorized Version', *Times Literary Supplement*, 4606 (12 July 1991), p. 19.
12 Imlah (1991), p. 19.
13 Vanessa Guignery, 'Excentricité et interlinguisme dans *Metroland* et *Talking It Over* de Julian Barnes [Excentricity and interlinguism in Julian Barnes's *Metroland* and *Talking It Over*]', *Études britanniques contemporaines*, 15 (December 1998), pp. 13–24.
14 Bayley (1991), p. 25.
15 Levenson (1991), p. 44.
16 In Rudolf Freiburg and Jan Schritker (eds), '*Do you consider yourself a postmodern another?*'; *Interviews with Contemporary English Writers* (Reihe: Erlanger Studien zur Anglistik und Amerikanistik, vol. 1, 1999), p. 52.
17 Elaine Showalter, 'Careless Talk Costs Wives', *Guardian* (5 August 2000), p. 16.
18 Thomas Sutcliffe, 'I met a man who wasn't there', *Independent*, 4302 (1 August 2000), Tuesday Review, p. 7.
19 Linda Hutcheon, *The Politics of Postmodernism* (London: Routledge, 1989), p. 79.
20 Tim Adams, 'The Eternal Triangle', *Observer* (23 July 2000), Review Section, p. 11.
21 Anthony Quinn, 'Money Can Buy Me Love', *Independent*, 1486 (20 July 1991), p. 26.
22 Imlah (1991), p. 19.
23 Bayley (1991), p. 26.
24 In Vanessa Guignery, 'Julian Barnes in Conversation', in Antoine Capet et al. (eds), '*Flaubert's Parrot' de Julian Barnes: 'un symbole du logos?*' (Rauen: Publications de l'Université de Rouen, 2002), p. 132.
25 William Hutchings, '*Love, etc.*', *World Literature Today*, 75.2 (Spring 2001), p. 329.
26 Jerry Brotton, 'Let's Talk about *Love, etc*', *Amazon.co.uk* (Sept. 2000).
27 Craig Hamilton, 'La Narration bakhtinienne dans *Talking It Over* et *Love, etc* de Julian Barnes [Bakhtinian narration in Julian Barnes's *Talking It Over* and *Love etc*]', *Imaginaires* (Université de Reims), 10 (2004), p. 187.
28 Dominic Bradbury, 'Talking it over about writing, etc.', *The Times*, 66895 (2 August 2000), p. 12.
29 Julian Barnes, ' "Merci de m'avoir trahi" [Thanks for betraying me]', *Nouvel Observateur*, 1675 (12 December 1996), p. 114.
30 Brotton (2000).
31 Barnes, ' "Merci de m'avoir trahi" ' (1996), p. 114.
32 Bryan Appleyard, 'Godlike Reader can Choose between Partial Versions', *Literary Review*, 157 (July 1991), p. 25.
33 James Wood, 'Bedizened by Baggage', *Guardian* (4 July 1991), p. 26.
34 Peter Kemp, 'His Best Friend's Girl . . .', *Sunday Times*, 8708 (14 July 1991), Section 6, p. 5.
35 Levenson (1991), p. 44.
36 Hamilton (2004), p. 179.
37 Showalter (2000), p. 16.
38 Todd (1996), p. 276.
39 Hateley, 'Erotic Triangles' (2001).
40 Matthew Pateman, *Julian Barnes* (Tavistock: Northcote House, Writers and their Work, 2002), p. 58.
41 Pateman (2002), p. 57.
42 Hateley, 'Erotic Triangles' (2001).
43 Merritt Moseley, *Understanding Julian Barnes* (Columbia, SO: University of Carolina Press, 1997), p. 139.
44 Vanessa Guignery, *Postmodernisme et effets de brouillage dans la fiction de Julian Barnes*

[*Postmodernism and Modes of Blurring in the Fiction of Julian Barnes*] (Villeneuve d'Ascq: Presses Universitaires du Septentrion, 2001), pp. 206–11.
45  Charles Nicholl, 'Oliver's Riffs', *London Review of Books*, 13 (25 July 1991), p. 19.
46  In Freiburg (1999), p. 60.
47  Barnes, ' "Merci de m'evoir trahi" ' (1996), p. 114.
48  Julian Barnes, *Something to Declare*, p. 286.
49  Julian Barnes, 'Curious Case of Infidelity', *Observer* (7 October 1984), p. 24.

CHAPTER EIGHT

1  John Bayley, 'Time of Indifference', *New York Review of Books*, 39:21 (17 December 1992), p. 30.
2  Patrick Parrinder, 'Sausages and Higher Things', *London Review of Books*, 15 (11 February 1993), p. 18.
3  Richard Brown, 'Julian Barnes', in Neil Schlager and Jos Lauver (eds), *Contemporary Novelists*, 7th edn (New York: St James Press, 1996; up-dated by Tobias Wachinger, 2001), p. 79.
4  Merritt Moseley, *Understanding Julian Barnes* (Columbia, SO: University of Carolina Press, 1997), p. 148.
5  In Rudolf Freiburg and Jan Schnitker (eds), '*Do you consider yourself a postmodern author?*' *Interviews with Contemporary English Writers* (Reihe: Erlanger Studien zur Anglistic und Amerikanistic, 1999), p. 61.
6  Julian Barnes, 'How Much is That in Porcupines?', *The Times*, 64472 (24 October 1992), p. 5.
7  Julian Barnes, 'Candles for the Living: Julian Barnes in Bulgaria', *London Review of Books*, 12:22 (22 November 1990), pp. 6–7.
8  Barnes, 'Candles for the Living' (1990), p. 7.
9  Matthew Pateman, *A Critical Study of the Fiction of Julian Barnes with Reference to Selected Theories of Narrative and Legitimation* (Dissertation, Leeds University, 1995), pp. 174–6; Vanessa Guignery, *Postmodernisme et effets de brouillage dans la fiction de Julian Barnes* [*Postmodernism and Modes of Blurring in the Fiction of Julian Barnes*] (Villeneuve d'Ascq: Presses Universitaires du Septention, (2001), pp. 506–11.
10  In Pateman (1995), p. 174.
11  In Michael March, 'Into the Lion's Mouth', *New Presence* (www.new-presence.cz) December 1997.
12  Maureen Howard argued, however, that Solinski was the eponymous 'Porcupine'. 'Fiction in Review', *Yale Review*, 81:2 (April 1993), p. 134.
13  Julian Duplain, 'The Big Match', *New Statesman and Society*, 5:228 (13 November 1992), p. 35.
14  Michael Scammell, 'Trial and Error', *New Republic*, 208:1/2 (4–11 January 1993), p. 37.
15  Scammell (1993), p. 37.
16  Scammell (1993), p. 38.
17  Barnes, 'How Much is that' (1992), p. 5.
18  Barnes, 'How much is that' (1992), p. 5.
19  Barnes, 'How much is that' (1992), p. 5.
20  Barnes, 'How much is that' (1992), p. 5.
21  Barnes, 'How much is that' (1992), p. 5.
22  Barnes, 'How much is that' (1992), p. 5.
23  Robert Stone, 'The Cold Peace', *New York Times Book Review*, 97 (13 December 1992), p. 3; Bayley (1992), p. 30.
24  D. J. Taylor, 'Poisonous Quills in a Show Trial from the East', *Independent*, 1891 (7 November 1992), p. 29.
25  Scammell (1993), p. 38.

26 Bayley (1992), p. 32.
27 Barnes, 'The Afterlife of Arthur Koestler', *New York Review of Books*, 47:2 (10 February 2000), p. 24.
28 Bayley (1992), p. 31.
29 Scammell (1993), p. 38.
30 Barnes, 'One of a Kind', *London Review of Books*, 4:3 (18 February to 3 March 1982), p. 23.
31 In Mira Stout, 'Chameleon Novelist', *New York Times* (22 November 1992), p. 69.
32 Barnes, 'How Much is that' (1992), p. 5.
33 Barnes, 'How Much is that' (1992), p. 6.
34 Linda Hutcheon, *A Poetics of Postmodernism: History, Theory, Fiction* (New York and London: Routledge, (1988), p. 114.
35 Bruce Sesto, *Language, History, and Metanarrative in the Fiction of Julian Barnes*, vol. 3 (New York: Peter Lang, 2001), p. 125.
36 Brian McHale, *Postmodernist Fiction* (New York and London: Methuen, 1987), p. 85.
37 Stone (1992), p. 3.
38 Howard (1993), p. 134.
39 Moseley (1997), p. 154.
40 Matthew Pateman, *Julian Barnes* (Tavistock: Northcote House, Writers and their Work, 2002), p. 66.
41 Brown (1996), p. 69.
42 Nick Hornby, 'Much Matter, Few Words', *Sunday Times* (8 November 1992), Section 6, p. 11.
43 In Claude Mourthé, 'Julian Barnes: un savoureux éclectisme [a savoury eclecticism]', *Magazine Littéraire*, 315 (November 1993), p. 101.
44 Hornby (1992), p. 11.
45 Moseley (1997), p. 156.
46 Barnes, 'Candles for the Living' (1990), p. 7.
47 Pateman (2002), p. 64.
48 Pateman (2002), p. 68.
49 Michiko Kakutani, 'Confrontation between Post-Soviet Bureaucrats', *New York Times*, 142 (10 November 1992), Section C, p. 19.
50 Scammell (1993), p. 37.
51 Jean-François Lyotard, *The Postmodern Condition: A Report on Knowledge*, trans. Geoff Bennington and Brian Massumi (1979; Minneapolis: University of Minnesota Press, 1984), p. xxiv.
52 Pateman (2002), p. 67.
53 Moseley (1997), p. 156.

## PARENTHESIS

1 John Walsh, 'The Best Lines', *Bookseller* (25 September 1992), p. 905.
2 James Wood, 'The Fact-checker', *New Republic*, 214:26 (24 June 1996), p. 41.
3 Steven Poole, 'Why Don't we Make it All Up?' *Independent on Sunday*, 447 (30 August 1998), Culture, p. 10.
4 Mark Lawson, 'Marmite for New Workers', *Independent*, 2643 (8 April 1995), Weekend, p. 26.
5 Henry Hitchings, 'Not Just Parroting Flaubert', *Financial Times*, 34737 (19 January 2002), Weekend, p. V.
6 Jason Cowley, 'Gauls, Please', *Observer* (6 January 2002), p. 15.
7 James Wood, 'Bedizened by Baggage', *Guardian* (4 July 1991), p. 26.
8 James Wood, 'The Facts of Life', *Guardian* (5 January 1996), Section 2, p. 16.
9 In Henry Porter, 'The Heart of a Man of Letters', *Independent on Sunday* (2 April 1995), p. 4.

10 In Christopher Hawtree, 'Novel Escape', *The Times*, 65475 (13 January 1996), p. 19.
11 Merritt Moseley, *Understanding Julian Barnes* (Columbia, SC: University of Carolina Press, 1997), p. 167.
12 Porter (1995), p. 5.
13 Hazel K. Bell, 'An index for Thalia', *The Indexer*, 22:3 (April 2001), pp. 147–8.
14 David Buckley, 'Little England, Big Apple', *Observer* (9 April 1995), Section R, p. 18.
15 Ian Buruma, 'Mrs Thatcher's Revenge', *New York Review of Books*, 43:5 (21 March 1996), p. 24.
16 Moseley (1997), p. 167.
17 Buckley (1995), p. 18.
18 Jeremy Paxman, 'London Calling', *Sunday Times* (9 April 1995), Section 7, p. 1.
19 Patrick Cockburn, 'I-*Spy* Things Unravelling', *Times Literary Supplement*, 4803 (21 April 1995), p. 32.
20 Moseley (1997), pp. 167, 168.
21 Moseley (1997), p. 169.
22 Cockburn (1995), p. 32.
23 Hilary Spurling, 'In Full Feather', *Daily Telegraph*, 45598 (19 January 2002), p. A3.
24 Gillian Tindall, 'Monsieur Barnes Crosses the Channel', *Times Literary Supplement*, 5157 (1 February 2002), p. 36.
25 Anne Haverty, 'Pursuing the F-word in France', *Irish Times*, 46295 (2 February 2002), Weekend Review, p. 8.
26 'A motor-flight through France', BBC Radio 4 (29 April and 9 May 2004).
27 Hazel K. Bell, 'Something to Indicate', *The Indexer*, 23:2 (October 2002), pp. 102–3.
28 In Hermione Lee, 'Julian Barnes: an English Frenchman?' Hampstead Town Hall, London (24 January 2002).
29 Spurling (2002), p. 3.
30 Hitchings (2002), p. V.
31 Claire Messud, 'Tour de France', *New York Times Book Review*, 107 (6 October 2002), p. 25.
32 Alain De Botton, 'The French Master', *Sunday Times* (30 December 2001), Section 7, p. 34.
33 De Botton (2001), p. 34.
34 In Carl Swanson, 'Old Fastery and Literary Dish', *The Salon Interview* (http://archive.salon.com/weekly/interview960513.htm), 13 May 1996).
35 Messud (2002), p. 25.
36 Cowley (2002), p. 15.
37 In Lee, London (2002).
38 Jane Jakeman, 'The Best Possible Taste', *Times Literary Supplement*, 5253 (5 December 2003), p. 29.
39 Judy Rumbold, 'What Jamie could Teach Julian', *Guardian* (15 October 2003), p. 5.

## CHAPTER NINE

1 In Rudolf Freiburg and Jan Schnitker (eds), '*Do you consider yourself a postmodern author?*': *Interviews with Contemporary Novelists* (Reihe: Erlanger Studien zur Anglistik und Amenkanistik, vol. 1, 1999), p. 61.
2 Matthew Pateman, *Julian Barnes* (Tavistock: Northcote House, Writers and their Work, 2002), pp. 74, 75.
3 Andrew Marr, 'He's Turned Towards Python', *Observer* (30 August 1998), Review section, p. 15.
4 In Vanessa Guignery, 'History in question(s): an Interview with Julian Barnes', *Sources*, 8 (Spring 2000), p. 70.
5 Patrick Parrinder, 'The Ruined Futures of British Science Fiction', in Zachary Leader (ed.), *On Modern British Fiction* (Oxford: Oxford University Press, 2002), p. 228.

6  Pateman (2002), p. 78.
7  Marr (1998), p. 15.
8  In Freiburg (1999), pp. 60–1.
9  Marr (1998), p. 15.
10  Anthony Thwaite, 'Buying up Buck House', *Sunday Telegraph* (23 August 1998), Sunday Review, p. 14; Richard Eder, 'Tomorrowland', *New York Times Book Review*, 104 (9 May 1999), p. 17.
11  Peter Childs, 'Julian Barnes: "A Mixture of Genres" ', in *Contemporary Novelists: British Fiction since 1970* (Basingstoke: Palgrave Macmillan, 2005), p. 85.
12  Marr (1998), p. 15.
13  Pateman (2002), p. 76.
14  In a private correspondence with the author of this Guide, on 26 February 2005, Barnes said he had never heard of, let alone read Williams-Ellis's book.
15  Ian Sansom, 'Half-Timbering, Homosexuality and Whingeing', *London Review of Books*, 20:19 (1 October 1998), p. 31.
16  In John Lanchester, 'A Vision of England', *Daily Telegraph*, 44540 (29 August 1998), p. A5.
17  Private correspondence, 26 February 2005.
18  William Ernest Henley, *England, my England*, Norton Anthology of English Literature, ed. M. H. Abrams, 5th edn, vol. 2 (New York and London: W. W. Norton, 1986), p. 1656.
19  D. H. Lawrence, *England, my England* (1922; Harmondsworth: Penguin, 1988), p. 8.
20  George Orwell, 'England, Your England', in *The Lion and the Unicorn: Socialism and the English Genius* (London: Secker & Warburg, 1941).
21  Vera Nünning, 'The Invention of Cultural Traditions: the Construction and Deconstruction of Englishness and Authenticity in Julian Barnes' *England, England*', *Anglia*, 119:1 (2001), p. 61.
22  Nünning (2001), pp. 59, 62.
23  Nünning (2001), p. 66.
24  Parrinder (2002), p. 230.
25  Eder, 'Tomorrowland' (1999), p. 17.
26  Valentine Cunningham, 'On an Island of Lost Souls', *Independent*, 3702 (29 August 1998), Weekend Review, p. 14.
27  James J. Miracky, 'Replicating a Dinosaur: Authenticity Run Amok in the "Theme Parking" of Michael Crighton's *Jurassic Park* and Julian Barnes's *England, England*', *Critique*, 45:2 (Winter 2004), pp. 164, 166.
28  Childs (2005), p. 85.
29  Nünning (2001), p. 65.
30  In Guignery, 'History in question(s)' (2000), p. 69.
31  Nünning (2001), p. 64.
32  In Guignery, 'History in question(s)' (2000), p. 65.
33  In Guignery, 'History in question(s)' (2000), p. 70.
34  Jean Baudrillard, *Simulacra and Simulation*, trans. Sheila Faria Glaser (1981; Ann Arbor: University of Michigan Press, 1994).
35  Miracky (2004), p. 163.
36  Guy Debord, *The Society of the Spectacle*, trans. Donald Nicholson-Smith (1967; New York: Zone Books, 1995), p. 12.
37  Pateman (2002), p. 79.
38  Miracky (2004), p. 165.
39  Parrinder (2002), p. 228.
40  Miracky (2004), p. 169.
41  Michael Wood, 'Tight Little Island', *New York Review of Books*, 46:11 (24 June 1999), p. 57.
42  Parrinder (2002), p. 228.
43  Miracky (2004), pp. 165, 168.

44 Penelope Dening, 'Inventing England', *Irish Times*, 45239 (8 September 1998), p. 12.
45 Marr (1998), p. 15.
46 John Carey, 'Land of Make-Believe', *Sunday Times* (23 August 1998), Section 8, p. 1.
47 Miracky (2004), p. 169.
48 In Guignery, 'History in question(s)' (2000), p. 72.
49 In Guignery, 'History in question(s)' (2000), pp. 71, 72.
50 Parrinder (2002), p. 230.
51 Cunningham (1998), p. 14.
52 Nünning (2001), pp. 62, 71.
53 In Guignery, 'History in question(s)' (2000), p. 71.
54 Miracky (2004), p. 169.
55 In Guignery, 'History in question(s)' (2000), p. 72.
56 Nünning (2001), p. 71.
57 Parrinder (2002), p. 230.
58 In Guignery, 'History in question(s)' (2000), p. 72.
59 Cunningham (1998), p. 14.
60 Nünning (2001), p. 70.
61 Miracky (2004), pp. 169, 170.

CHAPTER TEN

1 In Christopher Hawtree, 'Novel Escape', *The Times*, 65475 (13 January 1996), p. 19.
2 Julian Barnes, 'Lost for Words', *Guardian* (6 November 2003), p. 37.
3 In Nicholas Clee, 'Windows onto the French', *Bookseller* (27 October 1995), p. 27.
4 Michael Wood, 'Another Country', *New York Times Book Review*, 101 (21 April 1996), p. 12.
5 James Wood, 'The Fact-checker', *New Republic*, 214:26 (24 June 1996), p. 42.
6 Kate Kellaway, 'The Grand Fromage Matures', *Observer* (7 January 1996), p. 7.
7 James Wood (June 1996), pp. 41, 42.
8 Adrian Kempton, 'A Barnes Eye View of France', *Franco-British Studies*, 22 (Autumn 1996), pp. 96, 98.
9 Merritt Moseley, *Understanding Julian Barnes* (Columbia, SC: University of Carolina Press, 1997), p. 160.
10 Gerald Mangan, 'Très British', *Times Literary Supplement*, 4842 (19 January 1996), p. 24.
11 Michael Wood (1996), p. 12.
12 Michael Wood (1996), p. 12.
13 Michiko Kakutani, 'Fictional Fiction Writer Demonstrates his Magic', *New York Times*, 145 (16 April 1996), Section C, p. 15.
14 Julian Barnes, 'Evermore', with pictures by Howard Hodgkin (London: Penguin, 1996). A painting by Howard Hodgkin also appears on the Picador cover of *Something to Declare*.
15 James Wood (June 1996), p. 43.
16 Teresa Waugh, 'Very Clever', *Literary Review* 211 (January 1996), p. 26.
17 In Vanessa Guignery, 'History in question(s): an Interview with Julian Barnes', *Sources*, 8 (Spring 2000) p. 69.
18 Kakutani (1996), p. 15.
19 Thomas Mallon, 'As Young as You Feel', *New York Times Book Review*, 109 (27 June 2004), p. 7.
20 Michiko Kakutani, 'A Writer who Uses Death as His Protagonist', *New York Times* (22 June 2004), Section E, p. 1.
21 Kakutani (2004), p. 1.
22 Robert MacFarlane, 'The Greater and the Lesser Pain', *Times Literary Supplement*, 5267 (12 March 2004), p. 19.
23 James Wood (June 1996), p. 42.

24 Moseley (1997), p. 162.
25 Carl Swanson, 'Old Fartery and Literary Dish', *The Salon Interview* (http://archive.salon.com/weekly/interview960513.htm), 13 May 1996.
26 MacFarlane (2004), p. 19.
27 Stephanie Merritt, 'Things can Only Get Bitter', *Observer* (14 March 2004), Review Section, p. 16.
28 Peter J. Conradi, 'Sweet and Sour Tales of Death and Dying', *Independent*, 5435 (19 March 2004), p. 29.
29 Barnes, 'Hamlet in the Wild West', *Index on Censorship*, 23: 4–5 (September 1994), p. 102.
30 MacFarlane (2004), p. 19.
31 Kakutani (2004), p. 1.
32 Kakutani (2004), p. 1.
33 MacFarlane (2004), p. 19.
34 MacFarlane (2004), p. 19.
35 In Aidan Smith, 'Reflections on This Mortal Coil', *Scotland on Sunday*, 813 (21 March 2004), Arts & Books, p. 4.
36 Merritt (2004), p. 16.
37 MacFarlane (2004), p. 19.
38 Kakutani (2004), p. 1.
39 Merritt (2004), p. 16.

CONCLUSION

1 In Amanda Smith, 'Julian Barnes', *Publishers Weekly*, 236:8 (3 November 1989), p. 73.
2 Arthur Conan Doyle, *Memories and Adventures* (1924; Oxford: Oxford University Press, 1989), pp. 215–22.
3 Arthur Conan Doyle, *The Story of Mr George Edalji*, edited by Richard and Molly Whittington-Egan (London: Grey House Books, 1985), 124 pp.
4 Steven Poole, 'Why Don't We Make It All Up?' *Independent on Sunday*, 447 (30 August 1998), p. 10.
5 Kate Kellaway, 'The Grand Fromage Matures', *Observer* (7 January 1996), p. 7.

# SELECT BIBLIOGRAPHY

## FICTION

### NOVELS

(Details of the first UK editions, followed by details of editions quoted in this Guide where these are different from the first UK edition.)

*Metroland* (London: Jonathan Cape, 1980; London: Picador, 1990).
*Before She Met Me* (London: Jonathan Cape, 1982; London: Picador, 1986).
*Flaubert's Parrot* (London: Jonathan Cape, 1984; London: Picador, 1985).
*Staring at the Sun* (London: Jonathan Cape, 1986; London: Picador, 1987).
*A History of the World in 10½ Chapters* (London: Jonathan Cape, 1989; London: Picador, 1990).
*Talking It Over* (London: Jonathan Cape, 1991; London: Picador, 1992).
*The Porcupine* (London: Jonathan Cape, 1992; London: Picador, 1993).
*England, England* (London: Jonathan Cape, 1998).
*Love, etc* (London: Jonathan Cape, 2000).
*Arthur & George* (London: Jonathan Cape, 2005).

### UNDER THE PSEUDONYM OF DAN KAVANAGH

*Duffy* (London: Jonathan Cape, 1980).
*Fiddle City* (London: Jonathan Cape, 1981).
*Putting the Boot In* (London: Jonathan Cape, 1985).
*Going to the Dogs* (London: Viking, 1987).

All four are included in the edition quoted in this Guide: *The Duffy Omnibus* (Harmondsworth: Penguin, 1991).

### SHORT STORIES

'A Self-Possessed Woman', in *The Times Anthology of Ghost Short Stories* (London: Jonathan Cape, 1975), pp. 132–49.
'On the Terrace', *Punch*, 281:7355 (28 October 1981), pp. 746–8.
'One of a Kind', *London Review of Books*, 4:3 (18 February to 3 March 1982), pp. 23–4.
'The Writer who Liked Hollywood', *New Statesman*, 104:2675 (2 July 1982), pp. 18–20.
'The 50p Santa: A Duffy Detective Story' (as Dan Kavanagh), *Time Out* (19 December 1985 to 1 January 1986), pp. 12–13.
'Hamlet in the Wild West', *Index on Censorship*, 23:4–5 (September 1994), pp. 100–3.
*Cross Channel* (London: Jonathan Cape, 1996).
'Trespass', *New Yorker*, 79:36 (23 November 2003), pp. 87–93.
*The Lemon Table* (London: Jonathan Cape, 2004).

## TRANSLATIONS

Kriegel, Volker, *The Truth about Dogs* (London: Bloomsbury, 1988).
Daudet, Alphonse, *In the Land of Pain* (London: Jonathan Cape, 2002). Translation, introduction and notes.


## NON-FICTION

### BOOKS

*Letters from London, 1990–1995* (London: Picador, 1995).
*Something to Declare* (London: Picador, 2002).
*The Pedant in the Kitchen* (London: Atlantic, 2003).


### ARTICLES

(Only articles referred to in the Guide are included here.)
'Remembrance of Things Past', *Observer* (24 July 1983), p. 22.
'Curious Case of Infidelity', *Observer* (7 October 1984), p. 24.
'The Follies of Writer Worship', *New York Times Book Review*, 90 (17 February 1985), pp. 1, 16, 17.
'Playing Chess with Arthur Koestler', *Yale Review*, 77:4 (Summer 1988), pp. 478–91.
'Candles for the Living – Julian Barnes in Bulgaria', *London Review of Books*, 12:22 (22 November 1990), pp. 6–7.
'How Much is That in Porcupines?' *The Times*, 64472 (24 October 1992), pp. 4–6.
' "Merci de m'avoir trahi [Thank You for Betraying Me]" ', *Nouvel Observateur*, 1675 (12 December 1996), p. 114.
' "O Unforgetting Elephant" ', *New York Review of Books*, 44:1 (9 January 1997), pp. 23–7. (Review of *Ford Madox Ford: A Dual Life*, by Max Saunders.)
'European Solutions to Travel', *New Yorker*, 73:10 (28 April to 5 May 1997), pp. 90, 92, 93, 96, 97, 109.
'Out of Place', *Architectural Digest*, 54:5 (May 1997), pp. 36–8.
'Bitter Lemon Days', in David Harsent (ed.), *Another Round at the Pillars: Essays, Poems, and Reflections on Ian Hamilton* (London: Cargo Press, 1999), pp. 15–21.
'The Afterlife of Arthur Koestler', *New York Review of Books*, 47:2 (10 February 2000), pp. 23–5. (Review of *Arthur Koestler: The Homeless Mind*, by David Cesarani.)
'Holy Hysteria', *New York Review of Books*, 50:6 (10 April 2003), pp. 32–4.
'Lost for Words', *Guardian* (6 November 2003), p. 37.
'When Flaubert Took Wing', *Guardian* (5 March 2005), p. 30.


### PREFACES

Preface to Gustave Flaubert, *Dictionary of Accepted Ideas* (London: Syrens, 1994), pp. 5–11.
Preface to Gustave Flaubert, *Le Sottisier*, trans. Emma Ducamp (Mesnil-sur-l'Estrée: NIL éditions, 1995), pp. 7–16.
Introduction to Clive James, *Reliable Essays: The Best of Clive James* (London: Picador, 2001), pp. xv–xviii.


### INTERVIEWS

Brotton, Jerry, 'Let's Talk about *Love, etc*', *Amazon.co.uk* (Sept. 2000).
Clee, Nicholas, 'Windows onto the French', *Bookseller*, 4688 (27 October 1995), pp. 26–7.

Freiburg, Rudolf, ' "Novels come out of life, not out of theory": an Interview with Julian Barnes', in Rudolf Freiburg and Jan Schnitker (eds), *Do you consider yourself a postmodern author?' Interviews with Contemporary English Writers* (Reihe: Erlanger Studien zur Anglistik und Amerikanistik, vol.1, 1999), pp. 39–66.

Guignery, Vanessa, 'History in Question(s): an Interview with Julian Barnes', *Sources*, 8 (Spring 2000), pp. 59–72.

Guignery, Vanessa and François Gallix, 'Julian Barnes at the Sorbonne, 14th November 2001', *Études britanniques contemporaines*, 21 (December 2001), pp. 107–32.

Guignery, Vanessa, 'Julian Barnes in Conversation, 9 November 2001', in Antoine Capet et al. (eds), 'Flaubert's Parrot' *de Julian Barnes: 'Un symbole du logos?'* (Rouen: Publications de l'Université de Rouen, 2002), pp. 119–33. Also at www.cercles.com

Hayman, Ronald, 'Julian Barnes in Interview', *Books and Bookmen*, 25.8:296 (May 1980), pp. 36–7.

Ignatieff, Michael, 'Julian Barnes in 10½ Chapters', BBC2, 14 November 1994.

March, Michael, 'Into the Lion's Mouth', *New Presence* (www.new-presence.cz), December 1997.

Marr, Andrew, 'He's Turned towards Python', *Observer* (30 August 1998), Review section, p. 15.

McGrath, Patrick, 'Julian Barnes', *Bomb*, 21 (Fall 1987), pp. 20–3.

Mourthé, Claude, 'Julian Barnes: un savoureux éclectisme [a savoury eclecticism]', *Magazine Littéraire*, 315 (November 1993), pp. 96–102.

Poole, Steven, 'Why Don't We Make It All Up?' *Independent on Sunday* (30 August 1998), Culture, p. 10.

Smith, Amanda, 'Julian Barnes', *Publishers Weekly*, 236:18 (3 November 1989), pp. 73–4.

Stuart, Alexander, 'A Talk with Julian Barnes', *Los Angeles Times* (15 October 1989), Book Review, p. 15.

Swanson, Carl, 'Old Fartery and Literary Dish', *The Salon Interview* (http://archive.salon.com/weekly/interview960513.html), accessed 13 May 1996.

# CRITICISM

## BOOKS DEVOTED TO JULIAN BARNES

Guignery, Vanessa, *Postmodernisme et effets de brouillage dans la fiction de Julian Barnes* [*Postmodernism and Modes of Blurring in the Fiction of Julian Barnes*] (Villeneuve d'Ascq: Presses Universitaires du Septentrion, 2001), 735pp. (PhD thesis about all Barnes's books up to *England, England*. In French.)

Guignery, Vanessa, *Julian Barnes: L'Art du mélange* [*The art of mixing*] (Bordeaux: Presses Universitaires de Bordeaux, 2001), 140pp. (Comprehensive approach to all Barnes's books up to *Love, etc.* In French.)

Guignery, Vanessa, 'Flaubert's Parrot' *de Julian Barnes* (Paris: Nathan Université/Armand Colin, 2001), 136pp. (Analysis of *Flaubert's Parrot* for post-graduate students. In French.)

Henke, Christoph, *Vergangenheitsobsessionen: Geschichte und Gedächtnis im Erzählwerk von Julian Barnes* [*Obsessions of the Past: History and Memory in the Fiction of Julian Barnes*] (Trier: Wissenschaftlicher Verlag Trier, 2001), 326pp. (PhD thesis about all Barnes's books up to *Love, etc.* In German.)

Moseley, Merritt, *Understanding Julian Barnes* (Columbia: University of South Carolina Press, 1997), 198pp. (Well-informed study of all Barnes's books up to *Cross Channel*. One chapter on the Kavanagh books.)

Pateman, Matthew, *Julian Barnes* (Tavistock: Northcote House, Writers and their Work, 2002), 106pp. (Perceptive analysis of all Barnes's novels up to *Love, etc.*)

Sesto, Bruce, *Language, History, and Metanarrative in the Fiction of Julian Barnes* (New York: Peter

Lang, Studies in Twentieth-Century British Literature, vol. 3, 2001), 136pp. (Description of all Barnes's novels up to The Porcupine, except Staring at the Sun.)

BOOKS AND ESSAYS WITH KEY DISCUSSIONS OF THE FICTION OF JULIAN BARNES

(Where it is not clear from the essay title, the Barnes titles discussed are in brackets at the end of each entry.)

Bell, William, 'Not Altogether a Tomb: Julian Barnes: Flaubert's Parrot', in David Ellis (ed.), Imitating Art: Essays in Biography (London: Pluto Press, 1993), pp. 149–73.

Billen, Andrew, 'Two Aspects of a Writer', Observer Magazine (7 July 1991), p. 27.

Bernard, Catherine, 'A History of the World in 10½ Chapters de Julian Barnes et Le Radeau de la Méduse: L'image comme métaphore incongrue [Julian Barnes's A History of the World and The Raft of the Medusa: the image as an incongruous metaphor]', in Jean-Pierre Guillerm (ed.), Récits/tableaux (Lille: Presses Universitaires de Lille, 1994), pp. 245–57.

Brooks, Neil, 'Interred Textuality: The Good Soldier and Flaubert's Parrot', Critique: Studies in Contemporary Fiction, 41:1 (Fall 1999), pp. 45–51.

Brown, Richard, updated by Tobias Wachinger, 'Julian Barnes', in Neil Schlager and Josh Lauer (eds.), Contemporary Novelists, 7th edn (1996; New York: St James Press, 2001), pp. 67–9.

Buxton, Jackie, 'Julian Barnes's Theses on History (in 10½ Chapters)', Contemporary Literature, 41:1 (Spring 2000), pp. 56–86.

Candel, Daniel, 'Julian Barnes's A History of Science in 10½ Chapters', English Studies, 82:3 (2001), pp. 253–61.

Childs, Peter, Contemporary Novelists: British Fiction since 1970 (Basingstoke: Palgrave Macmillan, 2005), chapter 3, 'Julian Barnes: "A Mixture of Genres" ', pp. 80–99. (Flaubert's Parrot, pp. 86–92; A History of the World, pp. 93–9).

Clinton, Alan, 'Faking gestures: a Brief Guide to Art, Literature, and Politics', in Philippe Romanski and Aïssatou Sy-Wonyu (eds), Trompe(-)l'œil. Imitation et falsification (Rouen: Publications de l'Université de Rouen, 2002), pp. 299–376. (A History of the World.)

Connor, Steven, The English Novel in History: 1950–1995 (London: Routledge, 1996), pp. 232–8. (A History of the World.)

Finney, Brian, 'A Worm's Eye View of History: Julian Barnes's A History of the World in 10½ Chapters', Papers on Language and Literature, 39:1 (Winter 2003), pp. 49–70.

Gasiorek, Andrzej, Post-War British Fiction: Realism and After (London: Edward Arnold, 1995), 'Postmodernism and the Problem of History. Julian Barnes', pp. 158–65. (Flaubert's Parrot, A History of the World.)

Guignery, Vanessa, 'Palimpseste et pastiche génériques chez Julian Barnes [Palimpsest and generic pastiche in Julian Barnes]', Études anglaises, 50:1 (1997), pp. 40–52. (Flaubert's Parrot, A History of the World, Talking It Over.)

Guignery, Vanessa, 'Excentricité et interlinguisme dans Metroland et Talking It Over de Julian Barnes [Excentricity and interlinguism in Julian Barnes's Metroland and Talking It Over]'. Études britanniques contemporaines, 15 (December 1998), pp. 13–24.

Guignery, Vanessa, ' "My wife . . . died": une mort en pointillé dans Flaubert's Parrot de Julian Barnes [death by suggestion in Julian Barnes's Flaubert's Parrot]', Études britanniques contemporaines, 17 (December 1999), pp. 57–68.

Guignery, Vanessa, 'Du psittacisme à l'émancipation? La transtextualité flaubertienne dans Flaubert's Parrot de Julian Barnes [From repetition to emancipation? Flaubertian transtextuality in Julian Barnes's Flaubert's Parrot]'. Études britanniques contemporaines, 20 (June 2001), pp. 1–17.

Guignery, Vanessa, ' "Re-vision" et révision de l'histoire sacrée dans le premier chapitre de A History of the World in 10½ Chapters de Julian Barnes [Re-vision and revision of sacred history in the first chapter of Julian Barnes's A History of the World]', Alizés, 20 (July 2001), pp. 67–86.

Guignery, Vanessa, 'Le Narrataire ou le lecteur de l'autre côté du miroir dans *Flaubert's Parrot* de Julian Barnes [The narratee, or the reader through the looking-glass in Julian Barnes's *Flaubert's Parrot*]'. *QWERTY*, 11 (October 2001), pp. 167–76.

Hamilton, Craig, 'La narration bakhtinienne dans *Talking It Over* et *Love, etc* de Julian Barnes [Bakhtinian narration in Julian Barnes's *Talking It Over* and *Love, etc*]', *Imaginaires* (University of Reims), 10 (2004), pp. 177–92.

Hateley, Erica, '*Flaubert's Parrot* as Modernist Quest', *QWERTY*, 11 (October 2001), pp. 177–82.

Hateley, Erica, 'Erotic Triangles in Amis and Barnes: Negotiations of Patriarchal Power', *Lateral* (www.julianbarnes.com/Sr/erotic-triangles.html.www.latrobe.edu.au/www/english/lateral/hateley.html), 3 (2001). (*Talking It Over*.)

Higdon, David Leon, ' "Unconfessed Confessions": the Narrators of Graham Swift and Julian Barnes', in James Acheson (ed.), *The British and Irish Novel since 1960* (Basingstoke: Macmillan, 1991), pp. 174–91. (*Metroland*, pp. 175–7; *Before She Met Me*, pp. 177–9; *Flaubert's Parrot*, pp. 179–81.)

Johnston, Georgia, 'Textualising Ellen: the Patriarchal "I" of *Flaubert's Parrot*', *Philological Papers*, 46 (2000), pp. 64–9.

Kelly, Lionel, 'The Ocean, The Harbour, The City: Julian Barnes's *A History of the World in 10½ Chapters*', *Études britanniques contemporaines*, 2 (June 1993), pp. 1–10.

Kotte, Claudia, 'Random Patterns' Orderly Disorder in Julian Barnes's *A History of the World in 10½ Chapters*', *Arbeiten aus Anglistik und Amerikanistik*, 22:1 (1997), pp. 107–28.

Kotte, Claudia, 'The Moral Negotiation of Truth in Julian Barnes's *A History of the World in 10½ Chapters*', in *Ethical Dimensions in British Historiographic Metafiction: Julian Barnes, Graham Swift, Penelope Lively* (Trier: Wissenschaftlicher Verlag Trier, 2001), pp. 73–106.

Louvel, Liliane, 'L'Effet-Méduse ou la drôle "d'histoire" de Julian Barnes [The Medusa effect, or Julian Barnes's odd "history"]', in Claudine Verley (ed.), *L'Entre-deux, Cahiers forell*, 6 (March 1996), pp. 219–35.

Lozano, Maria, ' "How You Cuddle in the Dark Governs How You See the History of the World": a Note on Some Obsessions in Recent British Fiction', in Susana Onega (ed.), *Telling Histories: Narrativizing History, Historicizing Literature* (Amsterdam and Atlanta: Rodopi – Costerus New Series 96, 1995), pp. 117–34. (*A History of the World*.)

Millington, Mark K. and Alison S. Sinclair, 'The Honourable Cuckold: Models of Masculine Defence', *Comparative Literature Studies*, 29:1 (1992), pp. 1–19. (*Before She Met Me*, pp. 12–17.)

Miracky, James J., 'Replicating a Dinosaur: Authenticity Runs Amok in the "Theme Parking" of Michael Crighton's *Jurassic Park* and Julian Barnes's *England, England*', *Critique*, 45:2 (Winter 2004), pp. 163–71.

Monneyron, Frédéric, 'Lien, liage et déliages de la jalousie dans *Before She Met Me* de Julian Barnes [Bond, bonding and unbonding of jealousy in Julian Barnes's *Before She Met Me*]', in *L'Écriture de la jalousie* (Grenoble: Editions Littéraires et Linguistiques de l'Université de Grenoble, 1997), pp. 137–51.

Nünning, Vera, 'The Invention of Cultural Traditions: the Construction and Deconstruction of Englishness and Authenticity in Julian Barnes' *England, England*', *Anglia* 119:1 (2001), pp. 58–76.

Pateman, Matthew, 'Julian Barnes and the Popularity of Ethics', in Steven Earnshaw (ed.), *Postmodern Surroundings*, Postmodern Studies 9 (Amsterdam and Atlanta, GA: Rodopi Press, 1994), pp. 179–89. (All novels up to *The Porcupine*.)

Pateman, Matthew, 'Is There a Novel in this Text? Identities of Narrative in *Flaubert's Parrot*', in Michel Morel (ed.), *L'Exil et l'allégorie dans le roman anglophone contemporain* (Paris: Ed. Messene, Collection 'Dire le Récit', 1998), pp. 35–47.

Pédot, Richard, 'Voyage au centre de la métaphore: *Staring at the Sun* de Julian Barnes [A journey to the centre of a metaphor: Julian Barnes's *Staring at the Sun*]'. *Études britanniques contemporaines*, 15 (December 1998), pp. 1–11, 117.

Porée, Marc, 'Des choses cachées depuis la fondation de l'Arche [Hidden facts since the foun-
    dation of the Ark]', *Critique*, 522 (November 1990), pp. 900–10. (*A History of the World*.)
Raucq-Hoorickx, Isabelle, 'Julian Barnes's *History of the World in 10½ Chapters*: a Levinasian
    Deconstructionist Point of View', *Le Langage et l'homme*, 26:1 (March 1991), pp. 47–54.
Rubinson, Gregory J., 'History's Genres: Julian Barnes's *A History of the World in 10½
    Chapters*', *Modern Language Studies*, 30:2 (2000), pp. 159–79.
Salyer, Gregory, 'One Good Story Leads to Another: Julian Barnes's *A History of the World in
    10½ Chapters*', *Literature and Theology*, 5:2 (June 1991), pp. 220–33.
Scott, James B., 'Parrot as Paradigms: Infinite Deferral of Meaning in *Flaubert's Parrot*', *ARIEL*,
    21:3 (July 1990), pp. 57–68.
Shepherd, Tania, 'Towards a Description of Atypical Narratives: a Study of the Underlying
    Organisation of *Flaubert's Parrot*', *Language and Discourse*, 5 (1997), pp. 71–95.
Stout, Mira, 'Chameleon Novelist', *New York Times* (22 November 1992), Section 6, pp. 29,
    68, 69, 72, 80. (All novels up to *The Porcupine*.)
Todd, Richard, *Consuming Fictions: The Booker Prize and Fiction in Britain Today* (London:
    Bloomsbury, 1996), chapter 8, 'Domestic Performance: Julian Barnes and the Love
    Triangle', pp. 265–79. (*Metroland*, pp. 265–7; *Before She Met Me*, pp. 267–9; *Flaubert's Parrot*,
    pp. 269–71; *Staring at the Sun*, pp. 271–2; *A History of the World*, pp. 273–5; *Talking It Over*,
    pp. 275–9.)
White, Patti, *Gatsby's Party: The System and the List in Contemporary Narrative* (West Lafayette,
    IN: Purdue University Press, 1992), chapter 8, 'Stuffed Parrots', pp. 111–23. (*Flaubert's
    Parrot*.)

# A SELECTION OF REVIEWS OF JULIAN BARNES'S NOVELS

## DAN KAVANAGH NOVELS

Binyon, T. J., 'Wearing the Gold Stud', *Times Literary Supplement* (30 October 1981), p. 1260.
Kaufman, Gerald, 'Malice Aforethought', *Listener*, 118 (26 November 1987), p. 29.
Sutherland, John, 'Carrying On with a Foreign Woman', *London Review of Books*, 7 (7
    November 1985), p. 24.
Waugh, Harriet, 'With a Dagger in the Library', *Spectator*, 260 (27 February 1988), p. 30.

## METROLAND

Bailey, Paul, 'Settling for Suburbia', *Times Literary Supplement*, 4018 (28 March 1980), p. 345.
Blishen, Edward, 'Growing Up', *Times Educational Supplement*, 3334 (2 May 1980), p. 22.
Boyd, William, 'Late Sex', *London Magazine*, 20:7 (October 1980), p. 96.
Church, Michael, 'New Books. Fiction', *The Times*, 60586 (27 March 1980), p. 11.
Levin, Bernard, 'Metroland: Thanks for the Memory', *Sunday Times*, 8128 (6 April 1980),
    p. 42.
Parini, Jay, 'Two Clever Lads From London', *New York Times Book Review*, 92 (3 May 1987),
    p. 26.
Paulin, Tom, 'National Myths', *Encounter*, 54:6 (June 1980), p. 63.
Shrimpton, Nicholas, 'Bourgeois v. Bohemian', *New Statesman*, 99:2558 (28 March 1980),
    p. 483.
Williams, David, 'Paperbacks of the Month: Fiction', *The Times*, 60995 (1 August 1981), p. 9.

## BEFORE SHE MET ME

Abley, Mark, 'Watching Green-Eyed', *Times Literary Supplement*, 4125 (23 April 1982), p. 456.
Greenwell, Bill, 'Flashback', *New Statesman*, 103:2665 (16 April 1982), pp. 18–19.

Kakutani, Michiko, 'Books of the Times', *New York Times*, 136 (17 December 1986), p. C26.

Krist, Gary, 'She Oughtn't to have Been in Pictures', *New York Times Book Review*, 91 (28 December 1986), p. 12.

Mellors, John, 'Bull's Balls', *London Magazine*, 22:1–2 (April–May 1982), pp. 133–4.

Raphael, Isabel, 'Fiction', *The Times*, 61208 (15 April 1982), p. 8.

Shrimpton, Nicholas, 'Fiction – The Crocodile File', *Sunday Times*, 8233 (18 April 1982), p. 40.

Thwaite, Anthony, 'A Course in Creativity', *Observer* (18 April 1982), p. 31.


*FLAUBERT'S PARROT*

Brooks, Peter, 'Obsessed with the Hermit of Croisset', *New York Times Book Review*, 90 (10 March 1985), pp. 7, 9.

Coward, David, 'The Rare Creature's Human Sounds', *Times Literary Supplement*, 4253 (5 October 1984), p. 1117.

Fenton, James, 'A Novelist with an Experiment: Discuss', *The Times*, 61953 (4 October 1984), p. 13.

Kermode, Frank, 'Obsessed with Obsession', *New York Review of Books*, 32:7 (25 April 1985), pp. 15–16.

Rafferty, Terence, 'Watching the Detectives', *Nation*, 241:1 (6–13 July 1985), pp. 21–2.

Updike, John, 'A Pair of Parrots', *New Yorker*, 61 (22 July 1985), pp. 86–7.


*STARING AT THE SUN*

Banner, Simon, 'Word Painter's Brush with the Future', *The Times*, 62568 (20 September 1986), p. 10.

Bruckner, D. J. R., 'Planned Parenthood and the Novel', *New York Times Book Review*, 92 (12 April 1987), p. 3.

Fuentes, Carlos, 'The Enchanting Blue Yonder', *New York Times Book Review*, 92 (12 April 1987), pp. 3, 43.

Hennegan, Alison, 'Aerobatics', *New Statesman*, 112:2897 (3 October 1986), pp. 38–9.

Hulbert, Ann, 'The Meaning of Meaning', *New Republic*, 196:19 (11 May 1987), pp. 37–9.

Kastor, Elizabeth, 'Julian Barnes' Big Questions', *Washington Post*, 111 (18 May 1987), *Book World*, pp. 1, 9.

Lawson, Mark, 'The Genre-Bender Gets it Wrong', *Sunday Times*, 8460 (28 September 1986), p. 53.

Lehmann-Haupt, Christopher, 'Books of the Times', *New York Times*, 134 (28 February 1985), p. C20.

Lodge, David, 'The Home Front', *New York Review of Books*, 34:8 (7 May 1987), p. 10.


*A HISTORY OF THE WORLD IN 10½ CHAPTERS*

Coe, Jonathan, 'A Reader-Friendly Kind of God', *Guardian* (23 June 1989), p. 27.

Cook, Bruce, 'The World's History and Then Some in 10½ Chapters', *Los Angeles Daily News* (7 November 1989), p. L10.

Irwin, Robert, 'Tick-Tock, Tick-Tock', *Listener*, 121:3119 (22 June 1989), p. 26.

Kermode, Frank, 'Stowaway Woodworm', *London Review of Books*, 11:12 (22 June 1989), p. 20.

Locke, Richard, 'Flood of Forms', *New Republic*, 201:23 (4 December 1989), pp. 40–3.

Nixon, Robert, 'Brief Encounters', *Village Voice Literary Supplement*, 80 (7 November 1989), p.S5.

Oates, Joyce Carol, 'But Noah was Not a Nice Man', *New York Times Book Review*, 94 (1 October 1989), p. 12.

Rubin, Merle, 'From Nebulae to Noah's Ark', *Christian Science Monitor*, 82 (10 January 1990), p. 13.
Rushdie, Salman, *Imaginary Homelands: Essays and Criticism, 1981–1991* (London: Granta Books, 1991), pp. 241–3.
Saunders, Kate, 'From Flaubert's Parrot to Noah's Woodworm', *Sunday Times*, 8601 (18 June 1989), pp. G8–9.
Sexton, David, 'Still Parroting On about God', *Sunday Telegraph*, 1463 (11 June 1989), p. 42.
Taylor, D. J., 'A Newfangled and Funny Romp', *Spectator*, 262 (24 June 1989), pp. 40–1.

*TALKING IT OVER*

Appleyard, Bryan, 'Godlike Reader can Choose between Partial Versions', *Literary Review*, 157 (July 1991), pp. 24–5.
Bayley, John, 'Getting to Know You', *New York Review of Books*, 38:20 (5 December 1991), pp. 25–6.
Buchan, James, 'An Unsuccessful Likeness', *Spectator*, 266 (20 July 1991), pp. 25–6.
Holloway, David, 'Parroting On about Gillian and Oliver and Stuart', *Weekend Telegraph* (13 July 1991), p. xx.
Imlah, Mick, 'Giving the Authorized Version', *Times Literary Supplement*, 4606 (12 July 1991), p. 19.
Kemp, Peter, 'His Best Friend's Girl . . .', *Sunday Times*, 8708 (14 July 1991), Section 6, p. 5.
Levenson, Michael, 'Flaubert's Parrot', *New Republic*, 205:25 (16 December 1991), pp. 42–5.
Nicholl, Charles, 'Oliver's Riffs', *London Review of Books*, 13 (25 July 1991), p. 19.
Quinn, Anthony, 'Money Can Buy Me Love', *Independent*, 1486 (20 July 1991), p. 26.
Wheeler, Edward T., 'Breaking the Frame, Again', *Commonweal*, 119:9 (8 May 1992), pp. 22–4.
Wood, James, 'Bedizened by Baggage', *Guardian* (4 July 1991), p. 26.

*THE PORCUPINE*

Bayley, John, 'Time of Indifference', *New York Review of Books*, 39:21 (17 December 1992), pp. 30–2.
Duplain, Julian, 'The Big Match', *New Statesman and Society*, 5:228 (13 November 1992), pp. 34–5.
Eder, Richard, 'History, Take Two', *Los Angeles Times* (8 November 1992), Book Review, p. 3.
Hornby, Nick, 'Much Matter, Few Words', *Sunday Times* (8 November 1992), Section 6, p. 11.
Howard, Maureen, 'Fiction in Review', *Yale Review*, 81:2 (April 1993), pp. 134–9.
Kakutani, Michiko, 'Confrontation between Post-Soviet Bureaucrats', *New York Times*, 142 (10 November 1992), Section C, p. 19.
Parrinder, Patrick, 'Sausages and Higher Things', *London Review of Books*, 15 (11 February 1993), pp. 18–19.
Puddington, Arch, 'After the Fall', *Commentary*, 95:5 (May 1993), pp. 62–4.
Scammell, Michael, 'Trial and Error', *New Republic*, 208:1/2 (4–11 January 1993), pp. 35–8.
Stone, Robert, 'The Cold Peace', *New York Times Book Review*, 97 (13 December 1992), p. 3.
Taylor, D. J., 'Poisonous Quills in a Show Trial from the East', *Independent*, 1891 (7 November 1992), p. 29.

*LETTERS FROM LONDON*

Buckley, David, 'Little England, Big Apple', *Observer* (9 April 1995), Section R, p. 18.
Buruma, Ian, 'Mrs Thatcher's Revenge', *New York Review of Books*, 43:5 (21 March 1996), pp. 22–7.

Cockburn, Patrick, 'I-*Spy* Things Unravelling', *Times Literary Supplement*, 4803 (21 April 1995), p. 32.

Lawson, Mark, 'Marmite for New Workers', *Independent*, 2643 (8 April 1995), Weekend, p. 26.

Paxman, Jeremy, 'London Calling', *Sunday Times* (9 April 1995), Section 7, pp. 1–2.


*CROSS CHANNEL*

Kakutani, Michiko, 'Fictional Fiction Writer Demonstrates his Magic', *New York Times*, 145 (16 April 1996), Section C, p. 15.

Kellaway, Kate, 'The Grand Fromage Matures', *Observer* (7 January 1996), Section R, p. 7.

Kempton, Adrian, 'A Barnes Eye View of France', *Franco-British Studies*, 22 (Autumn 1996), pp. 92–101.

Mangan, Gerald, 'Très British', *Times Literary Supplement*, 4842 (19 January 1996), p. 24.

Waugh, Teresa, 'Very Clever', *Literary Review*, 211 (January 1996), pp. 25–6.

Wood, James, 'The Fact-checker', *New Republic*, 214:26 (24 June 1996), pp. 40–3.

Wood, Michael, 'Another Country', *New York Times Book Review*, 101 (21 April 1996), p. 12.


*ENGLAND, ENGLAND*

Carey, John, 'Land of Make-Believe', *Sunday Times* (23 August 1998), Section 8, pp. 1–2.

Cunningham, Valentine, 'On an Island of Lost Souls', *Independent*, 3702 (29 August 1998), Weekend Review, p. 14.

Dening, Penelope, 'Inventing England', *Irish Times*, 45239 (8 September 1998), p. 12.

Eder, Richard, 'Tomorrowland', *New York Times Book Review*, 104 (9 May 1999), p. 17.

Lanchester, John, 'A Vision of England', *Daily Telegraph*, 44540 (29 August 1998), p.A5.

Sansom, Ian, 'Half-Timbering, Homosexuality and Whingeing', *London Review of Books*, 20:19 (1 October 1998), pp. 31–2.

Wood, Michael, 'Tight Little Island', *New York Review of Books*, 46:11 (24 June 1999), pp. 56–9.


*LOVE, ETC*

Adams, Tim, 'The Eternal Triangle', *Observer* (23 July 2000), Review section, p. 11.

Bradbury, Dominic, 'Talking it Over about Writing, etc.', *The Times*, 66895 (2 August 2000), pp. 12–13.

Hutchings, William, '*Love, etc*', *World Literature Today*, 75.2 (Spring 2001), pp. 329–30.

Showalter, Elaine, 'Careless Talk Costs Wives', *Guardian* (5 August 2000), p. 16.

Sutcliffe, Thomas, 'I met a man who wasn't there', *Independent*, 4302 (1 August 2000), Tuesday Review, p. 7.


*SOMETHING TO DECLARE*

Cowley, Jason, 'Gauls, Please', *Observer* (6 January 2002), p. 15.

De Botton, Alain, 'The French Master', *Sunday Times* (30 December 2001), Section 7, pp. 33–4.

Haverty, Anne, 'Pursuing the F-word in France', *Irish Times*, 46295 (2 February 2002), Weekend Review, p. 8.

Hitchings, Henry, 'Not Just Parroting Flaubert', *Financial Times*, 34737 (19 January 2002), Weekend, p. V.

Messud, Claire, 'Tour de France', *New York Times Book Review*, 107 (6 October 2002), p. 25.

Spurling, Hilary, 'In Full Feather', *Daily Telegraph*, 45598 (19 January 2002), p.A3.

Tindall, Gillian, 'Monsieur Barnes Crosses the Channel', *Times Literary Supplement*, 5157 (1 February 2002), p. 36.

*THE PEDANT IN THE KITCHEN*

Jakeman, Jane, 'The Best Possible Taste', *Times Literary Supplement*, 5253 (5 December 2003), p. 29.
Rumbold, Judy, 'What Jamie could Teach Julian', *Guardian* (15 October 2003), p. 5.


*THE LEMON TABLE*

Conradi, Peter J., 'Sweet and Sour Tales of Death and Dying', *Independent*, 5435 (19 March 2004), p. 29.
Kakutani, Michiko, 'A Writer who Uses Death as His Protagonist', *New York Times* (22 June 2004), Section E, p. 1.
Kermode, Frank, 'Age Has Not Withered Him', *Guardian* (13 March 2004), p. 26.
MacFarlane, Robert, 'The Greater and the Lesser Pain', *Times Literary Supplement*, 5267 (12 March 2004), pp. 19–20.
Mallon, Thomas, 'As Young as You Feel', *New York Times Book Review*, 109 (27 June 2004), p. 7.
Merritt, Stephanie, 'Things can Only Get Bitter', *Observer Review* (14 March 2004), p. 16.
Smith, Aidan, 'Reflections on This Mortal Coil', *Scotland on Sunday*, 813 (21 March 2004), Arts & Books, p. 4.


## FILMS

*Love, etc*, dir. Marion Vernoux, with Charlotte Gainsbourg, Yvan Attal and Charles Berling. France: AFMD, 1996, 105 min. Adapted from *Talking It Over*.
*Metroland*, dir. Philip Saville, with Christian Bale, Emily Watson, Lee Ross and Elsa Zylberstein. England: Caro-Line, 1998, 96 min.


## WEBSITE

www.julianbarnes.com
An excellent website, established and updated by Ryan Roberts. It includes bibliographies, criticism, selected reviews, interviews, a biography, a discussion board, and links to other sites.

# Index